TRANSCENDENTAL
MEDITATION

TRANSCENDENTAL MEDITATION

Maharishi Mahesh Yogi
and the
Science of Creative Intelligence

JACK FOREM

New York Area Coordinator,
Students International Meditation Society

E. P. DUTTON & CO., INC.,   NEW YORK   1973

Published simultaneously in Canada
by Clarke, Irwin & Company Limited, Toronto and Vancouver

SBN: 0-525-47341-6 (Paper)
SBN: 0-525-22225-1 (Cloth)
Library of Congress Catalog Card Number: 72-96900

Grateful acknowledgment is given the following for permission
to use copyright material:

From GROUP PSYCHOTHERAPY WITH CHILDREN by Haim
G. Ginott. Copyright © 1961 Haim G. Ginott. Used with permission of McGraw-Hill Book Company.

From TOWARD A PSYCHOLOGY OF BEING by Abraham
H. Maslow. Copyright © 1968 Litton Educational Publishing, Inc.
Reprinted by permission of Van Nostrand Reinhold Co.

From HUMAN SOCIETY IN ETHICS AND POLITICS by
Bertrand Russell. Copyright © 1955 Bertrand Russell. Used with
permission of Simon and Schuster, Inc.

This book is dedicated to
my mother, Eva Dobkin Forem, and to
His Holiness Maharishi Mahesh Yogi

with immeasurable gratitude
for the gift of life
and the knowledge
of how to live it

and to anyone and everyone
who wants to live a better life
and create a better world

Acknowledgments

I would like to express my thanks to all those who helped me in this project, either with ideas, encouragement, typing, proofreading, or any of the myriad details which are involved in the making of a book. Particularly, I'd like to thank my mother, Jerry Jarvis, Judy Booth, Janet Hoffman, and the late Joseph T. Clarke. Without their inspiration and aid this probably would never have been completed.

Contents

Introduction

Why This Book Was Written

It was a cold November evening in Berkeley, with the wind whistling up from the Bay and climbing toward the hills. Huddling against the chill, I noticed some posters still up around campus as I hurried to enter Dwinelle Hall. When I arrived at the lecture hall, the talk had already begun. The room was so packed that dozens of people overflowed into the corridor, and, like them, I had to listen to the lecture over a loudspeaker.

The speaker's musical voice, with its slight Indian accent, was soft yet full of life, calm but extremely expressive. He was talking about life in contemporary society, noting that "as the rate of progress increases, as the pace of life becomes faster and man's aspirations literally expand to the moon and the stars, the responsibilities and pressures of life naturally become greater." But, he pointed out, man's capabilities are *not* expanding at an equivalent rate. "Because man has not been able to find sufficient energy and creative intelligence within himself to meet the demands of life, frustration, unhappiness and lack of fulfillment are increasingly common."

The speaker likened the situation to living in a building

in which all the walls had begun to crack. If the building is to continue to stand, the foundations must be investigated and strengthened. He proposed the technique of transcendental meditation (the practical aspect of the science of creative intelligence) as a way to restore balance to life, to give strength and dignity back to man. He described transcendental meditation as a way by which any individual could tap the inner source of thought, a reservoir of "unlimited energy, intelligence, power, peace and bliss." When a man utilizes this field of unlimited potential, he said, "all aspects of his life flourish, in the same way that the branches, fruits and leaves of a tree flourish when the roots maintain contact with the field of nourishment in the soil."

It was a beautiful message, and the audience—even those of us standing in the hall who had not been able to see the speaker—listened intently. He began answering questions. After a while a few people began to leave the hall, and I was finally able to get to the door and catch my first glimpse of His Holiness Maharishi Mahesh Yogi, sitting on the stage on a covered couch.

A small man with long, dark hair and beard just beginning to turn gray, wearing traditional white silk robes, the Maharishi moved and spoke with an extraordinary combination of gentleness and strength. His words were carefully chosen and his speech, though simple, was highly articulate. He had a quick and lively wit, and a hearty laugh.

One thing was obvious: He was a happy man. Serene. At peace with himself and the world. He received every question —some hostile, discourteous, provoking—with patience and answered thoughtfully, thoroughly. Here was a man who could see the suffering and confusion of modern life, understand it and explain it, yet could remain unhurt by it.

At one moment, discussing a point of philosophy, his intellect seemed to dominate; his voice rose, his bright, clear eyes flashed and his hands moved quickly and decisively. Answering a different question, he was the embodiment of love, fingers caressing the petals of a rose, his voice soft and full. He seemed complete in himself, a whole world, yet totally alert and responsive to those around him.

The Maharishi answered every question in terms of the technique of transcendental meditation. He outlined the physiological effects of its practice, reviewed the principles and showed the relevance of the technique to whatever specific problems, individual or social, concerned the questioner. He emphasized that he was not espousing philosophy or religion, or offering something to believe in or accept on faith. Rather, he said, transcendental meditation is a practical technique, based on verifiable, scientifically validated principles. It is easy to learn and has immediate and practical benefits for all aspects of life. And, although it was obvious that it was he who was bringing this message to the world, the Maharishi took no credit for himself, but expressed gratitude to his teacher for passing on to him this "wisdom of living the fullness of life."

These were my first impressions of Maharishi Mahesh Yogi. My first impression of transcendental meditation, gained a few weeks later when I took the course offered by the Students International Meditation Society, was that everything Maharishi had said was true.

Since that time almost six years have passed, and my continuing experience with transcendental meditation has brought ever-increasing richness into my life. My appreciation led me to India in early 1970, where I received training from Maharishi in the theoretical aspects of the science of creative intelligence and the art of imparting the technique of transcendental meditation to others. Having now spent a total of more than eight months with Maharishi, in India, Europe and the United States, I can see that my first impressions were, while accurate, far from complete in fathoming the integrity, vision and scope of this remarkable man.

This present study was begun several years ago as an objective study of the phenomenon of transcendental meditation and its results. But it would be untrue to claim that this is now a completely objective study. I *have* been faithful to critical standards of scientific accuracy in reporting scientific data and results from questionnaires or recorded interviews. But I have made no effort to conceal my enthusiasm for the science of creative intelligence and its potential value. When we find something good we want to share it, and that has been the guiding motivation in the preparation of this book.

The Search for Happiness

In all ages and places men and women have sought happiness and fulfillment of their potentialities as human beings. Over the years our struggles to achieve fulfillment have become increasingly complex, but not necessarily more effective. In our own age this search is more intense and yet appears to be more unsuccessful than ever before. We have talked about fulfillment so much, looked in so many different directions and tried so many things that we hardly know what we want any more. What, indeed, do we want out of life? What is happiness? What does it mean to be fulfilled?

One man tells us that happiness is money and material comfort, another espouses love. Someone tells us that freedom alone can give happiness. Others say real fulfillment comes from "being yourself," from acting spontaneously, from achieving a certain kind of wisdom or knowledge. Whom can we believe? Has any other age offered so many different answers to these same questions?

The search for greater happiness takes us from one activity to another. If we do something and are not fulfilled by it, we turn elsewhere. If we are not satisfied with one way of life, one occupation, one mate, one house or car, we look for another. But what are we really looking for? What is missing?

We live in a world of unsurpassed technology and material richness. Our medical, scientific and industrial achievements offer us health, comfort and abundance. We have invented subtle and powerful communications media to spread the diverse cultural achievements of centuries and close the distances of space and time. We can choose from a huge variety of occupations and life-styles. We can eat, wear, say and do just about anything, and go almost anywhere; the range of possible experiences open to us is enormous. And yet, despite all that we have, all our abundance, our freedom of choice, action and expression, we feel restless, dissatisfied, bored, tired. We don't feel really alive. We are not so happy as we could be, and we are always on the lookout for something more.

Because of this, throughout the world today the most advanced thinkers and researchers concerned with human life and human development are experimenting with systems and techniques designed to help individuals tap more of their creative power and become more aware, loving and alive. The last few years have brought to our attention numerous methods, chemical and mechanical, scientific and mystical, all claiming to improve the quality of life.

In addition to the traditional forms of psychoanalysis and psychotherapy, a "third force" in psychology, sometimes called the "Human Potential Movement," has sprung up. Writers, researchers and therapists in this area are exploring the effectiveness of countless techniques (such as psychodrama, dance therapy, transactional analysis, Gestalt therapy, sensitivity training, encounter groups, etc.) aimed at achieving the goal of "self-actualization." A resurgence of evangelical Christianity, a swarm of teachers of Yoga, saffron-robed Hare Krishna chanters, bio-feedback technicians with instruments enabling an individual to attempt to condition the output of his brain—the techniques and ideologies continue to proliferate and the individual seeking a practical, meaningful way to live a more creative, happier life is increasingly baffled as to which way to turn.

But one fact is obvious: This thirst for self-realization, for utilizing our full potential and living more of life is a dominant theme of our time. People of all ages and ways of life are concerned with this pursuit of full development, and to a large number of people it is an all-engrossing ideal, implicit in everything they think and do.

Maharishi and the Science of Creative Intelligence

Out of this chaos of experimentation and speculation the science of creative intelligence (SCI) and its practical technique, transcendental meditation (TM), are being given increasing attention by scientists, educators, students and professionals. The science of creative intelligence is entirely different from any other system or practice being taught anywhere in the world. Its results and the almost incredible speed at which it is spreading throughout the world indicate that it may be the answer to this intensive search for an effective method of unfolding full human potential.

The theoretical framework of SCI is derived from a combination of Western scientific methods of objective investigation and the ancient wisdom of subjective development proclaimed in the Vedas. It draws together knowledge of the nature, origin, development, range and application of creative intelligence in individual life and throughout creation, from the structure of the atoms to the motions of the stars. The practical aspect of the science of creative intelligence, transcendental meditation, enables the student to experience directly the source of creative intelligence within himself, and apply it to all aspects of his life. Because the practice of TM produces beneficial effects immediately and cumulatively, the student of SCI, at every step of his progress, enjoys the satisfaction of seeing his theoretical understanding continuously supported by practical experience.

Increasing scientific data show that the physiological, psychological and behavioral changes which result from TM are extraordinary. Physiologists (particularly at Harvard Medical School) have found that the practice produces a state of rest and relaxation deeper than sleep, allowing for the release of accumulated stress and strain. This freedom from the restrictions of stress allows an individual to enjoy life more fully, as indicated by studies showing increased learning ability, a marked decrease in drug, alcohol and tobacco usage, an increase of creativity and personal stability, quicker reaction time and more. These scientific findings are an objective verification of the principles of the science of creative intelligence and substantiate the subjective results of transcendental meditation reported by practitioners.

The science of creative intelligence is unique in a number of ways. First, it differs from other techniques and programs for self-development in that, while it is extremely exact, systematic and scientific, it is also entirely natural and easily mastered. Personal instruction takes only a few hours and after that the individual is free to practice TM on his own, for a few minutes a day. The practice requires no discipline or control, nor is it emotionally demanding. Most people would be willing to spend a great deal of time, money and energy to gain the kind of results reported by practitioners of TM, yet contrasted with other programs of self-development, the course of instruction in TM is ridiculously inexpensive. Nevertheless, it seems to be far more effective in accomplishing its professed goals than other practices.

This leads to another vital point of uniqueness: The *goals* of the science of creative intelligence are clearly defined— something which sets it apart from most current programs, whose goals are nebulous and ill-defined. Maharishi Mahesh Yogi's presentation of the possible states of development available to a man is articulate and thorough, and his delineation of the path to achieving this development is systematic and easily understood. His language is simple and precise, not hidden in the veils of mysticism. Many feel that the ideal of human development which he sets forth far surpasses the range of vision of modern psychology.

TM and Its Teachers: Expansion

The technique of TM was brought to the world in 1958 by His Holiness Maharishi Mahesh Yogi. A physics graduate of

Allahabad University in India, the Maharishi studied for 13 years with his master in the Himalayas before beginning to teach TM throughout the world. His teacher, Swami Brahmananda Saraswati, was Shankaracharya * of northern India. Recalling his beloved teacher, Maharishi says, "He expounded the Truth in its all-embracing nature. His quiet words, coming from the unboundedness of his heart, pierced the hearts of all who heard him and brought enlightenment to their minds. His message was the message of fullness of heart and mind." A picture of Swami Brahmananda Saraswati, or Guru Dev (Divine Teacher) as he is affectionately called, is behind Maharishi wherever he speaks.

Maharishi first began teaching TM in India. After two years, as he tells the story, he reflected on what he had already accomplished and what lay ahead. He realized that at his present rate of teaching it would take him 200 years to bring TM to the whole world. He decided to visit the West, where transportation and communication are so much more efficient and his message could spread more rapidly. Since that time, he has spoken and taught in over 60 countries, and almost half a million individuals have begun the practice of TM.

Maharishi's message—that it is easy to unfold the full potential of mind and heart and live a life of freedom, fulfillment and happiness—has been accepted around the world by people of all ages, but with special enthusiasm by youth. In the United States alone, since 1965, when the Students International Meditation Society (SIMS) was created to meet the demand of students throughout the country for instruction in TM, over 200 thousand individuals have begun meditating,† including students, teachers, business, professional and working people.

Centers of SIMS are now established at colleges and uni-

_____

* A position of highest spiritual authority.

† As of January 1973. "The vast acceptance of transcendental meditation throughout the world," Maharishi says, "is due to its effects, not only for the individual but for all that is dear to him: his family, his society, his nation, his world." [1]

versities across the country, including Harvard, University of California at Los Angeles, University of California at Berkeley, Yale, Penn State, Ohio State, University of Colorado, New York University and over 1,000 others. The number of individuals beginning the practice has increased consistently, more than doubling in each of the last five years.

The teaching of TM and SCI is, to a great extent, a grassroots movement. The main source of publicity for the movement has been satisfied practitioners, spreading news of the benefits by word of mouth. Virtually no other publicity, aside from posters on college campuses, is used. However, in order to meet the steadily increasing demand for the teaching on all levels of society, a five-branched organization has developed. Four organizations teach the practical aspect of SCI, transcendental meditation. The Students International Meditation Society (SIMS) focuses on the student community. The American Foundation for the Science of Creative Intelligence (AFSCI) offers courses to business and industry. The Spiritual Regeneration Movement (SRM) makes the teaching available to that segment of the population which has a particular interest in philosophical and spiritual values. The International Meditation Society (IMS) offers courses to the general public. Although lectures may place special emphasis on specific benefits relevant to the needs of a specific segment of society, instruction in the actual process of transcendental meditation is identical in these four organizations.

The fifth branch of the movement is Maharishi International University (MIU), which offers comprehensive courses in the science of creative intelligence, more extensive in theory than the more practically oriented courses offered by the other four. MIU is responsible for training all teachers of SCI and TM throughout the world, and for creating and supplying teaching materials—video and audio tapes, films, slides, charts and a variety of written materials—to guide and enrich the course presentations. It also offers undergraduate and graduate degree programs centered on examining all disciplines in the light of the science of creative intelligence.

Directing the activities of these five branches of the movement in every country of the world is an organizational and operational structure known as the "world plan." The objective of the world plan is to train, as quickly as possible, enough teachers of TM and SCI so that there will be one teacher for every 1,000 persons. The first phase of this bold project is to open 3,600 SCI teacher-training centers in the major population centers of the world, irrespective of political and geographical boundaries. This will provide one center for every one million people. Each of these centers will train 1,000 teachers and maintain their strength through refresher courses. In this manner it is hoped that the 3.6 billion people in the world will, within a few years, have the 3.6 million teachers needed to provide one teacher for every 1,000 persons. Already almost 4,000 teachers have been trained, and many of the 3,600 centers have begun their activities.

In inaugurating the world plan in January 1972, Maharishi said, "We do not go by what the world has been. We go by what the world should be. We are planning today for the happiness of every man on earth. We want to outdate the old expression, 'Life is a struggle.' We want to replace it with, 'Life is bliss,' to educate every man everywhere in the full value of life." He then proceeded to enumerate the seven goals of the world plan, which are as follows:

1. To develop the full potential of the individual.
2. To enhance governmental achievements.
3. To realize the highest ideal of education.
4. To solve the problems of crime, drug abuse and all behavior that brings unhappiness to the family of man.
5. To maximize the intelligent use of the environment.
6. To bring fulfillment to the economic aspirations of individuals and society.
7. To achieve the spiritual goals of mankind in this generation.

"These admittedly ambitious but necessary objectives," he concluded, "are now attainable and must soon be realized in every area of the globe. The active cooperation of outstanding men and women in the world is all that is necessary now with this knowledge of the Science of Creative Intelligence."

In the United States the first phase of the world plan has begun "from the level of fulfillment," Maharishi has said. For a population of 205 million, 205 world-plan centers have been designated and, although a large number of these areas do not yet have physical facilities, teachers are active and courses are being offered in all 205 areas.

Part of the world plan is the establishment of 36 administrative centers, each of which will be responsible for the smooth functioning of 100 centers. One such center is the national headquarters of the movement in the United States. This center, located in Los Angeles a few blocks from the sprawling University of California at Los Angeles campus, is a hub of activity. Coordinators, secretaries, bookkeepers and volunteer helpers often work from morning till after midnight, keeping pace with the expanding activity throughout the country. The national director maintains close contact with four regional coordinators (East Coast, West Coast, South and Midwest), each of whom helps to coordinate the activities of the world-plan centers in his region.*

It is interesting that, although the teaching of TM and SCI is well established in over 60 countries, it is expanding most quickly in the United States. Apparently its simplicity and naturalness make it readily acceptable to a society caught up in complexity and all too aware that life has become divorced from nature. Maharishi has often mentioned that the United States, because it is already enjoying such a high state of material prosperity, has the chance of leading the world to the "200 percent value of life—100 percent inner, spiritual glory and 100 percent outer, material values." This country, he contends, is the most creative country in the world. We are most willing to try something new and, if it works, to adopt

---

* Addresses of the major U.S. and international world-plan centers are included in Appendix C.

it and use it. Because of this progressive attitude, TM is catching on more quickly here than anywhere else in the world.

The life of a teacher of the science of creative intelligence is a highly satisfying one. What could be more rewarding than supplying knowledge and teaching a technique that results in immediate, positive changes in life? One traveling instructor described it this way: "You teach a course, and then go on to another school. When you come back, maybe a month later, everyone looks younger, brighter, happier. You've given them something real, something they can use on their own to improve their lives. It's a beautiful feeling."

Many of the 2,500 teachers in the United States hold full- or part-time jobs, and teach evenings or weekends. Many are students, and give courses at their own and neighboring colleges. Some travel, moving from one campus to another. Others work at one of the established world-plan centers, where courses in TM are offered every week and SCI teacher-training courses are regularly in progress.

A course in TM is always taught in a series of seven steps, including two introductory lectures, an interview with an instructor, and four one-and-a-half-hour sessions of personal instruction over four consecutive days. Following the course, centers are open and teachers are available to the meditator, for "checking" of meditation (private consultation to see that the practice is correct and all questions are answered), group meditation, advanced lectures on practice and philosophy, and other optional programs. Courses in TM offered by any of the five organizations are taught by qualified teachers, all of whom have received their final training as instructors from Maharishi himself.

From 1966 to 1970 all teachers were trained at the International Academy of Meditation in India, but the facilities allow for the training of only 300 teachers a year, and applications for the courses began to run into the thousands. In the last two years Maharishi has conducted teacher-training courses in the United States, Europe and Canada, using public facilities (university dormitories and lecture halls, and hotels) where he trained over 1,000 teachers in 1971 and about 2,000 more in 1972.

Until the fall of 1972, teacher training always began with a one-month course in the summer (summer 1972 courses in North America were held at Queen's University, Kingston, Ontario, and California State University at Humboldt). Course participants have represented a wide diversity of ages and backgrounds, but the atmosphere has always been exceptionally harmonious and the mood serious despite all the laughter and warm feelings shared by all present. Two or three lectures a day by Maharishi, video tapes, guest speakers, group meetings for discussion of the lecture points and teaching practice, and seminars for special-interest groups (educators, scientists, artists, etc.) have highlighted the course program.

At present this first step in teacher training is being offered by Maharishi International University in each of the 205 world-plan centers throughout the United States, and locally throughout the world. Based around a series of color video tapes of lectures by Maharishi and guided by a detailed syllabus and a teaching procedure designed by Maharishi and a group of educational consultants, these courses will allow many more teachers to be trained in all parts of the world.

This first course provides theoretical knowledge of the science of creative intelligence. Following successful completion of either the one-month course or its local equivalent, applicants are selected for a two-and-a-half-month advanced course, at which they learn to impart the technique of TM, the practical basis of SCI. The course pattern remains essentially the same as the one-month course, but includes intensified testing, as well as personal meetings with Maharishi to finalize the training.

In addition to the classes in TM and SCI offered at the world-plan centers, increasing numbers of colleges, universities and high schools are now offering the science of creative intelligence as a fully accredited course. These courses outline the dynamics of increasing creative intelligence through TM and show the science of creative intelligence as the unifying basis of all fields of man's concern. This is because the basis of all branches of knowledge and action is the knower, the actor, the individual. As knowledge expands in all fields and life becomes increasingly complex, man's mind, the container of knowledge, must also expand. The key to progress in all facets of living is expanded creativity, perception and understanding. The science of creative intelligence shows the way to this necessary development of mental potential.

In July and August 1971 the first International Symposia on the Science of Creative Intelligence were held at the University of Massachusetts and Humboldt State College, to explore the relationship of TM and SCI to various fields of knowledge. Scientists, philosophers, educators, physicians, artists spoke on their respective fields and joined with Maharishi in relating SCI to their area of concern. *Boston After Dark* reported on the University of Massachusetts symposium as follows:

> There was an extraordinarily wide range of speakers. Throughout the lectures, Maharishi sat cross-legged on a yellow couch onstage, the area around him festooned with flowers. Invariably, he would offer comments about the lecture just heard in the form of a reconciliation between their thought and his own. The exchange between Dr. Harvey Brooks, president of the American Academy of Arts and Sciences, and himself was a representative one.
>
> Dr. Brooks: "Technology has allowed us to choose to paint ourselves into a corner. Like the sorcerer's apprentice we may constantly need to develop better and better systems to feed our 'technological addiction.' " Maharishi: "Technology today demands that man be more practical. The inefficiency to cope with his own progress threatens to slow its expansion. SCI meets this challenge by enabling every man to use more of his full potential."
>
> This tendency to present everything in terms of SCI at first seemed manipulative; but it became apparent that the thought processes Maharishi is concerned with are indeed so fundamental and their application so broad

that they can hardly be extraneous to any discussion of consciousness. His points were, at the worst, obvious, but more often than not, analytically useful and poetically apt. The love feast of the Symposium was Buckminster Fuller's talk with Maharishi. To Fuller, "What makes Maharishi beloved and understood is that he has manifest love. You could not meet with Maharishi without recognizing instantly his integrity. You look in his eyes and there it is." [2]

Other notable participants in the symposia included Melvin Calvin, Nobel prizewinning biochemist from the University of California at Berkeley, Major General Franklin Davis, commandant of the U.S. Army War College, and about 40 others. The symposia were a great success and have given rise to several more such seminars in the United States, Canada and Europe. Eminent speakers at the 1972 symposia included Marshall McLuhan (world's foremost expert in communications media), Hans Selye (pioneer in stress research), Donald Glaser (Nobel prizewinning physicist who invented the bubble chamber), and Rusty Schweikart, NASA astronaut who was the first man to walk in space on the Apollo 9 mission and is backup commander of the Skylab project. A large number of these men are themselves practitioners of TM.

A Closer Look

On October 25, 1971, *Time* magazine reported a study by Drs. Benson and Wallace of Harvard. "They asked 1,862 drug users who had also tried TM for at least three months to fill out questionnaires. 'It was clear,' [Benson] says, 'that most were at one point heavily engaged in drug abuse. But practically all of them—19 out of 20—said that they had given up drugs.' " [3] The study found that not only did individuals stop or significantly decrease using drugs, but that they also stopped selling drugs and even changed their attitudes in the direction of discouraging others from using drugs. "Further, the subjects decreased their use of 'hard' alcoholic beverages and cigarette smoking. The magnitude of those changes increased with the length of time that the subject practiced transcendental meditation." [4]

Apparently drug users who start TM begin to live happier, more creative and productive lives, and consequently lose interest in drugs. Benson and Wallace are engaged in a large-scale study of high-school students to determine the long-range effects of TM on drug use, creativity, attitudes toward life and other psychological measurements. Meanwhile, encouraged by the already established data, innovative educational and community leaders throughout the country are beginning to include TM and SCI in schools and in drug-abuse prevention programs.

In May 1972 the House of Representatives of the State of Illinois became the first major legislative body in the United States to officially recognize the value of transcendental meditation and the science of creative intelligence. House Resolution #677 noted that "whereas . . . studies indicate that it shows promise of being the most positive and effective drug prevention program being presented in the world today; and . . . physiological experiments provide evidence that through the regular practice of T.M. (twice daily for 15–20 minutes) the main causes of hypertension, anxiety, high blood pressure, cardiac arrest, and other psychosomatic illnesses are removed; and . . . the whole thrust of the programs of SIMS and IMS is to aid in the practical development of happy and productive citizens," the House resolved "that all educational institutions . . . be strongly encouraged to study the feasibility of courses in Transcendental Meditation and the Science of Creative Intelligence (SCI) on their campuses . . . that the Department of Mental Health of the State of Illinois, Drug Abuse Section, be encouraged to study the benefits of T.M. and . . . to incorporate the course in T.M. in the drug abuse programs; and . . . that the State of Illinois give all possible cooperation to the new Center for the teaching of the Science of Creative Intelligence to be founded in Chicago, Illinois." *

When this can occur, and when a *Scientific American* article [5] can suggest that the state produced by TM is a "guidepost to better health"; when a superintendent of schools can report that his schools have opened their doors to "this unique and distinctive type of educational experience" because of evidence that

1. students improve their grades;
2. students get along better with teachers;
3. students get along better with parents;
4. students get along better with other students; [6]

when the Michigan Governor's Office on Drug Abuse can state, "We consider the Transcendental Meditation program a necessary ingredient to every drug abuse education effort seriously concerned with providing strong and useful alternative life styles for its participants"; [7] when educators, artists, businessmen, housewives, scientists and students all converge around a single focus; when SIMS-IMS, an organization that uses almost no publicity, has to train thousands of teachers to keep up with the demand for instruction in the science of creative intelligence and transcendental meditation, it is time to take a closer look at what this program is, what it does, and how it may be relevant to our lives.

---

* The full text of this Resolution appears in Appendix A.

CHAPTER 1

Fundamentals

I. THE GOAL OF LIFE

The Direction of Evolution

Scientists today who study the nature of life are increasingly impressed by the powerful tendency, inherent in all living things, to progress, to evolve, to move toward a state of fulfillment. A seed, for example, contains within it the whole structure of the tree. The tiny seed sends a shoot down into the ground and another up toward the light. Against all odds (rocky soil, no rain, lack of nutriments) this tiny seed with its delicate shoots strives to become a tree, to complete the cycle, to become capable of producing new seeds, which can produce new trees. Individuals of every species, plant or animal, move steadfastly through progressive changes toward maturity, toward whatever they can be. Everything that lives wants to grow, to unfold, until it reaches full development.

How is growth accomplished? Through a series of changes. Without change there can be no development. And indeed, the most characteristic quality of life as we know it is change. Life is eternally changing, and the inevitable flow of life from one event or state to another is an eternal truth. In spring buds appear on the trees, followed by leaves and flowers, and then the fruit. The fruit ripens and falls, the leaves dry and fall, winter comes with its snow. And in our own lives we are always moving from place to place, from home to school to job, reading one book and then another, holding to one idea and then discarding it for another, spending time with now this person, and later, someone else.

These changes in our lives are not random and purposeless. Every choice we make is for more happiness, more knowledge, more love, more insight or understanding, more energy or peace. What man ever makes a conscious choice for *less* of life? It is true that our actions may not always bring us the desired result, but that does not alter the motivation. The desire for expansion, for growth and development belongs to the very nature of life, and it is the basis of all progress and improvement.

Contemporary psychologists have observed and described this tendency toward fulfillment. "Life has an inherent tendency to grow, to expand, to express potentialities," [1] wrote Erich Fromm. Abraham Maslow, in his book *Toward a Psychology of Being,* wrote, "It looks as though there were a single ultimate value for mankind, a far goal toward which all men strive. This is called variously by different authors, self-actualization, self-realization, integration, psychological health . . . but they all agree that this amounts to realizing the potentialities of the person, that is to say, becoming fully human, everything that the person *can* become." [2] Man has within him, Maslow writes, "a pressure . . . toward unity of personality, toward spontaneous expressiveness, toward full individuality and identity, toward seeing the truth rather than being blind, toward being creative, toward being good, and a lot else." [3] Maslow further states that man demonstrates this "pressure toward fuller and fuller Being, more and more perfect actualization of his humanness in exactly the same naturalistic, scientific sense that an acorn may be said to be 'pressing toward' being an oak tree, or that a tiger can be observed to 'push toward' being tigerish." [4]

The noted psychotherapist Carl R. Rogers has also described what he sees as "man's tendency to actualize himself, to become his potentialities. By that I mean," says Rogers, "the directional trend which is evident in all organic and human life—the urge to expand, extend, develop, mature—the tendency to express and activate all the capacities of the organism." [5]

Every man wants to extend the range of his experience, to know more of life, to expand the boundaries of his knowledge and strengthen his ability to act.* Neither the mind nor the heart enjoys limitations; the natural tendency of life is to overcome limitations, to move toward unbounded love, unbounded awareness and unrestricted freedom of activity.

It is the universal experience of humanity that no matter what a man may achieve in his life, no matter what he may own or accomplish or see or do, it does not seem to satisfy him. He wants to achieve or know or be even more. From this it can be seen that the direction of man's life is toward the infinite: not only *more* happiness, *more* energy, *more* intelligence are desired and required for fulfillment, but, ultimately, *the most*.

Our Largest Untapped Natural Resource: Human Potential

Every action that a man performs requires energy. Every word, every act utilizes energy. But every display of energy we know of in human life is directed: every action is either *this* or *that;* it implies choice; it requires intelligence. It is impossible to conceive of an action which does not expend energy nor require intelligence to give it direction.

Therefore, as long as man has sufficient energy and intelligence to act effectively and accomplish his goals, his progress

---

* "Fulfillment," Julian Huxley wrote, "seems to describe better than any other single word the positive side of human development and evolution—the realization of inherent capacities by the individual and of new possibilities by the race; the satisfaction of needs, spiritual as well as material; the emergence of new qualities of experience to be enjoyed; the building of personalities." [6]

can be unrestricted. He can move ahead and fulfill his aspirations one after another. But without sufficient intelligence and energy to meet the demands of living, a man either fails to achieve the goals to which he aspires, or exhausts himself straining to achieve them. Most of us today find that the demands and responsibilities of life are so great that they absorb all our resources, and the charm and glory of life are lost in the mere maintenance of living. Frustration, tiredness, anxiety and dissatisfaction with life are found everywhere in the world.

However, these signs of suffering, whatever their nature or their ostensible "cause," are only symptomatic. Maharishi Mahesh Yogi, in full accord with a growing number of psychologists, holds that we have been unable to attain our goals, unable to live a fulfilled life and create a harmonious society because we have failed to make use of our full potential. We simply have not fully unfolded our own human resources.

That we do not even approach full development of our potential is common knowledge. Many psychologists estimate that we use, at best, only ten to fifteen percent of our mental capacity. "If there is one statement true of every living person it must be this: he hasn't achieved his full potential," writes William Schutz of Esalen Institute in Big Sur, California. "The latent abilities, hidden talents and undeveloped capacities for excellence and pleasure are legion. The consequences of this universal fate are many. Observers frequently refer to the human potential as our largest untapped natural resource." [7] Is it surprising that there is so much suffering in the world, with man utilizing such a limited portion of his mental potential? No wonder we experience frustration, inability to fulfill our desires, inability to reach intelligent solutions to situations that arise in society and in daily life. No wonder we are unable to live harmoniously with nature and our fellowmen. Since we live life with one-tenth of our potential, it is no surprise that the results are not thoroughly gratifying. Imagine trying to play an instrument (piano, guitar, flute) with one out of ten fingers!

Some commentators on the human predicament have suggested that it is our goals and desires which are the cause of our suffering. But all progress depends upon desires and aspirations, and the ability to fulfill them. Evolution rides on fulfilled desire. From the fulfillment of one level of aspirations we can move on to other, greater accomplishments. Frustration and suffering arise only if we are unable to progress. And restricted progress is the result of weakness, of using our inherent faculties only partially. Must we then conclude that man is weak and will always suffer? Or, if we truly have unused resources within us, could they, if tapped, put an end to suffering? If the pace and demands of contemporary society are too much for us, must we admit defeat and try to slow down the advance of civilization (or try to withdraw from it), or can we rise up to meet the challenge of its rapid progress?

The Need of the Age

"The great and urgent need of these times is transcendence," Charles A. Reich wrote in *The Greening of America*. "The last two hundred years have fundamentally and irrevocably altered the terms of man's existence. The price of survival is an appropriate consciousness and social order to go along with the revolution of science and technology that has already occurred. The chaos we are now experiencing is the inevitable and predictable consequence of our failure to rise to this necessity. . . . What is called for is a higher logic and a higher reason. The creation of a new consciousness is the most urgent of America's real needs." [8]

This need has been recognized by many. "I maintain that there is a desperate social need for the creative behavior of creative individuals," writes Carl Rogers. "Why be concerned over this? . . . In a time when knowledge, constructive and destructive, is advancing by the most incredible leaps and bounds into a fantastic atomic age, genuinely creative adaptation seems to represent the only possibility that man can keep abreast of the kaleidoscopic change in his world. Unless man can make new and original adaptations to his environment as rapidly as his science can change the environment, our culture will perish. Not only individual and group tensions but international annihilation will be the price we pay for lack of creativity.

"Consequently it would seem to me that investigation of the process of creativity . . . and the ways in which it can be facilitated, are of the utmost importance." [9] Man needs a way to tap his inner reservoir of energy and creative intelligence, to expand the conscious capacity of his mind, broaden his vision, and bring his new powers into the field of action. In order to improve the quality of life, the actions we perform must become more intelligent, creative and effective, more in harmony with nature and conducive to the growth and well-being of all.

But to do this, we must strengthen the root of action, which is the individual, the man who acts, because the quality of action is determined by our inner status, particularly by the strength of the mind. If the mind is strong and creative, capable of broad vision and deep insight, capable of comprehending the many aspects of a given situation, action will be spontaneously creative and strong. If the mind is capable of only limited vision, if it is dull, shallow and not very creative, action will be restricted. Just as we must provide a strong foundation if we want a strong building, if we want to enrich the field of action, we must strengthen the field of thought.

Is it possible to make thought more powerful? What can be done to strengthen and expand the mind? These are certainly not new questions. But have they ever been satisfactorily answered?

It is easy to see that the field of thought underlies the field of action, that doing arises from thinking. But what is that field from which thought arises, as action follows from thought? What is the source of thought?

To analyze this carefully, we must first consider the basic characteristics of thought. We know that thought flows.

Therefore it must have energy. Thought is an impulse which can, to some extent, be detected and measured by sophisticated laboratory instruments.* Thus, one quality of thought is that it has energy, which enables it to flow.

Thought also takes a direction. A thought may lead us to the library or the bank. It may lead from confusion to understanding. With every thought the mind expresses a choice; it is a constant searchlight of attention. This directional, choosing aspect of the mind we could summarize as intelligence. A thought, then, flows because of energy, and that flow takes a direction because of intelligence. Energy and intelligence are thus fundamental to both action and thinking.

It is logical to assume that this energy and intelligence must have a source. From somewhere must come all the tremendous creative intelligence and energy which are constantly expressed in thought and action, which constantly maintain the human organism in all its complexity, keeping the body and mind functioning. Somewhere, at some intimate, fundamental level of life, even deeper than thinking, a virtually unlimited source of energy and intelligence must exist.

Where exactly would such a field lie? Where is it located, and how could we come into conscious contact with it?

Trees: A Brief Handbook for Gardeners

If there is a tree in our garden with no leaves or fruit or flowers growing on it, even though it is springtime, we don't go from branch to branch and try to force growth. We don't water each individual flower, prop up the branches, paint the leaves green. We water the root. Why? Because "in all the operations of nature, development is from within. A tree, that is nourished by the rain of heaven and the moisture of the earth, assimilates its nutriment, not through its outer bark, but through the pores of its inmost parts. On this account the

---

* *Cf.* the currently emerging knowledge about various sorts of brainwaves, indicating differing activity of the mind.

gardener waters, not the branches, but the roots." [10] The problem of each branch is solved by watering the root, by providing nourishment at the source of the structure of the tree.

For clearly the outer, obvious structure of the tree—the trunk, branches, leaves, flowers and fruit—depends for its existence and sustenance upon an inner, less obvious aspect: the vast and intricate root system that reaches far under ground, receiving nourishment and water from the soil and bringing it to all parts of the tree. It is this third aspect—the huge field of nourishment—which supports and gives rise to the whole life of the tree from beginning to end. This is the basis of the entire tree; trunk, leaves, fruit and flowers are all an expression of the pure sap, the nourishment that is drawn in from the soil. The roots, then, serve as a link between the source of nourishment and its expression in the outer tree.

"If you have in your garden an apple tree that is not bearing fruit," Paul Tournier wrote in his book *The Meaning of Persons*, "you don't accuse it of having a false attitude. Love of life is one of life's natural fruits. Nor do you try to manufacture apples; they have to grow of themselves. What you do is to put all your energies into looking after your apple tree . . . providing the conditions favourable to its life. The natural sap, the current of life, must be set in motion again. True liberation depends, then, on this welling up of life." [11]

The wise gardener waters the root. The tender root tips, in touch with the soil, draw the necessary nourishment, which is distributed to all parts of the tree. This process—putting the outer structure into coordination with the source of nourishment—allows the tree to reach its full development of beauty and usefulness.

Man's life has a similar structure: an outer field of action, an inner field of thought and an innermost source of thought. As we have seen, the quality of man's outer life—all his actions, achievements and relations with the world—is as dependent upon his inner life—his mind—as the tree is upon its roots. But just as the real life nourishment of the tree lies beyond the roots, in the soil, beyond the finest, deepest level of thinking is the origin of thought, a vast reservoir of energy and creative intelligence, the basis of all thought and action. By consciously tapping that source, Maharishi teaches, we can spontaneously bring its richness to all the areas of our lives.

The tree of a man's life is composed of various branches, such as family, occupation, health, friendship, education. All these aspects of life, rather than being a source of problems and suffering, should bloom like the fruit and flowers of a healthy tree. They should—and they can—blossom and grow to ripe fullness, making life a constant joy and a blessing to each individual and those around him.

The Old Testament beautifully describes such a life: "He is like a tree planted by streams of water, that yields its fruit in its season, and its leaf does not wither. In all that he does, he prospers." [12]

II. SCIENTIFIC REALITY

The Ocean of Mind

The technique of transcendental meditation is defined as a way of allowing the attention to go from the gross, surface level of ordinary thought to increasingly subtle levels, until finally the subtlest level is reached and then transcended. The meditator's attention goes beyond (transcend = to go beyond) the finest level of thought to the source of thought, the inner reservoir of energy and creative intelligence.

Maharishi compares the occurrence of thought in the mind to the rise of a bubble from the bottom of a pond. The bubble is very small at the bottom and grows as it rises, becoming increasingly large until it finally bursts at the surface. The mind, Maharishi explains, is like an ocean. "The surface layers of the mind function actively while the deeper levels remain silent. The functioning surface level of the ocean of mind is called the conscious mind . . . and it is at this level that thoughts are appreciated as thoughts." [13] Thought, at its source, is very subtle and refined. As it rises through the different levels of the mind, it becomes increasingly gross, until it is perceived at the ordinary thinking level. In TM the meditator begins on the surface level of ordinary thought and follows the thought through finer and finer stages to its source. The following diagram illustrates the process:

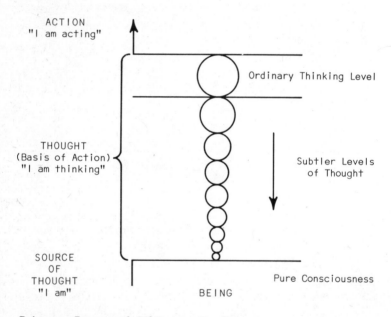

Science, Law and Ultimate Reality

Now let us define our terms more carefully. First of all, what are subtler or finer levels of thought?

All sciences begin their observations on the gross, surface level of life, the phenomenal, external aspects, and proceed toward the subtle. From the effect level to the causal level, from the surface level to the deeper levels is the direction of scientific investigation. From observing how a man walks and talks, we begin to look deeper within him, to his motivations, to the biological structure of his life, the chemical or genetic structure. A physicist begins on the surface level of an object and begins to look deeper, to the molecular level, atomic level, subatomic level. The goal of this search, in all sciences whether it be physics, chemistry, psychology, biology or botany, is to uncover the ultimate nature of life, to find out what life is, what man is, what the universe is, to locate the source, the stuff of creation.

The investigations of these sciences have revealed that there are different levels of creation, all present simultaneously. For instance, consider a leaf. It has a gross level, available to our sense perception. But we know that if we put it under a powerful microscope, we would discover that the leaf has a cellular level, utterly different from the gross, obvious level; finer than that, it has a molecular structure; going still deeper, we would arrive at the atomic level, then at a subatomic level, and so on. All these strata of creation coexist.

On one level we could say that the leaf, which seems to have certain dimensions and observable qualities, is really nothing but molecules. But penetrating deeper, the whole molecular structure dissolves and we could say that the true nature of the leaf is atoms in motion. And so on. At each level the perception is valid and correct. It does not invalidate the previous perception. The fact that there are atoms does not invalidate or preclude the existence of molecules or cells. But it does indicate that none of these levels of reality is the *ultimate* level—that these perceptions are not the ultimate perception of the essential nature of the object.

At the current stage of scientific knowledge we believe that the atomic level of life is omnipresent: it is present everywhere throughout material creation, at every moment, in ourselves and in every object, even though we are not ordinarily aware of it. It is only logical to assume that some level of life, finer than the finest levels of matter and energy, must be the ultimate, the source of all the tremendous energy and intelligence which give rise to the immensity of creation. This field, too, would be omnipresent, locatable in sun, sea, stone or flower, and, most importantly for our investigation, within man.

It is important to note that knowledge of each level of life has been and must be gained by extending our faculties of experience, our powers of direct perception. A theory may point to something, may suggest the existence of some law or level of life before it is verified by direct cognition, but it is only through direct perception, direct experience, that we can truly be said to know anything. This is the basis of science: empirical knowledge.

At this point it might be valuable to examine what we mean by experience and determine what the basic mechanics of experience are. Obviously, for any experience there must at least be a subject and an object, an experiencer and an object of experience—plus the faculties of perception which link the two. For instance, when I see or touch a table, I am the experiencer, or subject, and the table is the object of experience, brought to my awareness by the sense of sight or touch, through the nervous system and the brain. In the experience of a thought there is also the experiencer, who thinks, and the object of experience, the thought. For there are many thoughts, coming and going, but the thinker, I, remains. A thought, however subtle, is experienced just as is any of the more gross objects of manifest creation. A thought is just as much a part of reality as a leaf or a table, a subway or an elephant. If we could systematically reduce a thought to increasingly subtle levels just as we reduced the leaf to cells, molecules, etc., with our microscope, we would eventually arrive at the source of the thought.

And since thought is an energy impulse, a part of creation, it is at least conceivable that we could—by experiencing the subtle levels of a thought and then transcending the subtlest, finest level—directly perceive the ultimate constituent of reality. This field of life, as the source of all creation, the field from which all manifest creation rises, would undoubtedly have to be an unlimited ocean of energy, creative potential, intelligence and power.

We know this first of all from our consideration of the nature of thought, where we concluded that the origin or source of thought must be a field of unlimited energy and intelligence. And secondly, even the most superficial analysis of the nature of life must conclude that the basis or source of life must also possess these qualities in abundance. We know that energy is present everywhere; science has revealed that everything we once thought of as matter is nothing but "formless" energy. Even a rock, which seems to be the epitome of inertia and inactivity, is, we know, humming with tremendous energy and activity if we examine it on a subtler level. Excite the atomic structure of some "inert" rock, such as uranium, and you can produce an explosion of immense magnitude. So energy is found everywhere, even in the apparently lifeless aspects of creation; and the more deeply we penetrate, the more powerful is that energy.

We also know that life expresses intelligence on all levels. Everything proceeds according to law, from the motions of the galaxies to the motions of the electrons in their orbits. Apricot seeds do not grow into Chevrolets, nor do flowers spring fully formed out of the air, then turn to a bud, and then to a seed. There is an order, an intelligible structure, on all levels of creation. (This is the underlying assumption of science: that there *are* laws, which can be discerned and then applied.) This ordering aspect of life we summarize as intelligence.

Because everything, even at the minutest level, proceeds according to order and law, we must assume that the deepest level of life, the source of life or basis of creation, must be a source of intelligence just as it must be a source of energy. And because it underlies and gives rise to the whole complex and immense creation in all its diversity, its creative potential and power must be virtually unlimited.

"All This Is That"

Maharishi Mahesh Yogi calls this the field of Being, or pure creative intelligence. A thorough discussion of the nature of Being can be found in the first section of Maharishi's book, *The Science of Being and Art of Living.** Maharishi defines Being as pure, unmanifest existence, which underlies all that exists. Absolute and eternal in nature, the field of creative intelligence expresses itself in every form as the basis of all manifestation, just as hydrogen and oxygen, stable and unchanging, appear as water, ice or steam, or as the same pure sap expresses itself as the hard bark, the green leaf, the tender petal.

Everything in the relative field of life, the world of ever-changing phenomena with which we are all familiar, is nothing but various manifestations of Being, which is absolute and unchanging. There is a famous saying in the Upanishads which expresses this fact: "I am That, Thou art That, all this is nothing but That."

In the light of what modern physics tells us about the structure of life, such a statement is far from extreme. We know that there are subtler levels of life, yet the knowledge of these subtler levels does not invalidate the reality of the more obvious aspects. We still speak quite freely about tables and chairs, knowing all along that they are composed of molecules, atoms and subatomic particles, and that they are really over 90 percent empty space. Similarly, with the knowledge of Being, we can still speak of all the changing phenomena of life as real, but we can also begin to understand—and to experience—that Being is the essential constituent of all that is. Just as it is perfectly sensible to say that the atomic or subatomic level of life is omnipresent—locatable deep

---

* International SRM Publications, 1966. Available from SIMS-IMS National Center, or any SIMS-IMS center throughout the world. (See Appendix C.)

within the structure of anything in creation—we can at least intellectually accept the possibility of a still deeper, *deepest* level of life, which we could call Being.

According to Maharishi's definition, this field of pure creative intelligence is the source and basis of all creation, the source of all thought. Although it is present throughout creation, in its pure, unmanifest essence it lies beyond the realm of relative experience, subtler than the subtlest field of life, inaccessible to ordinary perception.* That is why it is said to be "transcendental," and the technique of experiencing it is thus termed "transcendental meditation."

Maharishi also refers to this field as pure consciousness, the basis of all experience. For clearly consciousness must underlie all experience. All experience, whether it be external or internal, happy or unhappy, implies an experiencer, a conscious being. In order to be happy, to be sad, in order to be aware of this or that, we have to be conscious. (We also have to *be*—the first, most fundamental aspect of life, before thought, feeling, speaking or acting, is *being*.) This field of Being or pure consciousness is what we locate when we trace a thought to its source. This is what Maharishi means by the knower, the subject or pure consciousness, the innermost level of one's own Self or Being.

Why is it that we do not ordinarily experience Being if it is the essential nature of the mind? Maharishi answers that it is because our attention is always projected outward through the senses. The mind, as pure consciousness, is the experiencer and does not experience itself. It is like the eye, which sees all the changing phenomena of the world—movement and play of light and shadow, form and color, all the drama of life—yet does not see itself. Although it lies at the root of all existence, Being, consciousness, is not ordinarily perceived in its purity.

---

* Just as, to experience the sap, we must go beyond the outer structure of the leaf or petal, or to experience the hydrogen and oxygen we must penetrate deeper than the surface phenomenon of the water or ice.

But throughout the ages, great philosophers and seers of the truth of life have experienced the field of creative intelligence and given us a record of their experiences. The idea that "the Kingdom of Heaven is within you" is certainly not a new one. Several beautiful, poetic descriptions of this ultimate field of life appear in an ancient Chinese classic, the *Tao Teh Ching,* where the word "Tao" (sometimes translated as the "Way") may be equated with Being.

> There was something formless yet complete,
> That existed before heaven and earth;
> Without sound, without substance,
> Dependent on nothing, unchanging,
> All-pervading, unfailing.
> One may think of it as the mother
>   of all things under heaven.[14]

> Tao is all-pervading, and its use is inexhaustible!
> Fathomless!
> Like the fountainhead of all things.[15]

> It is there within us all the while;
> Draw upon it as you will, it never runs dry.[16]

An extremely beautiful expression of the ultimate nature of life, of Being, is given by the American poet Walt Whitman:

> O Thou transcendent,
> Nameless, the fibre and the breath,
> Light of the light, shedding forth universes, thou
>   centre of them,
> Thou mightier centre of the true, the good, the loving,
> Thou moral, spiritual fountain—affection's source—
>   thou reservoir,
>
> .   .   .   .
>
> Thou pulse—thou motive of the stars, suns, systems,
> That, circling, move in order, safe, harmonious,
> Athwart the shapeless vastnesses of space,

How should I think, how breathe a single breath,
how speak, if, out of myself,
I could not launch, to those, superior universes? [17]

In the preface to his translation of the Bhagavad Gita,
Maharishi speaks of this level of Being and what happens to
human life when the knowledge of this essential field of life
is lost:

> The omnipresence of eternal Being, unmanifested and
> absolute; Its status as That, even in the manifested diver-
> sity of creation; and the possibility of the realization
> of Being by any man in terms of himself—these are
> the great truths of the perennial philosophy of the
> Vedas. . . .
> The truth . . . is by its very nature independent of
> time and can therefore never be lost. When, however,
> man's vision becomes one-sided and he is caught by the
> binding influence of the phenomenal world to the exclu-
> sion of the absolute phase of Reality, when he is thus
> confined within the ever-changing phases of existence, his
> life loses stability and he begins to suffer. When suffering
> grows, the invincible force of nature moves to set man's
> vision right and establish a way of life which will again
> fulfill the high purpose of his existence.[18]

III. TWO HUNDRED PERCENT OF LIFE

> Man is born to live a perfect life, encompas-
> sing the values of the transcendental Absolute—
> unlimited energy, intelligence, power, peace and
> bliss—together with the unlimited values of the
> world of multiplicity in relative existence.
> —MAHARISHI MAHESH YOGI

Thus, man's life has two aspects, the inner, unmanifest, unchanging, pure field of Being, and the outer, ever-changing
field of activity and experience. The outer without the inner
is like a building without a foundation, weak and baseless.

But what good is the foundation without the building? Wherever a man may live, whatever his goals may be, if he is to gain fulfillment, he must gain it by living both these aspects of his life simultaneously.

We have seen that just as the growth of a tree is dependent upon its hidden, inner aspect, so the growth and success of man's life depends on his inner development, his state of consciousness. It is timeless wisdom. One great teacher expressed it this way: "Seek ye first the Kingdom of Heaven and all else shall be added unto you." It is only because we have had no way to reach the "Kingdom of Heaven," no maps locating it, no guide, no vehicle, that so many of us have failed to arrive. Intellectually, many of us have a good idea of how we want to live. But the *idea* of water will not quench our thirst. The idea of how we want to live does not guarantee us the ability to live that way.

"So often we find in our particular civilization this curious assumption that exhortations and commands will of themselves help you to obey those exhortations and implement your good intentions," Aldous Huxley pointed out. "In fact, however, they don't, and you have to propose at the same time means by which to fulfill them." [19] As Meister Eckhart said, "People should think less about what they ought to do and more about what they ought to be. If only their being were good, their works would shine forth brightly."

The Natural Tendency

The purpose of transcendental meditation, then, is to connect the outer field of activity with the unbounded potentiality of the inner man, for the purpose of enriching all aspects of life. TM is not a philosophy or a religion, but a practical technique. The success of the technique, Maharishi explains, is that it utilizes the powerful natural tendency of the mind to move always in the direction of greater happiness.

As we have seen, all of life exhibits a progressive tendency, a movement toward fulfillment. The desire for more, for evolution, is grounded in the nature of life. It is the basis of all growth and progress.

We experience the functioning of this natural tendency of the mind countless times a day. For example, a student sitting over a boring textbook finds his mind spontaneously drifting to an interesting conversation, a song from down the hall, a thought of a weekend excursion. A man sitting in his living room listening to music hears a more beautiful melody coming from another room; his attention shifts to enjoy the more charming melody. No effort is needed to turn the attention; it shifts automatically to a field of greater enjoyment. The technique of TM utilizes this natural tendency of the mind. Just as the attention will shift from one melody to a more pleasing one, effortlessly and spontaneously, so the mind will experience increasingly more subtle states of thought if it is given the opportunity. TM provides that situation.

The habit of the mind has been to search outside, to be turned toward external objects of experience in its search for happiness. But our own experience tells us that nothing in the relative, ever-changing field of life is sufficient to give the mind the satisfaction it is seeking. This generation has discovered that the material surface of life is not enough. We may have all the money, cars, houses in the world: it does not satisfy us. A film or some beautiful music, a face or a sunset may hold our attention for a while, but soon the mind becomes restless, discontented. It wanders off again in search of something more.

As other great teachers have said before him, Maharishi explains that only within, in the unchanging field of life which he calls Being (or "bliss-consciousness") will the mind find fulfillment of its quest. Only Being, an unbounded ocean of energy, creative intelligence and happiness, a field of eternal fullness, nonchanging and absolute, can satisfy the mind.

In order to experience the field of Being, states Maharishi, it is only necessary to take a correct angle and allow the attention to move within. The laws of our own nature carry us to fulfillment. He likens the process to diving into a pool of water. The diver only needs to take a correct angle and then let go. The laws of nature—in this case gravity—complete the dive. Similarly, during the process of TM, the mind, motivated by its own natural tendency to move in the direction of the infinite—that is, toward ever-increasing happiness and satisfaction—is drawn by the increasing charm of subtler levels of awareness, until it reaches the field of pure creative intelligence.

"The ability is there," says Maharishi. "The field of the Absolute Being is there. It is only necessary to begin to experience it. The only one thing to be done is, transcendental meditation to be added as a part of the daily routine. That is all." [20] The entire process is spontaneous and automatic. The mind goes inward to experience the unity of life, and it comes out to enjoy the multiplicity of relative creation, enhanced by the values of the inner Absolute.

In this way the two wings of life, the relative and the Absolute, are brought together. The eternally seeking nature of man finds its fulfillment in the eternally unchanging, innermost essence of what we are. Thus the technique is entirely natural and based on the very structure of life.

This union of the two sides of life, the ever-changing and the never-changing, the limited and the unbounded, is the accomplishment of Yoga in the true sense of the word. "Yoga" is a Sanskrit word which means "union"—the union of the Absolute and the relative. This integration of life's inner and outer phases is an effortless process, involving neither concentration nor control.

TM: How You Do It, How You Don't

Before being instructed in TM, many people feel that it must be something very difficult, demanding powerful concentration. Nothing could be further from the truth. Those who have advocated techniques of concentration or control have not, Maharishi asserts, fully understood the nature of the mind. They observed the mind wandering, but did not grasp that it was wandering in search of fulfillment. If we observed the wanderings of a honeybee from flower to flower, without realizing that it wanders to find nectar, in order to make honey, we might conclude that it just flies around aimlessly. Similarly the mind does not just move about aimlessly —the mind only wanders, in search of greater happiness, until it is fulfilled. Efforts to control or fix the attention are difficult and unnatural; in fact, they are difficult *because* they are unnatural. The process of TM is so natural and automatic that conscious effort only hampers its success.

"What I am emphasizing," Maharishi said once, "is the possibility of elimination of stress and strain, worries and suffering from daily life, and that *with the material with which everyone is born*. I am saying that the mind is wandering by nature because it is progressive under the impulse of evolution induced by the cosmic intelligence responsible for the creation and evolution of everything. This tendency of the mind to flow toward more and more growth, toward fulfillment, is quite enough for the mind to meet the pool of Bliss lying within. Integration of outer and inner aspects of life is brought about in a natural way and therefore no one needs to suffer in life." [21]

Because TM is a spontaneous process of direct perception, faith or belief is irrelevant. Whether a man is a believer or a skeptic, if he follows the directions of the teacher, the process works, quite automatically. Because the technique is also not a process of contemplation or of rational, intellectual thought, no particular background helps or hinders the process. In distinguishing TM from techniques of contemplation, Maharishi points out that contemplation—thinking about some topic, perhaps an elevating one such as God or love— only utilizes whatever small portion of the mind is already available to us. It is like swimming on the surface of the ocean of mind. TM is a *vertical* process, opening the awareness to deeper levels of the mind. It is like diving to the depths of the ocean.

The technique, then, involves neither contemplation nor concentration, nor is it based on one's acceptance of any ideas or philosophy. It is not religious and is not helped or hindered by skepticism or faith in its efficacy. It is just a practice, natural, simple and innocent, utilizing the natural tendency of the mind to move in the direction of greater enjoyment. Because this tendency is present in everyone, any individual can practice TM with success and enjoy its benefits.

However, although it is easy, the technique is a highly specialized and delicate process, which must be learned from a qualified instructor, trained by Maharishi himself. The practice involves thinking a specific sound, called a "mantra," chosen for each individual at the time of instruction. During TM the mantra is used as the object of attention. Mantras have no meaning to the meditator, but the sound quality is conducive to producing the deep rest and refined awareness characteristic of TM.

Maharishi defines a mantra as "a sound, the effects of which are known." It is common knowledge that different sounds have different effects. Sound waves, being a physical reality, strike against objects of creation, fall upon the human nervous system and have various effects, some positive, some negative. Some sounds can shatter glass; some music can be soothing, some can make us want to get up and dance. Recent scientific investigation has found that different music played to plants under controlled conditions where factors such as temperature, nourishment and light were equivalent produced different effects: some music accelerated growth, other music actually killed the plants.[22] The proper mantra given to an individual produces effects which are life-supporting on every level.

"Because individuals differ in the quality of the vibrations which constitute their individual personalities," Maharishi explains, "the right selection of a thought for a particular individual is of vital importance." [23] During their advanced course of instruction, teachers of TM are trained in "the art of selecting a sound or word to correspond to the special quality of the individual." [24] Just as a doctor analyzes the blood of an individual to determine the correct blood-type before he gives a transfusion, the teacher of TM evaluates certain specific criteria, ascertained during an interview with the prospective meditator, before he selects the appropriate mantra.

The mantra must be suitable for the individual, and its use must be properly imparted, in a step-by-step procedure determined by the rate of progress of each individual. "The practice of transcendental meditation has to be imparted by personal instruction," Maharishi explains. "It cannot be imparted through a book." [25] The nature of the technique, and differences in the rate of learning of each person, require that the guide be present at every step of the way, to ensure that the technique is learned correctly.

After the two introductory lectures and an interview with a teacher, the actual course of instruction in TM consists of four one-and-a-half-hour sessions over four consecutive days. On the first day of the course the basic elements of the technique are imparted. The individual learns enough to meditate successfully on his own. In the subsequent sessions further instructions are given, based on the new meditator's experiences in meditation. The correctness of his practice is verified, and a more thorough explanation of the mechanics of the process is given, based on his direct experience. On the final day a brief vision of the ultimate goals of meditation is offered, and an invitation is extended to participate in advanced lectures and group meditations once the course is over. The four-day course provides an individual with sufficient knowledge and experience to meditate on his own, but he is urged to have his meditation periodically checked by a qualified meditation guide to insure that his progress is as rapid as possible and that maximum benefits are being derived from the practice.

Once again, it is important to emphasize that TM can be learned only through the personal guidance of a trained teacher. Information about where the technique can be learned can be obtained from any of the major world-plan centers listed in Appendix C.

The Forgetful Millionaire

> The current interest in transcendental meditation represents the increasing need of man to find a way to live a more fulfilling life. He feels increasingly restricted in his progress, and the ways that for centuries have been offered have failed to remove the restrictions.
>
> —JERRY JARVIS

Maharishi speaks of his work as a revival of the knowledge of life. What he means is that man has forgotten about the underlying, infinite nature of his life, thereby losing the dignity and stature which are rightfully his. Our image of what man is, our ideals of life are severely limited by our restricted knowledge of what we really are, what we can be, what we can know and accomplish. To discover that within every one of us is an infinite ocean of energy, intelligence, creativity, peace and happiness is invaluable.

But even more than this, Maharishi emphasizes that what is of most significance in his message is not the words or concepts, but the technique of transcendental meditation, which is a practical method by which any man can make these glorious concepts a *living reality*. Without the technique, the words would be a torment, as they have been for centuries: if we are told again and again that within us is the Kingdom of Heaven, that God is merciful and good, and yet we continue to suffer and feel miserable and unfulfilled, eventually we will grow skeptical of such claims. We may have faith and belief and hope; yet, if we continue to suffer, even that faith is lost. For surely, some experience is required to justify faith, to give it validity. How could we have faith in the light switch if every time we pressed it, the room remained in darkness?

This is why the technique of TM is the important aspect

of Maharishi's teaching: it requires no faith, no belief, no adherence to any philosophy; "faith" in the efficacy of the practice is a *result* of gaining its benefits in daily life. Without these effects, faith would be unwarranted and baseless.

"By not using his full potential," Maharishi writes, "man is unable to fulfill the purpose of his life. He suffers in many ways because he is not using the full conscious capacity of his mind or the great energy he carries within himself. He is not experiencing and expressing in his life the abundance of absolute bliss that he naturally possesses, the absolute field of creativity and power that lies within himself. He is like a millionaire who has forgotten his wealth and position and goes begging in the street.

"All suffering is due to ignorance of a way to unfold the divine glory which is present within oneself." [26] This "way," the technique of transcendental meditation, if adopted by humanity on a wide scale, could, Maharishi believes, render suffering obsolete in this generation.

CHAPTER 2

The Psychobiology of Consciousness

I have so much *more* energy now, I feel like Superman.

—STUDENT MEDITATOR

I. SCIENTIFIC RESEARCH ON TM

States of Consciousness

"For thousands of years men have speculated about the nature of human consciousness. Only within the last 50 years, however, have scientists gained the technical ability to describe the physiological and biochemical correlates of states of consciousness. This ability has enabled them better to understand the processes and the neural structures which underlie these states." [1]

So begins Robert Keith Wallace's *The Physiological Effects of Transcendental Meditation,* a landmark in scientific inquiry and in man's knowledge of himself and the possibilities of human experience. Wallace was the first American scientist to undertake an extensive examination of the state of consciousness experienced in TM. His findings, published in such authoritative journals as *Science, Scientific American, American Journal of Physiology* and elsewhere, suggest the potential applications of TM to human life and health.

Wallace's work is based upon previous research in what might be called the "psychobiology of consciousness." As a result of studies made in this century, we now know that for every state of mind there is a corresponding physical state of the human nervous system. Physiological psychology has demonstrated that when the mind is in a particular state of consciousness, the body and nervous system are set to a corresponding style of functioning. "Time was," writes Wilder Penfield, neurophysiologist at the Montreal Neurological Institute, "when the brain was considered to be the 'organ of the mind,' functioning as a whole during all conscious states. Such a point of view is no longer tenable. . . . We are differently conscious from moment to moment, and concomitant with that there is a differing pattern of neuron activation." [2]

When we are awake, metabolic rate, heart rate, cardiac output, etc., are within a certain range, and brain waves appear in certain patterns on the electroencephalograph (EEG). When we fall asleep, metabolic rate drops, heart rate and cardiac output decrease, and brain waves change. During dreaming another unique set of physiological correlates arises. Each shift in the state of consciousness is accompanied by a shift of biochemical functions of the body. If these physiological activities are monitored (using EEG, EKG * etc.), a physiologist can tell, even if he cannot see the person under examination, whether the individual is sleeping, dreaming or awake.

Until 15 or 20 years ago physiologists recognized only two states of consciousness, waking and sleeping. Dreaming was considered merely a variation of the sleep state. Extensive investigation of the dream state, however, revealed the magnitude of changes which took place: different brain-wave patterns, rapid eye movements, increased metabolic rate, etc. Dreaming came to be accepted as a third major state of consciousness. [3]

Demetri Kanellakos, senior research engineer at Stanford Research Institute in California, in a paper presented at Stanford University on January 27, 1970, summarized the situation as follows:

---

* Electrocardiograph.

The human nervous system can exist in different states and can change from one state to another state in a short time. For each of the major states of the human nervous system, a different set of physiological and biochemical conditions exist. The major states of the nervous system that have been suggested up to now are (1) the wakefulness state; (2) the state of deep sleep; and (3) the dreaming state.[4]

In light of these findings on consciousness and its physiological correlates, it is clear that, if the experience of transcendental meditation is real and not illusory, if it is significantly different from the ordinary experiences of life, its reality and its uniqueness should be scientifically verifiable. Is TM based on faith and belief, is it a mood, or is it a unique state of awareness, a direct and valid perception, with measurable effects and significant implications?

A Wakeful Hypometabolic State, or, TM, O_2, EEG, GSR and the MDs

Dr. R. K. Wallace, writing in the March 27, 1970, issue of *Science,* reported the study he conducted at UCLA Medical School, in which

> oxygen consumption, heart rate, skin resistance, and electroencephalograph measurements were recorded before, during, and after subjects practiced a technique called transcendental meditation. There were significant changes between the control period and the meditation period in all measurements. During meditation, oxygen consumption and heart rate decreased, skin resistance increased, and the electroencephalogram showed specific changes in certain frequencies. These results seem to distinguish the state produced by transcendental meditation from commonly encountered states of consciousness and suggest that it may have practical applications.[5]

In his conclusion Dr. Wallace remarked that "physiologically, the state produced by transcendental meditation seems to be distinct from commonly encountered states of consciousness, such as wakefulness, sleep, and dreaming, and from altered states of consciousness, such as hypnosis and autosuggestion." [6] In his Ph.D. thesis Wallace referred to TM as a "proposed fourth major state of consciousness."

This is a very provocative proposal—it suggests that the human nervous system is capable of setting itself to function in such a way that an individual can experience an entirely new state of consciousness, as different from ordinary experience as the waking state is from deep sleep.

Wallace's conclusions stem from the dramatic changes which he and Dr. Herbert Benson of Harvard Medical School, who collaborated with Wallace on further studies in 1970 and 1971, found taking place during TM.* Wallace and Benson found that "oxygen consumption decreased in all subjects within 5 minutes after the onset of meditation. The mean decrease was about 45 cm^3/min, or *about a 20 percent decrease* from the control period." [8] In the *American Journal of Physiology* Drs. Benson, Wallace and Wilson reported that "after 6–7 hours of sleep . . . O_2 consumption usually decreases about 15%." [9] This means that the metabolic rate, or the rate at which the system consumes energy, is more sharply reduced during TM than during sleep. This occurs within five to ten minutes, rather than after six or seven hours. (See Figures I and II.)

Wallace found that during TM "there is a mean decrease in cardiac output of about 25%," whereas "during sleep there

---

* The tests were conducted as follows: "During each test the subject served as his own control, spending part of the session in meditation and part in a normal, nonmeditative state. Devices for continuous measurement of blood pressure, heart rate, rectal temperature, skin resistance and electroencephalographic events were attached to the subject, and during the period of measurement samples were taken at 10-minute intervals for analysis of oxygen consumption, carbon dioxide elimination and other parameters. The subjects sat in a chair. After a 30-minute period of habituation, measurements were started and continued for three periods: 20 to 30 minutes of a quiet, premeditative state, then 20 to 30 minutes of meditation, and finally 20 to 30 minutes after the subject was asked to stop meditating." [7]

FIGURE I

LEVELS OF REST

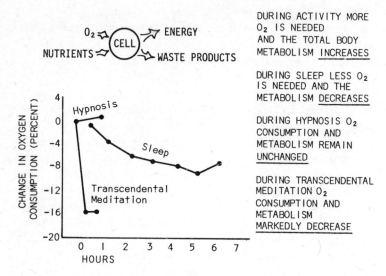

DURING ACTIVITY MORE O_2 IS NEEDED AND THE TOTAL BODY METABOLISM INCREASES

DURING SLEEP LESS O_2 IS NEEDED AND THE METABOLISM DECREASES

DURING HYPNOSIS O_2 CONSUMPTION AND METABOLISM REMAIN UNCHANGED

DURING TRANSCENDENTAL MEDITATION O_2 CONSUMPTION AND METABOLISM MARKEDLY DECREASE

Adapted from "The Physiology of Meditation" by Robert Keith Wallace and Herbert Benson. Copyright © 1972 by Scientific American, Inc. All rights reserved.

is a mean decrease in cardiac output of about 20%." [10] Also, "The heart rate of each of the subjects decreased during meditation, with a mean decrease of 5 beats per minute." [11]

Skin resistance increased markedly. The GSR * showed an average increase of about 250 percent during TM, going as high as 500 percent, as opposed to a 100 percent to 200 percent increase during sleep.[12] (See Figure III.) This is an interesting measurement. The GSR is commonly used in the "lie detector" test. It measures how easily an electrical current passes across the skin, usually on the palm of the hand. When a person is relaxed, the skin is dry and the current passes relatively slowly. The resistance to its flow is high. When ten-

---

* Galvanic skin resistance.

sion increases, sweating occurs; because of the moisture, the resistance drops; the current moves more easily. High GSR indicates a high level of relaxation and calm. TM, because it produces such a deep state of rest and relaxation, naturally produces a high GSR, higher even than deep sleep.

Further GSR studies indicate that meditators are less irritable and jittery than nonmeditators. The GSR amplitude

FIGURE II

EFFECT OF MEDITATION on the subjects' oxygen consumption (*black*) and carbon dioxide elimination (*broken line*) was recorded in 20 and 15 cases respectively. After the subjects were invited to meditate both rates decreased markedly (*gray area*). Consumption and elimination returned to the premeditation level soon after the subjects stopped meditating.

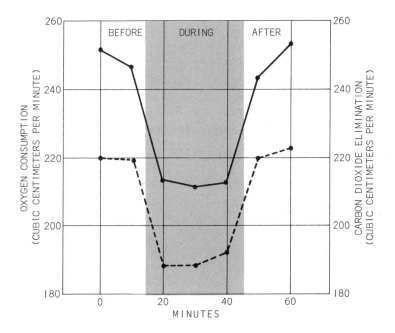

From "The Physiology of Meditation" by Robert Keith Wallace and Herbert Benson. Copyright © 1972 by Scientific American, Inc. All rights reserved.

FIGURE III

SKIN RESISTANCE

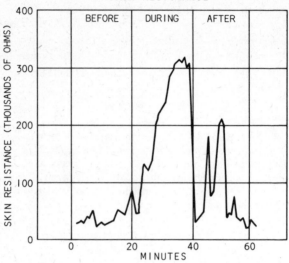

DURING TRANSCENDENTAL MEDITATION SUBJECTS
SHOWED AN INCREASE IN SKIN RESISTANCE
UP TO 500%

DURING STRESS OR ANXIETY
SKIN RESISTANCE
DECREASES

DURING SLEEP
SKIN RESISTANCE
INCREASES MODERATELY

DURING TRANSCENDENTAL
MEDITATION
SKIN RESISTANCE
INCREASES MARKEDLY

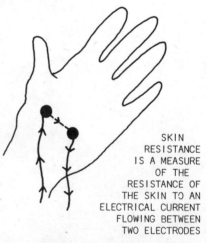

SKIN
RESISTANCE
IS A MEASURE
OF THE
RESISTANCE OF
THE SKIN TO AN
ELECTRICAL CURRENT
FLOWING BETWEEN
TWO ELECTRODES

typically shows a sharp decrease for a few seconds and then returns to normal when a person is subjected to a sudden unexpected stress, such as a loud noise. But if the stress is repeated often enough, eventually one "habituates"—he gets used to it and stops reacting. Generally the calmer a person is, the more quickly he habituates to a repeated stress that he knows to be harmless. Dr. David Orme-Johnson of the University of Texas, El Paso, subjected a group of meditators and nonmeditators to repeated loud noises of about the level of those of a boiler factory. The meditators habituated after far fewer repetitions than did the nonmeditators. It took the nonmeditators a mean of 26.1 repetitions to stop producing corresponding changes in their GSR amplitude, while the meditators habituated after a mean of 11 such trials.

Also indicative of a person's general anxiety level are the number of spontaneous changes he produces in his GSR amplitude during a period when he is sitting quietly and not exposed to any environmental stresses at all. Under these conditions individuals produce an average of 35 spontaneous GSR changes in ten minutes. Meditators produced fewer than ten. Furthermore, Dr. Orme-Johnson found that when he took some of the subjects who had produced the greatest number of GSRs per unit time and had them instructed in the practice of TM, they went down to 10 to 15 GSRs in a ten-minute period within a few days after they had started meditation.[13]

This relaxation is shown in another measurement. A 1969 study, "The Biochemistry of Anxiety," showed that a high concentration of lactate ion in the blood can produce anxiety symptoms in normal individuals, and that it regularly produces such symptoms in persons with a known history of anxiety neurosis.[14] During TM the blood-lactate concentration was found to decrease an average of 33 percent and to remain low for a considerable length of time thereafter.[15] (See Figure IV.) Wallace and Benson note that "it is significant that patients with hyper-tension . . . show higher blood-lactate levels in a resting state than patients without hypertension, whereas in contrast the low lactate level in transcen-

FIGURE IV

RAPID DECLINE in the concentration of blood lactate is apparent following the invitation to start meditating (*gray area*). Lactate is produced by anaerobic metabolism, mainly in muscle tissue. Its concentration normally falls in a subject at rest, but the rate of decline during meditation proved to be more than three times faster than the normal rate.

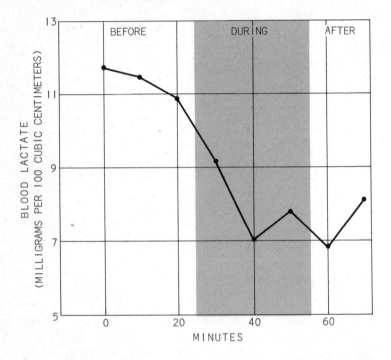

dental meditators is associated with low blood pressure. All in all, it is reasonable to hypothesize that the low level of lactate found in subjects during and after transcendental meditation may be responsible in part for the meditators' thoroughly relaxed state." [16]

Another unique finding of these researchers concerns brain-

FIGURE V

INCREASE IN INTENSITY of "slow" alpha waves, at eight to
nine cycles per second, was evident during meditation (*gray area*)
in electroencephalograph readings of the subjects' frontal and
central brain regions. This is a representative subject's frontal
reading. Before meditation most subjects' frontal readings showed
alpha waves of lower intensity.

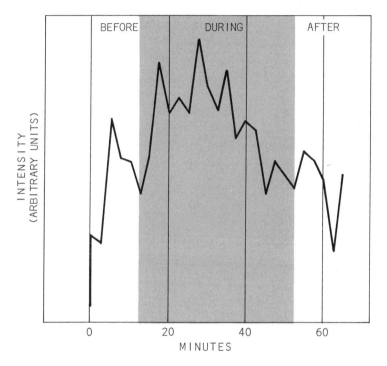

From "The Physiology of Meditation" by Robert Keith Wallace and
Herbert Benson. Copyright © 1972 by Scientific American, Inc. All
rights reserved.

wave patterns. At rest, with eyes closed, most individuals
show alpha wave activity of the brain. Alpha waves seem to
indicate a relaxed, comfortable state of mind and body. All
studies on TM have found that the regularity and amplitude
of the alpha waves increased during TM in all subjects tested.

(See Figure V.) In some individuals, lower-frequency alpha waves and low-voltage theta waves appeared.[17]

These patterns are similar to those reported by other investigators as occurring in expert Zen meditators of 15–20 years' practice,[18] yet they appeared in TM meditators of only a few weeks' time.

In their *Scientific American* article Benson and Wallace ask, "How do the physiological changes during meditation compare with those in other relaxed states, such as sleep and hypnosis?" Their answer: "There is little resemblance." [19] In addition to the differences in metabolic activity already mentioned, the EEG patterns occurring during TM clearly distinguish this state from sleeping or dreaming. There are no slow (delta) waves, sleep spindles, or REM * activity; rather, alpha-wave activity predominates.[20]

The physiological state attained in TM is also different from states induced by hypnosis or autosuggestion. Studies of hypnosis show no consistent pattern. Even in cases where complete relaxation has been suggested, no noticeable decrease in oxygen consumption occurs, as opposed to the 20 percent decrease observed during TM.[21] The EEG patterns during hypnosis are usually identical to wakefulness patterns, although they are markedly different during TM.[22]

There has been a great deal of recent interest in biofeedback procedures, notably for the conditioning of alpha-wave production. Dr. Wallace points out that such procedures (along with hypnosis) "seem to produce altered substates of wakefulness or to involve selectively controlling and manipulating a particular aspect of the organism. The waking, dreaming, sleeping *and transcendental* states may be distinguished from these other states because of the unique and well-integrated combination of physiological changes which occurs during these four major states of consciousness." [23]

In other words, manipulation or effort to control one physiological function, such as breathing or alpha activity, could conceivably cause strain and create an imbalance in the sys-

---

* Rapid eye movement.

tem, as opposed to the balanced, integrated style of functioning characteristic of a natural state of consciousness. There may be a danger inherent in singling out one effect (alpha waves occur as the *result* of relaxation) and trying to turn it into a cause. Conversely, "The physiologic changes during transcendental meditation," Benson and Wallace comment, occurred spontaneously and "simultaneously and without the use of specific feedback procedures." [24]

For many of us the word "meditation" might imply a sort of passivity, something not particularly lively in nature. Two researchers at the University of Texas in Austin tested this hypothesis. They gave a standard reaction-time test to a sampling of meditators and nonmeditators. (Reaction time, by measuring the speed of response to a given stimulus, gauges the alertness of mind and the coordination of mind and body.) They found that the transcendental meditators had a consistently faster reaction time—by about 30 percent—than the nonmeditators.

The meditators were then asked to meditate for 20 minutes while the nonmeditators were simply to close their eyes and rest. The tests were administered again. The nonmeditators reacted *more slowly* than before their rest period, by about ten percent. The meditators' speed *improved* by about 15 percent. This indicates that merely closing the eyes and resting can be dulling to the mind, whereas the dynamic process of TM is enlivening and refreshing, producing greater awareness and alertness. [25] (See Figure VI.)

The Value of Rest

Naturally, all these significant physiological changes have their effects on individuals practicing TM. Kanellakos [26] mentions increased tranquillity and relaxation, coupled with decreased mental and physical tension; increased energy and efficiency; elimination of such stress-caused symptoms as insomnia, worry and poor posture, resulting in better and less sleep and a sense of well-being; loss of desire for (or complete elimination of) the use of tobacco, alcohol, hallucino-

FIGURE VI

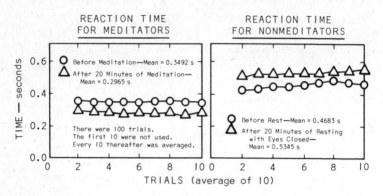

SOURCE: R. Shaw and D. Kolb (1971)

genic and depressant drugs, etc., and improved health, i.e., decreased susceptibility to disease.

In his doctoral thesis Dr. Wallace reported a questionnaire answered by 394 individuals practicing TM, of whom 117 noted fewer colds, 29 fewer headaches, 19 a decrease in allergic reactions, seven an improvement in hypertension conditions, and 84 an improvement or cure of miscellaneous problems such as overweight, acne, asthma, ulcers, insomnia and multiple sclerosis; 333 noted an improvement in mental health, and 22 had been able to discontinue psychiatric treatment as a result of the beneficial effects of TM.[27]

The significant factor in producing these changes is the deep state of rest enjoyed during TM. We know from personal experience the value of rest as the basis of activity; we know that if we don't get enough sleep, we become tired and less alert, which results in reduced enjoyment and decreased efficiency of functioning. Deep sleep allows the body to throw off fatigue, tension and stress, and allows the system to rejuvenate itself so that it can function better during the waking state. Without sleep, this rejuvenation could not take place, the body would rapidly deteriorate and the person would soon die.

During dreaming other processes take place which relieve the *mind* of stress and tension. Experiments with dream deprivation have shown that a person needs to dream. If he is denied dreaming, he rapidly develops psychotic symptoms, such as hallucination, disorientation and uncoordinated mental activity. Apparently, the physiological and biochemical changes which occur during TM "relieve the strains and stresses accumulated on the nervous system itself more efficiently than during either dreaming or sleeping." [28] It seems that more sensitive areas of the nervous system are enlivened and rejuvenated by TM. Thus, deprivation of the state of transcending leaves the nervous system filled with deep-rooted stresses which deprive a man of the opportunity to use his full range of capabilities. As a result, he feels unfulfilled. TM, by providing the depth of rest necessary to dissolve accumulated stress, allows for greater efficiency of functioning and hence greater enjoyment of life.

Kanellakos, using an example he borrowed from Dr. Vanselow of Kiel University, writes, in an unpublished essay:

> For example, suppose I am crossing a street and suddenly a car comes hurtling at me out of nowhere, screeching on its brakes and stopping a few inches before it hits me. My heart begins to beat fast. I sweat. Adrenalin and cholesterol rush through my whole system preparing me to flee from danger. But there is no reason to run. The car didn't hit me after all. So I just walk on. However, my nervous system was overwhelmed with sensory inputs and a lot of strain was stored biochemically in the nerves—in the same way that information is stored in a computer. That part of my nervous system in which this stress is stored is no longer available for me to use. Furthermore, let's say that two weeks later I am sitting in my living room reading the paper and a car outside slams on its brakes. The stored memory of the earlier experience, triggered by the outside noise, causes my heart to beat fast and my adrenalin and cholesterol to rush through my system, just as it did before. It is twenty minutes before I can settle back to

reading my paper again. This not only wastes time and energy; it also stores *new* strain in my nervous system.

The more dramatic the experience, the more deeply it is stored in the nervous system—on more unconscious, sensitive, and subtle levels, where the rest gained from sleep and dreaming cannot get at it. But during TM, the physiology of the whole body settles down to a lower and lower level, giving the body a more deep, profound rest, while the mind remains alert. Eventually I reach the level where this particular stress is stored . . . it is released painlessly, usually without my even being aware of it. The body, given the appropriate restful condition, will automatically throw off stress. . . .

Let's say that the next day I am sitting in my living room reading a paper and a car outside slams on its brakes. I look up from the paper and think, "A car outside has just slammed on its brakes like that time when one almost hit me" and I calmly go back to reading the paper. Not only have I not wasted any time or energy being upset, but also I have not stored new strain for a future time.

This decreased susceptibility for acquiring stress is evidenced by Dr. Orme-Johnson's tests of GSR habituation (see above).

The value of rest is evident throughout nature. All of life exhibits the cycle of rest and activity. Waves rise and fall, day and night follow in succession, the eyelids blink, even plants rest in the night and continue the photosynthesis process in the daylight. Progress cannot continue indefinitely without rest. Exhaustion overtakes us if we try to force the body to continue functioning when it is tired.

Furthermore, we have all experienced the phenomenon of being *more* awake or *less* awake at different times. We know that the times we most enjoy life, when we work most efficiently and respond most completely, occur when we are most fully awake. It is obvious that sufficient rest is the basis of clarity of mind and alertness. Just as we walk on two feet, each foot alternately active and inactive, so progress in life has two phases, activity and rest. "Action," says Maharishi, "rests on rest." Profound rest gives rise to the most dynamic, creative activity. TM provides a rest physiologically deeper than that of sleep. This enlivens the active phase of the cycle. By pulling the bow string back to a point of maximum potential the arrow can be shot forward with maximum skill and effectiveness. The value of the deep rest of TM is found later, enriching activity with broadened awareness, increased energy and freer expression of our creative intelligence. A lively feeling of relaxation and calm well-being is enjoyed, a balanced and dynamic state of life.

Maharishi Mahesh Yogi calls the state produced in TM "restful alertness," because even though the body is resting so deeply, the mind is fully awake (as the brain-wave patterns indicate). "In this quiet state both the mind and the nervous system are alertly poised. . . . It is this restful alertness of the nervous system which represents its most healthy state and is the basis of all energy and action." [29] Wallace and Benson conclude their article in *Scientific American* by suggesting that the state produced by TM, what they call a "wakeful hypometabolic state, . . . representing quiescence rather than hyperactivation of the sympathetic nervous system, may indicate a guidepost to better health. It should be well worthwhile to investigate the possibilities for clinical application of this state of wakeful rest and relaxation." [30]

How is this deep rest produced? Maharishi offers this explanation: "As the mind begins to experience subtler states of thought during TM it engages itself in correspondingly less activity, and as a result breathing simultaneously begins to be shallower, more refined and reduced in amplitude." [31]

The diagram on page 60 illustrates the gradual refinement of mental activity during TM, which takes place as the attention shifts from the surface level of thought through increasingly subtle or refined levels to the source of thought.

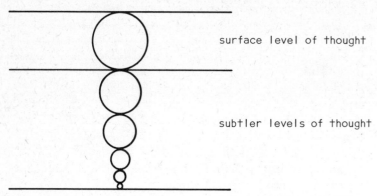

surface level of thought

subtler levels of thought

source of thought, Being

Maharishi continues,

> Physiologically it is clear that for this [shallower breathing] to take place there must be a fall in the level of carbon dioxide in the plasma. . . . The production of most energy for activity in the body finally involves the oxidation of carbon and its elimination as carbon dioxide.
>
> Greater activity needs greater energy, which is produced by the increased oxidation of carbon and its elimination as carbon dioxide. Less activity needs a smaller amount of energy, which results from less oxidation and elimination of carbon dioxide.
>
> This shows that when during TM less carbon dioxide is eliminated by softer breathing, the process of oxidation must be less, which naturally produces lesser amounts of energy.[32]

This means, as the physiological experiments revealed, that

> the activity of the body and the nervous system is reduced during transcendental meditation. This explains why the whole body becomes calm and quiet as the mind proceeds to experience finer states of a thought.
>
> This quietening of the body naturally allows an unusual degree of rest, which conserves energy to a considerable degree.[33]

Maharishi also adds this footnote:

> Unless one produces this state for a few minutes daily, by means of Transcendental Meditation, one has no chance of providing any rest for the inner machinery of the body, which otherwise functions twenty-four hours a day for the whole of one's life as long as breath flows. It is obviously to the advantage of health and longevity that the ever-functioning inner machinery of the body be allowed a few moments of rest and silence each day through this regular practice.[34]

This deep rest, then, is produced in an entirely natural way, by allowing the attention to fall on increasingly more refined, quieter levels of mental activity. There is no conscious effort to relax, no manipulation of the body, no attempt to control the breathing. The state of rest enjoyed in TM is purely a result, a by-product, of the inward journey of the mind. But it is a very real and significant phenomenon, which results in very real and significant changes in a person's life.

II. APPLICATIONS

"The significance of the physiological effects is twofold," states the *Mensa Journal;* "the body is allowed a new kind of rest, and clearly the effects are not trivial. . . . It is now not unreasonable for intelligent people to give sympathetic consideration to subjective reports on TM. By 'subjective report' is meant that of a meditator who speaks of a beneficial result which he attributes to the technique." [35]

Reduction of Stress

Subjectively, almost everyone remarks that he or she feels "less tense, less worried." Most mention that they had previously experienced some kind of tension, some degree of strain. Students, even, spoke of the "anxiety I felt about school and my future." But "now," said one man, "I feel a certain easiness, everything is smoother." "The main benefit of meditation for me," said another, "is the almost total reduction of serious worry. That means worry in the sense of nonproductive, nervous disruption. I can still be deeply concerned about important matters."

One man stated that "for the first time since I can remember, I can relax, really relax, without drugs or drink." A girl wrote, "Before I began meditation I used drugs, methedrine and narcotics. The effects of the drugs were that I was incredibly tense. Physically, my shoulders were up so high that one could barely see my neck." She said that, immediately after receiving instruction in TM, "my shoulders had dropped, all the tension in my face was gone so that my whole facial structure had changed, and most important to me, I was completely at ease. My tension didn't come back."

A Yale student reported that the reduction of tension resulted in a "tremendous relief of eye strain that once threatened my college career." A teacher reported having "severe headaches" which recurred daily; "this lasted eight years and in the later years became intense migraines. Nothing I could take medically or do would help. I had multiple tests run—nothing proving anything specifically. It was obvious, to me at least, that these headaches were just from tension—a great amount of tension and stress I didn't seem able to control.

"From my very first meditation," she continued, "I have not had a recurrence of those painful headaches at all. This astounds me—I can imagine the amount of tension released." It is not astounding, however, in view of current medical opinion, which holds that most headaches are caused by stress. In fact, if (as so many contemporary researchers suggest) 80 percent or more of all diseases are caused or complicated by stress (are "psychosomatic" in origin), the deep rest of TM, allowing for a release of deep-rooted stress, should result in a growing freedom from all forms of illness.

In *The Science of Being and Art of Living* Maharishi Mahesh Yogi discusses this exciting prospect:

> It is lamentable that for centuries past the problem of ill-health has been considered primarily on the physical level. Thanks to recent advances in medicine, investigations into the causes of disease have revealed that for a great majority of ailments the disease may be of physical nature though its cause is not physical. Such findings have emphasised the validity of mental phenomena as the cause of disorders in the physical body.
>
> The least that can be said about the problem of health in the world today is that the measures so far adopted are insufficient to maintain the health of the people. Even in countries where medical science is most advanced and psychiatrists and psychoanalysts are the fashion of the day, the health record shows that a large number of people suffer from weak hearts and die of heart failure, and that the number of mental patients is fast increasing.
>
> To build more hospitals to alleviate sickness and suffering for people who have already fallen ill is a laudable act of charity. But it is infinitely more important to find ways and means of preventing people from falling sick and of ensuring that they will always enjoy good health.[36]

Better Health

A large number of meditators do make a point of mentioning improved health and resistance to disease. "I haven't had any sort of cold since beginning meditation," one said. "I feel much better physically all the time." A student wrote, "Before TM I was very troubled with life. Health was a serious problem. After 17 months of TM severe asthma is completely gone. Perfect health."

A Los Angeles girl wrote, "About a year and a half ago, I was hospitalized for an examination of an abdominal condition, and was told that I was on the verge of a serious ulcer. No such problem today. I have always suffered from muscle strain in the lumbar sacral area of my back because of a trampoline accident—no more pain."

A woman in her late thirties reported, "I was very ill with arthritis. For years no doctor had been able to help it much, and I was depressed because of the vision of a future of increasing illness. Gradually, through meditation, I have been getting better. I no longer need to use *any* drugs to help it, and have almost no arthritic symptoms."

"I was a fairly happy person but I did have my anxieties," said a forty-two-year-old guidance counselor. "I liked my career but it was often full of counseling disturbed teenagers. I have always had great empathy for my counselees—but unfortunately I absorbed their problems. By the end of the day, I was tired, often under great tension. My physical examination the June before my initiation found me in rather unbalanced condition. My cholesterol count was up, my thyroid was sluggish and I needed hormones. After five months of meditation, I had my yearly physical. Everything was normal and my femininity index was up. My doctor said, 'I don't know what you have been doing but you are fifteen years younger biologically than you were a year ago!' "

More Energy

Of all the improvements reported by meditators in the area of health, the factor of increased energy was probably the most frequently mentioned. "I think the most profound change which came about through meditation is my increased energy," one student wrote. "Before meditation I lacked the energy to do the things I wanted to do." "I used to be thin, always tired and exhausted, lazy, pale, etc.," wrote a twenty-year-old girl. "I now have color and quite a bit of energy." A teacher said that "a full day's work no longer leaves me exhausted as it used to. In fact, I haven't been exhausted of energy once since I began meditation."

One man, meditating two and a half years, said, "I was a dull person, barely alive, my energy level was very low and had to be fortified with drugs. I had an irrational temperament, a disorderly mind and saw first the negative side of the world. . . . I could go on but it's too incredible to think of how long I existed in this state. Since TM it's been an entirely different experience for me. I have experienced a constant unfolding of new abilities, changed attitudes, more virtues than I could hope for. I've really gotten to like myself and the world I live in. My energy has been the most dramatic change. I was like a plant trying to exist in barren soil with minimal nourishment, transplanted to the best possible place and it rejoices and shoots up."

A Replacement for Sleep?

Many people wonder if the deep rest gained during TM might serve as a replacement for sleep. Using TM in place of sleep, however, would be like using apples to replace oranges: it won't work; they are two different things. Sleep is a state of consciousness with its own particular characteristics and its own value to life. Likewise, TM is a unique state. The two states are distinct and are not interchangeable.

Practical experience, however, shows that meditators frequently require less sleep. Not only that, but they report falling asleep more quickly and easily, and sleeping more deeply. This seems to be a natural result of the deep rest and relaxation. A more relaxed person falls asleep more readily than a tense person, whose mind often races busily along for hours before it settles down. Also, a more relaxed person gathers up less stress during the day—he gets less tired, has more energy and can accomplish more, having more time available for what he wants to do.

One student, working part time, had this to say: "Physically, I believe meditation has affected my health in that I need less sleep and yet produce a more effective day. I feel more alert when taking tests and working. After a hard day of physical work, I may be tired, but after my evening meditation, I am ready for an active night of play or study." Another wrote that after beginning meditation, "I slept immediately and woke up alert: something quite unusual for me." A twenty-four-year-old girl, a singer and songwriter, wrote with evident enthusiasm, "I get a good night's sleep *every* night!"

Skeptics and Enthusiasts

Such experiences are the rule rather than the exception and are undoubtedly the main factor in the rapid spread of TM. Enthusiasm of meditators is high. Scientists, highly skeptical of anything bearing a name such as "transcendental meditation," are a bit slower to catch fire. But the physiological studies are convincing, and once a man begins the practice, he finds himself an enthusiast.

"I began to meditate with skepticism and doubt," writes A. James Morgan, M.D., director of Adult Treatment Services at Pennsylvania Hospital in Philadelphia, and he goes on:

When the fragile method was taught to me it seemed impossible that this delicate thing could hope to accomplish anything beyond being a delightful way to relax twice a day. I began because the consensus of the testimonies I heard was too unanimous to be rejected and compelled me to try it first hand. It was clear that there could be no danger in such a natural, delicate and guileless procedure and so I began, expecting nothing. The effects were as others reported. They were immediate and increased with time. I began to feel more alert and awake at work and even through the evenings after particularly busy days. I no longer say, "What a grueling day" even though I am now doing much more than I had previously. Work just doesn't seem tiring. I have more energy with which to relate to people, and not feeling drained, I no longer feel put upon by the endless details and trivia with which I frequently must deal.

The possible uses of the technique as an adjunct to psychotherapy are exciting indeed. I cannot imagine any possibility of harm to any patient if meditation is practiced as taught. The general reduction in tension and increased alertness should complement any psychotherapeutic procedure . . . and I expect that transcendental meditation will emerge as a most welcome addition to our therapeutic armamentarium.[37]

After reporting on the physiological studies on TM, Sidney H. Scott wrote in the *Mensa Journal,*

> From my own experience of about three years' practice of TM, I can attest to the truth of some of these claims, particularly the remarks about tranquillity, tensions and functional disorders. At no time has the technique given rise to any distressing symptoms, of, say, oxygen starvation. I would stress the comment about non-adoption of new beliefs. Any person, whatever his belief or non-belief, may engage in TM without any offence to his principles. I believe that one who tries such an experiment is likely to find it a rewarding venture. In order to give the thing a fair trial, I continued with it, as I was instructed, in the face of an early skepticism amounting at times to hostility. My views have changed completely.[38]

"Much lip service is paid today to the concept of 'treating the whole man,' " Dr. Anthony Campbell, medical editor of the London *Hospital Times,* has noted, "yet few people seem to know exactly what this ought to imply. . . . There seems at least a fair chance that transcendental meditation . . . acting simultaneously on the physiological and psychological levels, is the long-sought answer to a very deep rooted malaise of our time." [39]

"The Answer to Future Shock"

A reporter for *The Albany Student Press,* reacting to a TM lecture on the State University campus, wrote that "TM people think that the answer to Future Shock has arrived in their movement." [40] The remark was an extremely perceptive one.

In his best-selling book *Future Shock,* Alvin Toffler defines future shock as "the shattering stress and disorientation that we induce in individuals by subjecting them to too much change in too short a time." [41] Toffler's research indicates that, because of the rapidly accelerating pace of change, future shock "may well be the most important disease of the future." [42] Indeed, "the malaise, mass neurosis, irrationality, and free-floating violence already apparent in contemporary life are merely a foretaste of what may lie ahead unless we come to understand and treat this disease." [43]

Toffler further defines future shock as the "distress, both physical and psychological, that arises from an overload of the human organism's physical adaptive systems and its decision-making processes." [44] This overload on the system is what Maharishi refers to as stress. In the last 20 years research on the human organism has revealed that a complex series of changes takes place in the body countless times every single day, in response to changes in the environment around us. Worry, anticipation, upset, conflict, uncertainty, even joy or laughter trigger what is called the "adaptive reaction," * an integrated response of nervous system and endocrine glands. We have experienced this countless times: the pupils of the eyes dilate, the muscles tense, blood vessels constrict, the palms sweat, breathing becomes deeper and faster, blood pressure goes up, the heart pounds. This response pattern of the system is natural and highly useful as a mechanism of adaptation. But it uses up a tremendous amount of energy and is exhausting to the system.

With the rate of change so rapid, this adaptive response is called into operation innumerable times each day, resulting in an accumulation of stress and tiredness. "Just a mere contact with the complex human situation almost automatically

---

* Sometimes also called the "adaptation response" or the "orientation response." Some researchers distinguish among these states according to intensity, but for our purposes we shall generalize and count them as one basic response pattern.

brings this about, this stimulation of the whole endocrine system," said René Dubos, author of *Man Adapting*. "There is absolutely no question that one can overshoot the stimulation of the endocrine system and that this has physiological consequences that last throughout the whole lifetime of the organs." [45] The accumulation of stress within the system reduces an individual's ability to function, lowers his energy level, reduces his ability to act and enjoy. It is the enemy of life. Increasingly medical science is showing that stress is the greatest factor in such problems as heart disease, ulcers, migraine, asthma, ulcerative colitis and other ills. The problem of stress is rapidly coming to the forefront of medical research. In 1950 Dr. Hans Selye, internationally recognized as the pioneer in stress research, published his first paper on the subject. It was the only technical paper published on stress that year. In 1971 there were over 6,000 separate reports on stress research.[46] It is estimated that at least one-third of America's adult population suffers from hypertension, high blood pressure or related stress-caused ailments.[47]

The application of the science of creative intelligence to the problem of stress is obvious. We have seen that what occurs physiologically during TM is an integrated response of the system, repeatable and predictable, just as the adaptive response is organized and repeatable. TM, however, moves in the opposite direction: muscles relax; blood flow in some areas of the body increases (indicating a dilation of the blood vessels); breathing becomes shallower and slower; heart rate slows down and cardiac output decreases; changes in blood chemistry indicate less anxiety. (See Figure VII.)

The immediate effect of allowing the system to receive this degree of rest is apparent: it reduces the burden of stress and fatigue under which a person is laboring and gives him immediate relief and refreshment. Maharishi has declared, however, that these immediate effects are only a small part of the story. Continuing regularly in the practice of TM, he maintains, gradually frees the system from the built-up stress and strain of the past. Deep-rooted exhaustion and strain far

FIGURE VII

Brief Comparison of TM and Stressful Reaction

Body Function	Stressful Reaction	TM Effect
muscles	tense	relax
blood vessels	constrict; extremities cold	relax; extremities warmer; blood flow increases in forearm
heart	pumps faster and pumps more blood	slows down and cardiac output down 25% (20% in sleep)
breathing	quicker and heavier	slower and shallower; oxygen intake down 17 to 20%
blood chemistry	increased adrenalin; more lactate ion	decrease of lactate by at least 30%
skin resistance	decreases; more perspiration	increases more than during sleep

below the surface level, which inhibit the full use of our faculties and keep us a prey to our own weaknesses, are dissolved, allowing action to be increasingly more spontaneous and energy and creative intelligence to be more fully displayed.

The subjective reports of meditators certainly attest to this growing freedom. Whether or not it has a physiological basis medical science will ascertain. A team of researchers at the Illinois Masonic Medical Center in Chicago has already begun work on a ten-year study of metabolic changes in meditators,[48] and other long-term studies are underway elsewhere.

A few years ago Maharishi's claim that TM produced a unique, physiologically measurable state of consciousness might have seemed extravagant. Today it is scientific fact. Will further research bring to light the existence of a fifth, or even further states which become possible to an evolving man as he enlivens deeper areas of the mind and nervous system and brings his full potential into play?

The answer to future shock, then, does not lie primarily in manipulating the environment, in creating new social structures and institutions. Nor does it lie in slowing down the rate of change, a suggestion that seems neither feasible nor likely, in view of the momentum of change that has been created and man's inherent desire to progress as rapidly as possible. Maharishi long ago pointed out that slowing down the rate of change or attempting to live a more simple life "in nature" does not provide a realistic solution to the situation before us. Rather, "man should be able to cope with his progress so that progress makes life increasingly meaningful. The only new course to be taken is to make men more intelligent, and this requirement of our age is going to be met by the Science of Creative Intelligence, which makes man more progressive and at the same time more fulfilled." [49] The answer, then, lies within man himself.

CHAPTER 3

Families and Friends

LEADER: Suppose it is one of those mornings when everything seems to go wrong. The telephone rings, the baby
cries, and before you know it, the toast is burnt. Your
husband looks over the toaster and says: "My God!
When will you learn to make toast?!" What is your
reaction?

MRS. A: I would throw the toast in his face!

MRS. B: I would say, "Fix your own damn toast!"

MRS. C: I would be so hurt I could only cry.

LEADER: What would your husband's words make you
feel toward him?

PARENTS: Anger, hate, resentment.

LEADER: Would it be easy for you to fix another batch
of toast?

MRS. A: Only if I could put some poison in it!

LEADER: And when he left for work, would it be easy
to clean up the house?

MRS. A: No, the whole day would be ruined.

LEADER: Suppose the situation is the same: the toast is
burnt but your husband, looking over the situation,
says, "Gee, honey, it's a rough morning for you—the
baby, the phone, and now the toast."

MRS. A: I would drop dead if my husband said that to me!

MRS. B: I would feel wonderful!

MRS. C: I would feel so good I would hug him and kiss him.

LEADER: Why?—that baby is still crying and the toast is still burnt?

PARENTS: That wouldn't matter.

LEADER: What would make the difference?

MRS. B: You feel kind of grateful that he didn't criticize you—that he was with you, not against you.

LEADER: And when your husband left for work, would it be difficult to clean up the house?

MRS. C: No! I'd do it with a song.[1]

It is this song that meditators, and those who meet and interact with meditators, are starting to sing. Concrete, positive changes in the area of interpersonal relationships are—aside from relaxation and increased energy—some of the most immediate changes noticed by those practicing transcendental meditation.

The Unwanted War

Be it happy or sad, loving or angry, what we are is expressed through our words and actions. Given a choice, who wouldn't choose to be positive, loving, good? No one wants to be miserable or to make others unhappy. Dr. Haim Ginott began his best-selling book *Between Parent and Child* by noting that "no parent wakes up in the morning planning to make his child's life miserable. No mother says to herself, 'Today I'll yell, nag, and humiliate my child whenever possible.' On the contrary. In the morning many mothers resolve: 'This is going to be a peaceful day. No yelling, no arguing, and no fighting.' Yet, in spite of good intentions, the unwanted war breaks out again. Once more we find ourselves saying things we do not mean, in a tone we do not like." [2]

In spite of our values, our desires and resolutions, we sometimes find ourselves acting in ways we do not like. We yell, argue, feel jealous or afraid, and afterwards we are sorry, we feel that we acted in spite of our understanding, our intentions, our "better" self. Why did we do it?

Suppose you are a high-school student. Last night you didn't get enough sleep, and today you failed an English test, you saw your girlfriend or boyfriend with someone else the whole day—by the time you get home you feel pretty tired and miserable. The moment you open the door your mother greets you with: "Now, you wipe your shoes and hang up your coat and stay out of the living room, we're having company tonight." How do you feel? And how do you react? If you had slept well, gotten an A on the exam, spent the day with that special person, you might have laughed at this barrage, hugged Mother, told her not to worry, and given her a chance to relax. Instead, you snap back at her, stomp to your room, slam the door and turn the stereo on full blast.

Or suppose you are that wife who burns the morning toast —or the husband who receives it. You have so much on your mind, decisions to make, financial questions, family problems, you tossed and turned half the night and reluctantly respected the alarm clock's authority—little by little stress builds up until it explodes. Any trivial incident can set it off. You're not really angry about the *toast*—a moment's thought shows you that it is quite insignificant. But it becomes the focal point for your built-up tension.

We rarely become angry or upset when we are fresh and rested, energetic, enjoying a fine day. Anger, or any expression of negativity, is easily seen to be the result of an accumulation of stress. Certainly everyone would like to act better—with more love, patience, understanding—but tension or stress blocks our better feelings, pinches the heart, and we find ourselves yelling. "Resolutions about not becoming angry are worse than futile," Dr. Ginott notes; "the peaceful home, like the hoped-for warless world, does not depend on a sudden benevolent change in human nature. It does depend on deliberate procedures that methodically reduce tensions before they lead to explosions." [3]

Behavior Changes: "Better Than I Had Hoped!"

Because TM produces such a profound state of healing rest and relaxation, it is just that "deliberate procedure" which can most efficiently free an individual from the restricting influence of stress and strain. However, this can be viewed as a real change in human nature—or rather, in human *behavior:* it is a way of allowing our authentic human nature to express itself, released from the bondage of stress and tension, which have nothing to do with what we really are. Stress, after all, is not natural to life. It is an imposition on the body and nervous system, from some unduly heavy pressure of experience which leaves a deep impression on us, but which can be removed by deep rest. TM provides that rest, allowing the system to normalize itself. As a result, very definite "benevolent" changes do occur.

"The major difference in my life," a young woman said, "has been an inner attitude of tranquility, which makes it easier for me to accept people and things as I find them. I still have lapses of uptightness, but I've only been meditating six months, after all. I don't seem to feel anger, nor to be suppressing anger. It just isn't there."

"Prior to beginning meditation," one man remarked, "I had a helluva problem with a woman I loved, caused largely by personal feelings of defensiveness and mild persecution, the latter due to general lack of self-confidence. Prior to meditating, all of my efforts to correct this problem were transitory, superficial, and foolish. After ten days of meditation, the problem solved itself, because my self-confidence became (as if magically) renewed and quite securely strong. I give meditation 100% credit, and I do not do this çasually, as I'm exceptionally analytical about it all."

Quite a number of meditators remarked that negative feelings of all kinds just vanished. "This has been the most noticeable change," said a student. "Things that used to irritate me just pass by now. I feel myself more tolerant of people who used to upset me or make me angry. It almost seems as though I can't get upset any more. People are so much easier to get along with." As for feelings of jealousy or grasping on to others, a young man said this: "Actually, I started meditating because I was in love with a meditator and I hoped to bring her back to me. But, through meditation, I learned to open my heart and let her go. Better than I had hoped!"

Such experiences give us great cause to be optimistic about what human nature really is when it is given full expression. And it shows us that what we need is not a new set of values or constant reminders or efforts to act in accordance with the values we hold to be good. What *is* necessary is a way to allow our own inherent strength and love to find expression, a way to live our own highest values spontaneously and naturally.

This is exactly what the science of creative intelligence is bringing about.

Steven is a second-year medical student at NYU Medical School in New York. I spoke with him one rainy afternoon, in the corridor of one of the medical school buildings, about his experiences with TM.

"How did you get involved with TM?"

"It was at the end of my junior year at college. I went to a lecture on Christianity, given by some reverend up at school. Someone asked the reverend how to actually *get* the experience of love and understanding he was talking about, and the reverend didn't really have any answer. He really didn't know.

"After the meeting I spoke to the boy who asked the question, and he sounded like he had some technique or something; I asked him if he did and he said yes, and he mentioned that it was Maharishi's technique. He told me where to go to hear about it, to the SIMS Center, and I did. I heard the lecture; it was very interesting and sounded very logical. The technique sounded like it had possibilities so I tried it and obviously it works. The changes I've undergone since I've been meditating—I've been meditating for about a year and a half—have been in all aspects of my life. For instance, I used to be a little hypertensive all the time, and had a stutter and was always nervous, always felt a little odd in my stomach whenever I was in any kind of stressful situation. Since I've started to meditate, and in increasing amounts afterwards, I've been much more settled and quiet and less anxious about stressful situations. This is something that accumulates as time goes on and you find that you're able to function in a better way."

Being a medical student, he easily got me into a discussion of the physiological effects of TM, something that deeply impressed and fascinated him. Then he returned to his own personal experiences.

"Prior to meditating I often found that what other people said and did would upset me—whether it was my mother, a friend, a school teacher, or whoever. Now I notice that very rarely if at all will something that someone else says or does upset me. I seem to have more awareness of myself and of others, so that I know what is me and what is someone else. I know when someone else has some problems, some particular hang-up or anxiety that he's taking out on everybody else, and it doesn't upset me any more. I just realize that this is what this person is going through and I find it easy to be understanding and to help him with whatever it is. I've noticed this with my mother and father, too. I had moved out from them at the end of my junior year because they were very hard to live with. They didn't have any attitudes like mine and, you know, they told me what to do and when and how and everything and I just had to move out. There was a tremendous amount of friction because whenever they would say something to me and tell me to do this and do that, it just upset me so much and I'd have all this conflict and there would be fighting—but now, even though they may be doing the same thing sometimes, since I began to meditate, what they said and did no longer upset me nearly as much. I just realized that this is the way they are, this is their life, this is their style, this is the way they're made up psychologically, and it didn't upset me. Because I'm looking at them more clearly, I'm able to understand them more and it's really nice being able to love them and appreciate them just for what they are, no more, no less, just love them for what they are as your parents with their own makeup.

"This works with my friends also. I don't have any kind of conflicts or fights with my friends any more. If they feel a certain way, fine, that is their attitude, and if they say something about me, I just look at it and see what it is. This is true with everybody I meet, in all situations, and it is so valuable because you're able to enjoy all your interactions with other people just so much more. Whenever you're with someone, you're always learning such new things about them, about yourself and about the interaction between the two. This makes it such a joy to be with people, to be actively involved in all situations, because it never upsets you and you're learning more and growing all the time."

Surprise!—Growth Is Natural

As I spoke to more and more meditators, one fascinating and significant concept kept reappearing. They frequently said that they had "noticed" some aspect of growth, or that they had witnessed some positive changes, without trying to make them occur. One girl, for instance, said that she had "noticed a self-development which has led to greater self-confidence; this has led to a lessening of fears surrounding emotional encounters with other people." One person even expressed surprise at his progress: "I am surprised at how much better I get along with people," he said, "especially people who have different values, philosophies of life and religions. It is much easier to accept each person as he is."

This spontaneous unfolding of life is one of the glories of the science of creative intelligence. Growth through this process of transcendental meditation is never forced or contrived, but comes as innocently and naturally as the dawn.

"Before, I was extremely shy and reticent when I was around people," wrote one girl. "Gradually I noticed a more harmonious feeling with others and now I have absolutely no problems getting along. I'm much more at home with people, less easily irritated, more appreciative of their being there. My close relationships have become more intimate. I seem to be able to make friends with nearly anyone."

Another young man said that as he "started becoming less insecure and hung-up, I became drastically more tolerant of both myself and others. I have learned to know and love myself enough to give this love to others." One girl felt this growing respect and self-respect to be the most important aspect of meditation. She said, "I'd like very much to see everyone meditating. If everyone could just feel more satisfied with himself. It's feelings of inferiority that ruin everything. How can there be an 'inferior' person? Maybe there can be inferiority in money or looks or power or intelligence, but an inferior person *inside?* I don't think so. People are so fantastic inside. . . . The basic personhood that we all have should bring enough joy."

Communication

Another vital aspect of good relationships which meditators find improved is the ability to communicate with others. They see this from two sides: their ability to express themselves, and their understanding and perception of others.

Obviously the ability to express oneself clearly depends first of all on clarity of thinking. Clarity of expression is a consequence of lucid thought. A girl at Berkeley told me, "I'm more logical and can express myself more clearly. . . . The whole way I think has cleared." A nineteen-year-old student wrote, "My thought process is more powerful and logical, and I am able to express myself clearly and efficiently."

If we can think and speak clearly what is on our minds and in our hearts, we are on the way to good communication.

The next step is freedom to disclose these thoughts and feelings; we need the courage and spontaneity to express ourselves. "I am more able to feel what I really am feeling, rather than what I think I should feel," said one man, meditating about a year; and a business student wrote, "I am better able to act on my feelings, thus making use of them, instead of being frustrated."

"Communication has become so natural and easy," a young woman wrote. "Not having to protect the self-identity/self-image any more, I am more confident of myself by 'being,' in a positive way. My husband and myself are closer, a real 'heaven on earth' as Maharishi has said is possible. My family welcomes us more readily and happily than ever before."

What about the receiving end of the communication process? "I am more sensitive to the needs and feelings others have," one person said. "I find that I'm more genuinely interested in other people, I'm a better listener, and I'm more sensitive to how other people are," a sociology teacher wrote. "A depth of understanding is present that was not there before."

How is it that a person *can* begin to perceive with more depth and clarity? A teacher of the science of creative intelligence suggested that a primary reason is "the expansion of consciousness that is gained through TM. As thought is repeatedly appreciated at subtler levels, deeper, previously unused portions of the mind become enlivened and available for use. Because we're using more of the mind, thought and perception become more refined and understanding becomes more profound. On a simple, sensory level, people often say that colors seem brighter, music is more charming, food tastes more delicious."

"What do we find on the gross level of creation?" Maharishi asks in *The Science of Being and Art of Living*. "We find gross things to see with the eyes, gross words or sound to hear with the ears. . . . The subtle fields are beyond our ordinary range of experience. We know that there are forms much finer than those which the eyes can see and that these may be observed through the microscope. We know that there are sounds which the ears cannot hear but which may be heard with the help of amplifiers. This shows that there exist subtle strata of creation with which we are not familiar because our ordinary capacity for experience is limited to the gross." [4] As we have seen, the practice of TM allows the mind to appreciate the more subtle or refined levels of thought, which refines the faculties of perception and enriches all aspects of experience. This explains at least in part why meditators find that they are more perceptive of nuances of feeling and behavior both in themselves and others.

Giving and Receiving

Meditators report that as they grow in strength and love, they naturally have more to give. Based on a principle of giving, relationships become more constructive and life-supporting. "I give more of myself to others, and likewise receive more," a student commented. "My personal relationships have become healthier and much more positive." Another said, "The nature of my thought and action seems to have changed, tending to be more useful and positive." This is an area which concerns us all. We want our relationships to be beneficial and conducive to the well-being of all involved. But too often they are quite the opposite. As one woman expressed it: "Before meditating I was unsure, afraid that I was a diseased cell in the body of the universe that should be surgically removed. Now I am serene."

This alone—whether we call it serenity, happiness, inner fulfillment—is the basis of positive, mutually beneficial relationships. "The first fundamental in the art of behaviour is: meet with warmth and meet to give," Maharishi writes. "If all people in society behaved on this level of giving, social behaviour could only result in the advancement and glorification of everyone's life." [5]

However, he points out that "a sincere sense of giving can only arise on a level of contentment. Only contented hearts and minds can think in terms of giving." [6] A meditating teacher expressed a similar discovery: "How can a person give love if he doesn't first have love within himself? How can a person bring peace and harmony to his environment if he isn't first peaceful and harmonious? It makes all the sense in the world to take the mind to an awareness of its own essential nature in bliss consciousness. Having gained that awareness, that joy, and that lightness of heart one very naturally spreads love and enthusiasm to his surroundings." This inner fullness provides a foundation for a naturally giving, spontaneously supportive relationship with life.

Love

The quality of love is so important to modern life that it cannot be overestimated. Indeed, "all love," writes Maharishi, "in every phase of every drop of it, is significant to life." [7] Speaking of the growth of love in her life, one woman wrote, "I am aware of increased mental capacities. I have greater clarity of mind and can grasp things more readily, but I am even more aware of the increased emotional capacity— because the contrast from before the time I began meditation is *so* great. I have become a very loving, compassionate, and tolerant person. I feel very warm and loving inside and this feeling is easily transmitted to other people. These feelings just arrive spontaneously. Before meditation I was considered a cold person. Now I feel as if there were a glowing warm fire in my heart which acts to make me warm and to make other people warm."

This increase in love is not a matter of pretense or mood-making. It has to be real, for, as Maharishi points out, love is the most innocent quality of life. It cannot be contrived; either it is there or it isn't. Love is the spontaneous expression of a full heart, and "lack of love denotes lack of life-content." Because real love can only be innocent and spontaneous, "the show of love without genuine love is a shame to life." [8] A girl at the Santa Barbara campus of the University of California verified this: "I find that everywhere I meet or run into people, I just naturally look for the 'good' in them. It's a beautiful thing. Before, I used to pretend that I loved people; after all, it was the 'happy' thing to love everyone. But it was so insincere that looking back on it I'm ashamed of how hypocritical I was."

"Whereas I was able to love only those I knew," a physicist said, "I find now that I have more love for strangers. I feel more akin to them."

"I believe that I am more compassionate and tolerant," a teacher said, "and also more loving toward those around me. This is a particularly difficult area as I have been rather selfish in the past."

Love helps us see and accept others, just for being. A twenty-year-old woman said, "My younger brother has always been a sore spot with me because about a year after his birth, my other brother, my dearest companion, was killed. At the time, in my ignorance and grief, I couldn't understand why my friend had been taken and this screaming child was kept. But meditation opened my heart and showed me the wonderful little being that still must develop on this earth. For this one great awareness, I feel that meditation never has to give me anything else. I am truly thankful."

"Those who are restricted in their ability to love," Maharishi writes, "those whose love flows only in restricted channels of isolated objects or individuals, those who can only like this or that, those who have no awareness of universal consciousness in their hearts, are like small ponds where the love can flow only as ripples and not as waves of the sea. . . . To enjoy the ocean of love, we have to improve the magnitude of our hearts and gain the depth of an ocean, unfathomable and full." [9] This melting and opening of the heart is certainly one of the most important results of transcendental meditation.

There are some people who believe that "meditation" is a selfish practice, taking a person away from life, making a person introverted and perhaps apathetic. This may be the case with other techniques and ideologies, but it is obviously not true of transcendental meditation. TM clearly serves to increase an individual's level of dynamic activity; it increases his concern for others and his desire to help create a better world. For instance, a twenty-year-old man said that because of his use of "the strongest hallucinogens available, intellectual and spiritual growth had ceased and I had ceased creative action. I was irresponsible and self-indulgent and little capable of helping others. After TM I'm thinking clearly, growing intellectually, growing more aware and involved with others and desirous of contributing to society."

Another young man, now working as a Youth Corps counselor, said that since beginning meditation, "I have become more and more integrated and have entered the field of activity in an effort to live as full a life as possible and to do my part in the total responsibility of man." Can we look forward to a world in which actions are motivated by love and are performed by individuals who have fully developed their minds and their powers of perception and understanding?

Tributes to Love

In these days of tremendous social upheaval, when so much in life, present and future, is impersonal, unstable and uncertain, it is only natural that we put great energy and hope into our personal relationships. TM, by developing inner stability, expanded awareness and a more loving heart, provides many people with a foundation for more successful, meaningful relationships. The deep, natural rest and relaxation brought about by the practice dissolves restricting stress and tension, which cause fear, inhibition, jealousy, anger, depression and other forms of negative reactions in life. Behavior becomes more spontaneous and joyful.

"My wife and I have worked out the many personal differences that have arisen," said one meditator. "Our love grows deeper and deeper. We are further developing tolerance and compassion for each other, for everyone and everything. We are happier than ever but not as happy as we shall be." Another admitted that before he started TM his "love life was very unstable. My fiancée and myself were in love, but we constantly fought and argued, never reaching any agreement. We both started meditating and now I look forward to our marriage. We are now at peace within and are able to function harmoniously as friends, lovers, man and woman. I feel that meditation saved our relationship, not to mention our lives."

"I guess the biggest or most pronounced difference in my 'love life' since I began meditating is the difference in the quality of my love, the quantity of my love and my attitude towards loving and being loved," said Celeste, a beautiful and effusive girl whose warmth and happiness are contagious. "First off, I *enjoy* the whole thing much more, I enjoy a relationship and I think that's because the feelings I have are more of an uplifting type than an undermining type.

"What I mean by 'uplifting' is that the feeling of being with someone, of working with someone, is a joyous feeling, an exhilarating, 'happy-inside' feeling. An 'undermining' feeling to me is a feeling which disrupts the flow of my life, the results being toward non-productivity, toward need and anxiety, toward the fear of losing and then being worse off than before.

"A positive love flows freely when you're feeling good inside, there's no worry at the time, you're not thinking, 'Gee, I love him a lot, I hope he loves me too or I'll be miserable.' You're just *feeling,* and the feeling is wonderful and the other person feels it too . . . everyone feels it! The feeling shines from your face. The negative or 'undermining' love leaves you more with thoughts like, 'Where is he tonight?' 'Will he love me tomorrow?' and even when the good feeling comes it's partially choked and overshadowed by the underlying fear. I remember a thought I used to have about A., someone I was very attached to for several years; I kept thinking, 'It's not worth it.'

"Now, as I see it, a good healthy relationship is not made

up of just feeling. The way these feelings are expressed is *very* important. I was so anxious to be with A. at every moment, to cuddle him and have his attention, that I never left him to his own thoughts, to his own privacy. . . . I never gave him any time to himself. He resented that, I remember, and the resentment became a force that made him want me less, which made me, in growing insecurity, demand more from him which in turn annoyed him more. The relationship almost self-destructed at points.

"Now I find that I actually enjoy loving someone while he's in one room working and I'm in another, even while he's away for days at a time. I can give him love in many ways, for instance by letting him be alone, by not draining him with my suspicions and fears. I feel full inside with my love and don't need to be told every minute in every way, 'I love you.' Of course I enjoy receiving his love, but it's comfortable and easy, and that's the best thing.

"I'm pretty sure that this change is due to some growth inside me. I know that meditation has strengthened my ability to act more naturally and at the same time more spontaneously. I feel more whole all the time, so whatever happens I'll still be whole. If someone comes and goes I won't drown in misery as I used to think I would. That kind of thought doesn't even come to me any more. And that's why I'm free to love more. I don't feel, by any means, that I want to be alone, or that I 'couldn't care less' if my boy friend stays or goes. I have a strong tendency toward marriage, and I'm glad that marriage is taking on a fuller look, a happier and workable image. A friend of mine told me the other day that she used to derive joy out of doing her husband's laundry, and that now it's just a chore. My spontaneous reaction was to tell her to start meditation. Meditation really can get you feeling fresh and whole, and a man needs someone fresh and abundant with love. Who needs to have their stress and tiredness bog them down, and who needs to feel that life is getting commonplace and wearisome? A relationship is as strong and viable as the people who make it."

Families: "A Connection Started to Flow"

A fundamental area of human relationships is the family. Despite changing values and standards, the family remains the basic social unit. It is there that, in our early years, we learn behavior patterns and mold our future modes of relating to others. Later, we invest huge amounts of time, energy, emotion—even money—in a family that we create. In a world of rapid change, we would hope that the family could be a source of stability and security, but instead we find such failures of love and communication within families, such deep resentments and misunderstandings between generations that too often the family is only a source of stress and frustration, rather than of harmony and shared love. Young people cannot seem to accept their parents' values or ways of living, and parents cannot understand why or what their children are looking for.

But we know all this, it's nothing new. What *is* new is strong evidence that it can be different. Here is part of a dialogue recorded in a family of five. They are all practicing TM. The father (fifty-nine) and his three children (Peter, twenty-five; Ruth, twenty-one; and Michael, twenty) take part in this section of the discussion.

RUTH: Before we started meditation there wasn't much communication.

PETER: Ruth had been taking dancing lessons for years and I didn't even know it. Nobody could talk to anybody.

MICHAEL: Peter was hibernating in the house in a little room; no one could go in.

PETER: My mother would come in and I'd yell at her; Michael would ask if he could come in, and I wouldn't let him.

RUTH: In the family as a whole, no one had reached each other. Everyone was doing his own thing; we didn't know how to express care for each other. We were all caught in our own behavior patterns. Nobody knew anything about anyone else.

MICHAEL: We cared, but no one could do anything about it. Now the family is getting closer and closer.

RUTH: Maharishi said that a family is a field of joy. I just started realizing that it's also a source of love. This is its ideal state, and this is what meditation is bringing our family to. Every aspect of the family has developed so much; we have so much open, good feeling for each other. It is really fantastic to discover that a family is for this—to help each other grow and evolve—it exists and it's there to tap.

FATHER: During the years prior to this, there had been a good deal of tension in the family. I felt that I had lost the children. I had a great longing for them. All of a sudden a connection started to flow—warmth came out and a feeling of closeness. In a home full of tension it takes love away from everybody.

RUTH: I very quickly developed some very strong natural emotions. There's a natural field of love.

"There's a natural field of love . . ." It isn't that all of a sudden the whole family begins to agree on all their values and ideas, but rather, as we saw above, that when people begin to feel inner fullness and strength, when they feel their own worth, they begin to accept themselves and others more easily and are no longer threatened by differing life-styles. "My relationship with my family has changed as I no longer fear them as a threat to my freedom," a girl wrote. One student said, "Family—they haven't changed their views—nor have I radically changed mine—but our *views* seem to make little difference. Their attitude toward me, and mine toward them, is changed." A twenty-two-year-old student, after relating his experiences since beginning meditation, added: "I forgot to mention this but living with my parents turned out to be not so bad. Meditation helped give me more understanding so our relations improved considerably. In fact, my mother even started meditating."

"I no longer argue with my parents during my weekly

visits with them," a girl said. "I have established my own 'inner independence,' so I no longer have to fight for it or prove it." A girl in Philadelphia said, "My mother has started to meditate, my sister also. Our relations have gotten tremendous. We're very improved, there's more sincerity between us, a true bond that was not so noticeable before, a real closeness and appreciation of who we all are. It's a delight to get together with them now, we laugh all the time."

Parents who are meditating profit just as much—as parents —from the relaxation and broadened awareness that meditation brings. A man wrote, "I seem to accept myself and others much more fully than I used to and I get along better with my wife and children, and enjoy them more than I did before beginning meditation."

As Ruth said above, the family is a source of love, something to be enjoyed, something to help all the members toward a better life.

"My ability to love is much deeper and I can see it being reflected in my little boy especially, and in my husband," a woman commented. Another young mother said, "My six-year-old son wants to meditate because 'it's made a big change in you—we used to have millions of fights!'"

It is certainly true that children, with their great sensitivity, feel a difference in their parents. One mother told about how one day, because of excessive demands on her time, she skipped her evening meditation. Missing the boost of energy and refreshment (on a day she especially needed it), she found herself cross with her little boy. Right away he asked, "Mommy, have you meditated yet?" "He knew darn well," she exclaimed, "that if I had, I wouldn't have acted that way. So I turned the heat off on the stove and went to meditate!" Many meditators have told related stories. They all seem to express an important discovery: that how we feel inside is more important than a few minutes' apparent saving of time; if we are rested, fresh and at ease, we are able to be more efficient in our activities and more of a positive influence on those around us.

"At home I've become so much more liveable. I admit I used to be so obnoxious," a nineteen-year-old girl said. "Anything my mother said, I'd usually either ignore her or snap back at her. But once I started meditating, and especially in the last couple of months, we've been sitting down and really having long, serious talks. Mutual respect and the love I never really saw before are growing. She understands that I'm finally doing something that is really important to me and is taking a serious interest in it."

Mrs. Johnson, age fifty, is a mother of four; two of her sons are in college. Before starting TM, she practiced hatha yoga for a while. She enjoyed it, but "it was very hard work," and now she and her husband, a television actor, are practicing TM. "When I went into this," she told me, "I had a lot of anxieties and fears and of course they were focused mostly on my family. I feel that I'm a better mother to my children now because I'm able to leave them alone. My anxiety about my children, trying to manipulate them the way I think they should go, made for very unhappy situations in the home. Now I'm finally able to let my children alone! The family life has really improved tremendously."

"For the first time in my married life," a thirty-six-year-old housewife reported, "I am enjoying my role and responsibilities as a cook, wife, mother, housewife—and mainly due to my new capabilities and accomplishments. I hated cooking before, and was too tired to do a good job of it for my family. Now I'm an excellent cook, love it, and have energy sufficient for it; good meals appear almost by themselves. . . . Our family used to argue a lot," she continued; "now we don't. We speak more softly, with more love, understanding and patience. We enjoy each other more. The children have benefited so much, it still seems miraculous."

One meditator's comment sums up the whole thing very well: "So short a time ago my family was filled with tension, stress and strain. It has become a source of joy."

CHAPTER 4

Education and the Science of Creative Intelligence

The aim of American education in an age of rapid change should be to do what it can to help everybody gain complete possession of all his powers. . . . This is the only possible aim. It is now clear that the only thing we can do is what we ought to have been doing all along.

—ROBERT M. HUTCHINS

Dreams and Nightmares

It was the great dream of nineteenth- and early twentieth-century educators that universal free education and increasing numbers of students attending colleges and universities would mean an end to ignorance and hence to prejudice, hatred, covetousness and other symptoms of narrow vision. This dream has turned into a nightmare of sit-ins, riots, teacher strikes and college presidents dying of heart attacks, not to speak of the widespread increase in crime and violence and the obvious continuation of bigotry, corruption and all forms of suffering on all levels of society. If, then, this generation has become thoroughly disillusioned with what one student called "the fading paradise of academia and academics," it is good that we have, because it was truly an *illusion* that knowledge of history, physics, literature would enable us to love, to recognize and live lives attuned to higher values, to attain true freedom and create a world at peace.

Certainly all the branches of knowledge have their fascination and their important place in the growth and maintenance of a society. Because each branch of knowledge offers efficiency in life in a specific field, each branch is important both to the individual seeking a comprehensive understanding of life and to the well-being and progress of society. But in an age of such rapid change as ours, knowledge given or gained today may be obsolete or irrelevant tomorrow. What is considered "fact" today may be proven wrong tomorrow.* The accumulation and manipulation of knowledge is not truly education.

In the words of Aldous Huxley, "Twentieth-century educators have ceased to be concerned with questions of ultimate truth or meaning and (apart from mere vocational training) are interested solely in the dissemination of a rootless and irrelevant culture, and the fostering of the solemn foolery of scholarship for scholarship's sake." [1] Throughout the country and the world students are complaining—and increasing numbers of educators are concurring—that their education is "rootless and irrelevant." It seems superficial; it does not provide a true and meaningful basis for life. They are not satisfied with "the solemn foolery of scholarship"; they want more than intellectual knowledge, more than vocational or professional training, more than words and concepts, more than indoctrination into a society and culture which they are finding increasingly difficult to believe in and support.

---

* Dr. Robert Hilliard, a top educational broadcasting specialist for the Federal Communications Commission, says that "at the rate at which knowledge is growing, by the time the child born today graduates from college, the amount of knowledge in the world will be four times as great. By the time that same child is fifty years old, it will be thirty-two times as great, and 97 percent of everything known in the world will have been learned since the time he was born."

But what exactly *do* they want? The classrooms, meeting rooms and educational journals abound with questions and proposed answers. What can we ask of education? Where is relevant education to be found? How can it be created?

The Purpose of Education

Perhaps the answer lies embedded in the very meaning of the word "education," which comes from the Latin root *e-ducere,* "to bring or lead out." It implies a bringing out and developing of an individual's full capacity for life. "Instruction is the process of pumping information into the person, it literally means 'to build into'; whereas education means the process of nourishing or rearing," writes Ashley Montague in *The Direction of Human Development.* "We must recognize that today, in the western world, we have far too much instruction and all too little education. We are far too busy filling up the young with what we think they ought to know, to have much time left over for helping them become what they ought to be." [2] Or, as Kant said, "The idea of an education which will develop all man's natural gifts is certainly a true one. . . . Under the present system of education man does not fully attain the object of his being." [3]

In *The Science of Being and Art of Living* Maharishi Mahesh Yogi gives his definition of the purpose of education:

> The purpose of education is to culture the mind of a man so that he can accomplish all his aims in life. Education, to justify itself, should enable a man to use the full potential of his body, mind and spirit. It should also develop in him the ability to make the best use of his personality, surroundings, and circumstances so that he may accomplish the maximum in life for himself and for others. [4]

When we consider how far we are from accomplishing these basic and sensible aims, we may begin to realize the root cause of our discontent with present educational systems.

When we realize that, as Maharishi continues, "there are tremendous latent possibilities which are never unfolded by young people during their student life," [5] we can see why students are dissatisfied with what is offered by current educational institutions. Students are being asked to absorb and produce more and more, to live in a world that is uncertain, often meaningless, often repugnant. As the demands on them increase, nothing is offered to increase their abilities, to provide added intelligence, energy or emotional stability. There is no course to provide the students with what they really want and need. If there were a complete and successful method of self-development available in the schools by which an individual could "gain complete possession of all his powers," education would fulfill its purpose and the schools would be at peace.

Students have every right to expect that their education help them to develop, harmoniously and completely, their faculties for mental, physical and spiritual experience. True education should certainly help an individual discover and create meaningful values, meaningful goals and a direction in life. It should allow him to discover and become who he really is and prepare him to solve the problems and answer the questions that life poses.

In addition, students today, recognizing that the educational process is a most vital factor in the development of any society or civilization, demand that their education be socially relevant, that it provide a meaningful way to implement their ideals and be of use in the world. They ask that education give them the tools to create badly needed social change.

Broadly speaking, then, education has two purposes or functions: the cultivation and development of the individual and the improvement of society. Which of these two goals is most important? It is difficult to say, for they are mutually dependent. However, the very basis of our democratic society, that which distinguishes it from any form of collective or totalitarian system, is an insistence on the preeminence of the individual. "Democracy is a system that creates the economic, political and cultural conditions for the full development of the individual," says Erich Fromm in *Escape from Freedom.*[6] And the wisdom of this insistence is clear, for the better the individual, the better society will be. What, after all, *is* a society, if not individuals? Of course, a better society will offer more opportunity for individual development. It works both ways, and the two are inseparable. But how is society to become "better"?

The answer is obvious: "From the Emperor down to the mass of the people, all must consider the cultivation of the person the root of all else."[7] We are not quite faced with the old chicken/egg paradox. Indeed, as Robert Hutchins says in his book *The Conflict in Education,* "Society is to be improved, not by forcing a program of social reform down its throat, through the schools or otherwise, but by the improvement of the individuals who compose it. As Plato said, 'Governments reflect human nature. States are not made of stone or wood, but out of the characters of their citizens: these turn the scale and draw everything after them.' The individual is the heart of society."[8]

It is easy to see which must come first, and yet the modern world seems to be dealing with the problem upside down. Don't we realize that we cannot legislate fulfilled human beings? We cannot write a law requiring hungry men to be full or angry men to be peaceful.

"I believe," said John Dewey, "that all reforms which rest simply upon the enactment of law, or the threatening of certain penalties, or upon changes in mechanical or outward arrangements, are transitory and futile. . . . Only by being true to the full growth of individuals who make it up, can society by any chance be true to itself."[9]

The Missing Element

If the outer structure and expression of life is based on the inner state of consciousness—as so many great thinkers have told us and as we ourselves are realizing more and more—why is it that we have tended to turn outward, dealing always with structures and forms, handling problem situations with whatever capabilities we have, instead of attempting to improve our capacity for effective, intelligent action? Why has inner development, the basis of all success and happiness in life, the most fundamental aspect of our education, been neglected?

The answer, stated bluntly, is overwhelming: *There simply has been no successful way to raise the level of human life.*

The dream of individual fulfillment and social harmony through education has failed because, although every person in our country goes through approximately 12 years of schooling, he is not given *education*—he does not come into complete possession of all his powers for living a full, useful and harmonious life. In a sense, then, we could say that *education has been missing from our society*. What we have called education has been incomplete and baseless. It has not provided an individual with a foundation for successfully living in the world.

This problem becomes intensified when we consider it in terms of higher education, which seems to present an unresolvable dilemma. On one hand, individual academic disciplines have—through the knowledge explosion—reached a point of refinement requiring a very high degree of specialization on the part of the scholar if he is to advance to the frontiers of his field and thereby fulfill the aspirations of scholarship. On the other hand, this specialization can apparently only be gained at the expense of knowledge in other fields of activity—fields which may be equally or even more relevant to his broader goal of living a fulfilled life in today's challenging world. A man may be a great scientist, make important discoveries and advance science, yet when he comes home from the laboratory he may not be able to deal with his family in a competent and loving manner. Individual development has largely been out of balance, incomplete. The pace and style of living today *necessitate* specialization: no one can learn everything and be an expert in all fields of knowledge. But this specialization should not be at the expense of a harmonious development of the personality.

Fulfillment in life requires efficiency in all fields of life's activity; fulfillment of scholarship means efficiency in a highly specialized branch of learning. Unfortunately there seems to be not enough time for both, and this conflict can only deepen with the further expansion of knowledge. The result is that institutions of higher learning are becoming increasingly unable to carry out their traditional responsibility of equipping the student with the intelligence and will to understand himself and solve the problems of his day. In the wake of this impotence have come the tensions which threaten the very foundations of higher education and, indeed, of broader components of Western civilization.[10]

What is missing from education, then, is an effective system or technique to improve our capacity for creative, intelligent action. We have known no successful process to expand the ability of the heart for love and human kindness, no way to help an individual attain full use of his potential for dealing effectively with all situations of life.

This, essentially, is all that is lacking. This statement is not an apology for the status quo: no doubt the current forms of education must, and will, change. But the changes must begin from within, with a development in the level of consciousness of the individuals who create the forms. The solution to the problem lies in the same place as the *source* of the problem: the individuals who make up society. If they experience no significant growth, we will see only futile shifting on the same level, only random change and experimentation, action and reaction mistaken for improvement and progress. "No man ever achieves his real self until he is his best self," writes Montague. "Man's self is the means of whatever ends he achieves, and the ends he seeks to achieve are largely determined by the nature of the self. . . . Hence the pressing necessity of realizing that healthy human development and survival depends upon our ability to help human beings fulfill their potentialities." [11]

That there is a pressing need for depth education, education of the whole man, is being increasingly recognized in America. Even in the sciences, where specialization is most extreme, the greatest minds have emphasized the importance of full human development. In *Out of My Later Years* Albert Einstein wrote that "the school should always have as its aim that the young man leave it as a harmonious personality, not as a specialist. The development of general ability for independent thinking and judgment should always be placed foremost." [12]

Swarthmore College's *Critique of a College* declares that the college must strive to develop an atmosphere in which a student can "find out who he is and what he really ought to become." [13] Franklin Patterson, president of Hampshire College, states that, as he sees it, the goal of his college is to help students "live fully and well in a society of intense change," a society which will offer "more options, more complex dilemmas, more possible joys, more chance of surprise and wonder, . . . more demands, more satisfactions, and more of a fighting chance to be human than men have known before." [14]

The 1968 study by the Hazen Foundation, called *The Student in Higher Education,* criticizes "American higher education for not being more concerned about the total personality development of its students," and asks that the American institution of higher learning "do more than ever before to educate the 'whole man.' " Significantly, the members of the Hazen committee note that "men of good will and intelligence have always sought this end, and there are educators today still seeking it." [15] Certainly the need for a way to unfold the full potential of man is the greatest need of the age, and it is the legitimate province and fundamental function of education.

The Science of Creative Intelligence:
Emergence of a New Science

> The thing in this world which is of most su-
> preme importance, indeed the thing which is of
> most practical value to the race, is not, after all,
> useful discovery or invention, but that which lies
> far back of them, namely, "the way men think." [16]
>
> —ROBERT A. MILLIKAN

The science of creative intelligence is emerging in response to this challenge of our times. The student support which is generating this emergence is based in part on a growing realization that despite all the elaborate theories and intellectual structures, the ultimate answer to basic fulfillment will be simple, not complex; inner, not external; natural, not synthetic.

The point of departure of SCI lies in its basic premise: there exists a source of creative intelligence which can be contacted by any individual, through the technique of transcendental meditation, and applied to all fields of life. Creative intelligence is defined by Maharishi Mahesh Yogi as "the impelling life force which manifests itself in the evolutionary process through creation of new forms and new relationships in the universe."

"A *science*," says a Maharishi International University brochure, "is taken to be a systematic investigation, by means of repeatable experiment, to gain useful and verifiable knowledge. *Creativity* is the cause of change and is present everywhere, at all times. *Intelligence* is a basic quality of existence exemplified in the purpose and order of change. *Creative Intelligence,* then, is the single and branching flow of energy (creativity) and directedness (intelligence) observable in all phenomena, and the *Science of Creative Intelligence* is the study of the nature, origin, range, growth and application of creative intelligence." "This science," the brochure continues, "arose from the major discovery that there exists throughout creation and in every human being an inexhaustible source of intelligence, energy and happiness, and that this source can be easily and systematically drawn upon by everyone for spontaneous use in daily life."

Courses in SCI include two aspects, theoretical and practical. The intellectual content of SCI includes an exploration of the premises that creative intelligence can be logically explained, directly experienced, scientifically verified, artistically actualized and fully unfolded and applied to all fields of knowledge and activity. The practical phase, sometimes called the "laboratory work," is transcendental meditation, by means of which this inner field of energy and intelligence can be experienced. TM brings the mind into contact with this field (sometimes referred to as Being, source of thought, or pure consciousness, as well as creative intelligence). The practical aspect verifies and gives substance to the theory, while the theory gives breadth and profundity to the experience. With these two aspects—experience and understanding—knowledge is complete.

The thrust of SCI is toward unfolding the full value of the subjective phase of knowledge. All knowledge includes two sides, a subjective and an objective, the knower and the known. Objects of knowledge abound; the "knowledge explosion" doubles every few years the amount of knowledge available to man. But man's mind, the container of knowledge, does not expand at an equivalent rate. In order for man not to be overwhelmed by the fast pace of life, the burden of decisions and responsibilities, too much fragmented knowledge, too much input of information, an increase in subjective development is imperative.

"Who Sees the Flower?" or, Getting to Know the Knower

The basis of all knowledge is the knower. "Knowledge," Maharishi explains, "is the product of the union of the knower and the known. The process of knowing connects the knower with the object of knowing." [17] Without the knower there is no knowledge, and without *knowledge* of the knower, of the subjective aspect of the process of knowing, knowledge is baseless. Without an experience of the experiencer, experience is baseless. Without knowing who it is that lives and enjoys, life itself is found to be baseless.

It may seem strange, at first, to suggest that the subjective phase of knowledge is ordinarily beyond the range of our experience. But what exactly *is* the experience of a man who says, "I see a flower"? We cannot doubt that he sees the flower—or rather, that the flower is being seen—but *who* sees the flower? Who is the "I"? Is it the eye, the retina of the eye, the optic nerve, some area of the brain—who is the "I" that sees the flower?

What we find when we examine carefully is that this "I" is very elusive. It is interesting that we can always locate the object of experience, but locating the subject is not so easy. It is easy to locate the flower that we see or smell, the music that we hear, some stiffness that we feel in our neck—it is even easy to locate our thoughts (I am thinking about my friend Joe)—but *who* is having all those experiences? We say, "I see," "I do," "I like," and yet we don't know who that "I" is, where it is located. For many centuries we have heard the dictum, "Know thyself," but we haven't been able to do so. Knowing *about* the self is not the same as knowing the self. We may know, "I like ice cream," "I don't like spinach"; "I can play the guitar but I'm too shy to play before others." This still doesn't locate that "I" who is at the basis of all experience and activity.

The science of creative intelligence intellectually locates the "I," the self, and defines it as a field of pure consciousness, a field of energy and creative intelligence, the source of all thought. On the practical side, through the process of transcendental meditation, the individual learns to reduce an object of knowledge systematically until the subject, the experiencer (the pure consciousness or Being) comes to full awareness.* This strengthens the subjective phase of life, opening the awareness to a broader range of comprehension and providing a basis of true self-knowledge for all thought and action.

"Knowledge," Maharishi has said, "is structured in consciousness." This phrase from the Rig Veda has been chosen as the motto of Maharishi International University. It means that whatever knowledge we gain, by whatever means—direct perception, intellectual analysis, inference—is always dependent upon our state of consciousness. When we see a room, that perception, the knowledge of who and what is in the room, is structured in our consciousness. It is based on awareness. When consciousness changes, knowledge changes. The room, blue and well-furnished in the waking state, may become golden and floating through space in the dream state of consciousness. To a child the complex workings of a watch may be mysterious and marvelous. To the same child, now a grown-up watchmaker, the watch is a well-understood object, looked at totally differently. Knowledge is different in different states of consciousness.

In order for the object to be experienced in its full value, Maharishi explains, in order for maximum truth of the object to be cognized, it is obvious that the subject has to be most fully developed, most completely alert. In order for knowledge to be unchanging, the subject must be unchanging: he must have a stable vantage point from which to observe and experience. When the pure field of creative intelligence becomes stabilized in one's awareness, that nonchanging, unbounded field of pure consciousness provides a platform from which all knowledge that is gained will be most useful, most profound, most complete and most fulfilling. Such knowledge can lead to profound action, resulting in significant achievement and fulfillment.

If the mind is not fully developed, it cannot be established

---

* See Chapter 1, page 28.

in that unbounded awareness. If education does not accomplish the full development of the mind, it cannot be said to be complete. Then knowledge will be incomplete. Action based on incomplete, ever-changing knowledge will not lead to significant achievement, and fulfillment will not be gained. SCI, by bringing to conscious awareness the source of thought, unfolds the full value of creative intelligence. This subjective development enhances all facets of activity, leading to life in fulfillment.

Did Newton Create Gravity? or, What Science Does

Thus, SCI brings to light, both theoretically and practically, the inner field of creative intelligence, and demonstrates how all aspects of knowledge and experience can be enriched and fulfilled by contact with it.

The phrase "brings to light" is significant, for it makes clear that SCI does not create anything new, it only brings to the light of our attention the knowledge of this unbounded field of creative potentiality. This is the case with any science. Physics, for instance, did not create the molecular and atomic strata of life; physicists discovered the reality of those levels and gave practical application to that knowledge. Nor was it the work of Copernicus and Galileo that made the earth revolve around the sun—theirs was a discovery of the mechanics of the universe that completely revolutionized man's way of seeing and understanding.

Newton did not create the force of gravity, but his discovery of it was both theoretically revealing and practically useful. Freud did not create the unconscious level of the mind; his discoveries, however, opened the door to a significant expansion of knowledge about the nature of man.

Clearly, then, science brings to our awareness aspects of life which already exist. Similarly, the science of creative intelligence reveals what has hitherto been beyond our experience and presents this new knowledge in a systematic way.

Life: Its Structure and Creative Intelligence

The science of creative intelligence asserts that there is a structure to life, that underlying the myriad, ever-changing, ever-evolving forms and phenomena of life is an "impelling life-force," an unbounded field of pure creative intelligence, which gives rise to the ever-new face of manifest creation. "The infinite expanse of the universe, its growth through immeasurable periods of time, the boundless range of its changes, and the rational order that pervades it all, seem to demand an infinite intelligence behind its manifestation," wrote David Starr Jordan, former president of Stanford University.[18]

Indeed, the "strongest and noblest driving force behind scientific research," said Albert Einstein, is "a deep faith in the rationality of the structure of the world" and "a longing to understand even a small glimpse of the reason revealed in the world." [19]

And certainly, from cosmos to electron, from galaxy to the atom, order is found. Life is organized, structured. Any living thing develops and is structured according to an organizational plan, a norm. There is some tremendously powerful ordering principle at work, maintaining any life and allowing it to progress, integrating it as a personality, an individuality. A living thing is an organized system of structures and functions, not a mass of independent, uncoordinated parts. For instance, when we eat, we take in a wide diversity of elements in our food. The system breaks these down even further to a myriad of molecules and then distributes them and builds them into the system: this protein goes here and this vitamin goes there, each occupying a precise place in the whole. As tissues wear out, matter leaves the organism. There is a constant turnover in the system, but, by a self-regulating process far beyond our comprehension or control, the organism maintains itself and its individuality.

"Development," said Yale biologist Edmund Sinnott, "is

not an aimless affair; each stage follows precisely its predecessor. . . . Each organism has its particular series of norms, its special cycle of progressive and creative development. Continual change is the keynote of this cycle; not unguided change but change that moves toward a very definite end—the mature individual and the completion of the cycle." [20]

Sinnot cites as an example how the growing shoot tip of a plant, if cut off and put into water or moist sand, will regenerate its entire root system. "Not only will isolated bits of stem do this but often leaf stalks, flower stalks or bits of the leaf blade. Many cases have been found where an entire plant will grow from a single cell, and presumably every cell has the power to do this if proper conditions could be provided." [21]

"This tendency in every living system to integrate its materials and processes in conformity with a norm which it persistently seeks to reach," Sinnott continues, "emphasizes the essentially teleological character of development and function. The unity of the organism seems to inhere in the end toward which it is moving. . . . Such a conception puts 'mind,' of a sort, into all animals and even into plants, and makes it coextensive with life. . . . *Life* itself is the creative process by virtue of its organizing, pattern-forming, questing quality, its most distinctive character." [22]

This most basic aspect of life is what Maharishi calls "creative intelligence." "Order in nature," Maharishi explains, "and man's power of ordering show that intelligence is at the core of every physical existence and every human mind. The understanding of the nature of intelligence, therefore, can be the common ground of all knowledge." [23] Albert Einstein had a very similar view of reality, based on an orderly cosmic structure, a "nobility and marvelous order which are revealed in nature and the world of thought," which he felt were only barely and partially apprehendable and expressible by man. [24]

The science of creative intelligence not only delineates this underlying "infinite intelligence," it shows the way to expand the conscious capacity of the mind to incorporate this field within direct experience and to contact it regularly. This results in "a natural and balanced development of all aspects of individual life. By enlivening the pure field of creative intelligence on the level of the individual, it is feasible to consider the possibility of a state of life in which one can be fully at home in all fields of knowledge and activity." [25]

Gaining the Advantage of Knowledge

Maximum efficiency in various fields of life is the promise of the different branches of learning. But man's goal is complete fulfillment, efficiency in *all* aspects of life, not just one or two or 20. We have seen that on the level of the different branches it is not possible to gain that fulfillment. Man does not have the time or the capacity to assimilate and master the enormous amount of available knowledge.

But maximum effectiveness in life *can* be gained by applying a well-known and obvious principle: handle the level of cause in order to have most influence on the level of effect. Handle the atomic level and maximum power over the surface level is gained. Nourish the root of the tree and all the branches thrive. On the level of the branches and leaves it is impossible to care for the life of the tree effectively. But from the level of the root it is possible.

We have seen that all fields of life spring from one source: Being, the underlying, unbounded ocean of creative intelligence and energy. This is the root of the tree of life, the ultimate cause of all the innumerable effects which constitute the relative field of life. If we can handle the level of Being, by contacting it, then spontaneously it nourishes the various branches of life, strengthening all aspects of thought, speech and action. Spontaneously the effect is taken care of, and life grows in freedom.

Overall effectiveness in life is the goal of education, but wholeness cannot be gained by amending the parts. The holistic value of education can *never* be gained by studying one branch and then another and then another. But by contacting the root of all knowledge and action, even without studying all the branches of learning, man gains the advantage of them: effectiveness in living and growth toward fulfillment. The apparent isolation or fragmentation of different spheres of knowledge or activity is due to narrowness of vision. As the capacity of the individual increases, the possibility for creative and integrative understanding increases; different avenues of man's concern are seen in a broader context, and the individual gains the ability to be more "at home" with life. To a fully expanded mind, "no field will be foreign or irrelevant and the application of knowledge will naturally flow in channels which are of maximum benefit to oneself and one's surroundings." [26]

The primary purpose of gaining knowledge is to use it, to gain some advantage from that knowledge. That there exists an atomic level of life is fascinating; utilizing the tremendous energy that can be gained by manipulating that level is practical and may prove crucial in solving man's energy requirements as population grows and natural resources are depleted. That there exists a structure to life, an outer, limited surface value and an inner, unbounded basis of energy and intelligence, is also fascinating; individuals *tapping* that inner source can gain the advantage of it: they can grow spontaneously toward the fulfillment of life.

The Real News Is Good News

I think this is the real news, that there is coming to the Western world through Maharishi what is really news, due to the fact that there have been people contemplating and isolating themselves for thousands of years, not apparently trying to bring advantage to many except in quite mysterious ways . . . but really only looking out for their own personal salvation. I'm sure what makes Maharishi beloved and understood is that he has manifest love. You could not meet with Maharishi without recognizing instantly his integrity. You look in his eyes and there it is. . . .

That Maharishi has been spontaneously engaging the love, understanding and support of the young is the most important manifestation we can have of that beautiful integrity. So, I'd like to say to the news that the great news is that young America has its arms open for the truth and love, tenderness, compassion, and for the only way in which we can know the truth, through our minds.

Our young world at first manifested great abhorrence for the non-truth, the superficial misleading information about customs, and now that young world has gone beyond just being dismayed and being disapproving of the non-truth, but is demonstrating in this wave of inspiration by Maharishi, demonstrating its yearning and its determination for humanity to survive on this planet. Very deep forces are operative here, the forces of the great intellect of the universe itself. This is the news. It's not easy to report in the newspaper this kind of news, but this is the news! [27]

Thus spoke Buckminster Fuller, scientist, architect, poet, mathematician, inventor, philosopher, creator of the geodesic dome. The occasion was the First International Symposium on the Science of Creative Intelligence, conducted at the University of Massachusetts in Amherst in late July of 1971. Before the symposium, Maharishi and Buckminster Fuller had never met. For two days they shared the stage, explaining to each other and a rapt audience their respective visions of man and the universe. When they had finished it was obvious to all that each man was deeply moved by the other. In response to Fuller's expressed appreciation of him and his movement, Maharishi said, "You are a great inspiration. . . . The message Mr. Fuller brings is the message of a fuller life."

Fuller, a man of broad and acute vision, a global ecologist before environment was anyone's concern, innocently subscribed the message of SCI by his repeated assertion that "I'm personally very deeply convinced that I have no faculties with which all human beings are not endowed. I do not think I am any exception whatsoever in this matter."

The Amherst symposium and a shorter one held a month later at Humboldt State College in the redwood country of Northern California were marked by lively exchanges between great minds. Nobel laureate Melvin Calvin, professor of chemistry at Berkeley, traced the molecular history of living organisms from the simplest to the most complex organizational structures, relating his ideas to SCI:

> Maharishi has recently said: "The whole of individual and cosmic life is fundamentally creative because it goes on and on; it is progressive, evolutionary; and the whole of life is fundamentally intelligent because it proceeds systematically, containing its own order and *unfolding in an overall orderly way."* . . . This seemed to focus my attention on that part of our more recent work in which we were concerned with the processes of chemical evolution. . . .
> The important idea here is that the structure of an atom is such that if one has those atoms present under the proper conditions (in the laboratory or in the primeval earth) with an energy input, they will combine in only certain kinds of ways.
> . . . Therefore there must be a molecular mechanism to decide which molecules are dominant over other ones. This requires the concept of stereospecific autocatalysis, [which] means that molecules are capable of inducing their own generation in a highly geometrically specific fashion.[28]

Maharishi, delighted by this concept, replied:

> It is so beautiful. One expression of an outstanding scientist innocently reveals the essential nature of creative intelligence. . . .
> The functioning of creative intelligence is such that under similar circumstances, similar results occur. Just this phenomenon explains why there is harmony in creation, not chaos. The apple tree only grows into apple fruit; it doesn't produce guavas. But if the circumstances

changed, grafting could produce guavas. The infinite flexibility of creative intelligence maintains its stereo-specific quality.

There is something definite; nothing is random, and it is this specific value of creative intelligence which automatically carries out evolution everywhere.[29]

Frank Barron, a noted authority on creativity and professor of psychology at the University of California at Santa Cruz, emphasized in his talk that "if we are to understand Man, the microcosm, we must understand him in relation to the cosmic matrix out of which his being emerged and in which his existence is immersed." Maharishi's reply was:

It is in the individual intelligence that the universal intelligence works. It is in the waves that the ocean moves. Within this range of individuality and universality is stationed the integration of man, the fullness of what he is and his possibilities. The Science of Creative Intelligence enlivens this natural co-existence in man: it arrests universality within the boundaries of individuality and moves infinity in his every breath.[30]

Some found the talk by Major General Franklin M. Davis, Commandant of the U.S. Army War College, and the replies by Maharishi most provocative. Davis, who is finding TM personally useful ("My friends and colleagues and my wife say it has improved my disposition, and my doctor says it's knocked my blood pressure down ten points"), seemed most optimistic about its application for others: "Transcendental meditation is the only thing I'm aware of aside from 'don't-do-it' lectures that offers promise in the mounting drug abuse problem."

Commenting on General Davis' talk, Maharishi expressed the view that the *real* purpose of the military is "victory before war—that is, to keep war from happening, or to end it quickly if it does happen"—in short, to maintain and protect a state of peace.

Such interchanges may have been the highlight of the symposium for some. Others may have been more deeply engrossed in the smaller seminars, in which the speakers discussed their fields with interested course participants, or by the harmony and creative understanding that pervaded the atmosphere. For whatever reason, everyone felt the symposia to be exciting and deeply meaningful events—"the real news," as Buckminster Fuller expressed it.

Results I: What the Students Say

Any discussion of the science of creative intelligence should not obscure the fact that its results—expansion of the mind, deep physical rest with the attendant release of stress, and changed behavioral patterns toward a more harmonious and loving response to life—are due to the practice of transcendental meditation; they are *not* the product of the intellectual analysis which constitutes the theoretical phase of SCI. In itself, the technique of TM has nothing whatsoever to do with analysis or rational thought. It is purely a process of direct perception at subtler or earlier stages of the thought process, until the source of thought, the field of Being or pure creative intelligence, is brought within the range of conscious experience.

Now that we have taken a thorough look at the theoretical framework of SCI, it would be interesting to examine the applied values of TM and SCI by exploring some personal experiences, particularly related to education, either in the more usual sense of schooling or in the broader sense of unfolding a more comprehensive vision and appreciation of life.

First of all, what do some of the students who have taken SCI for credit feel about its value?

One of the students remarked that the class was "more relevant to life than any other class I've been in." Another said it offered "freedom to think and create," while another expressed gratitude that it "offered many uncoverings of self that other classes can't even come close to." Several mentioned the value of SCI as a basis for knowledge, remarking that it "gave a reason to other classes," "offered us the key to other class offerings," or gave new ability to "relate the material to all fields of learning."

What about the value of TM alone, without the theoretical framework?

Mary * is a teenage girl, living in Southern California. Like many other high-school students, she always resented the fact that she *"had* to go to school. I usually did very little 'assigned' work, and spent most of my time reading or studying only subjects that interested me. As a result of this, I had about a C average. I hated grades and 'busy-work' assignments and regular classes. I ditched class regularly, and generally read my own books during classes. I was very frustrated and unhappy.

"Since beginning meditation"—she had been meditating about six months—"I have felt less 'forced' and 'trapped.' I still spend most of my time reading my own books and doing research in subjects of my own interest, but I also listen and take part in class. I find myself even liking the lectures. I feel much more interest for the required courses and am learning much more. The initiative is there now."

A nineteen-year-old boy majoring in religious studies summed up his remarks on TM this way: "All aspects of my activities [in school], be it reading, understanding, discussing or researching, have found steady improvement. I've always had good grades, but for the first time I've found learning to be joyful solely for the sake of learning."

A girl in Berkeley told me, "I've been in school two years while meditating. At the beginning I was average to mediocre. Every time I had a paper, I was miserable for about two weeks—it was an emotional trauma. In school this last quarter I had lots of papers to write and they just flowed out of me with no trauma. I feel my intellect has grown with meditation. I'm more logical and can express myself more clearly. I got A's this time which I never got in college before. The whole way I think has cleared."

———————

* All names are changed in the following anecdotes.

Paul is a filmmaker who has been meditating for a little over a year and a half. He is not a student, but his experience with transcendental meditation exemplifies TM's ability to satisfy the principal aim of education: enabling a person to live a life of fulfillment. A definition of fulfillment, given by William Schutz of Esalen Institute, seems to be tailor-made for the following story. "Fulfillment," Schutz writes, "brings to an individual the feeling that he can cope with his environment; the sense of confidence in himself as a significant, competent, lovable person who is capable of handling situations as they arise, able to use fully his capacities, and free to express his feelings." [31]

"Before I began meditation I was very nervous and tense (I smoked two packages of cigarettes a day). I was exhausted in the evening after the day's work. I usually had trouble sleeping. The main problem was that I felt I had stopped growing and was going nowhere, and my ideals all seemed very intellectual and impractical. I felt little confidence in myself and my ambitions and was ashamed of the very moral side of my character which I could never ignore and which, it seemed to me, would probably ruin my chances for success in life. I had a great desire for something more in life having experimented with drugs for a year and found, at least intellectually, that life held more than met the eye. Drugs became quite boring to me, however, and I stopped taking them about six months prior to meditation.

"Now, just over a year and a half later, the progress I've made in every element of life seems nothing less than astounding to me. At work, I have such great energy that I'm able to be of great service to all with whom I work and I take great pleasure in this service. I find that I am so clear-sighted now that no matter how hard I'm working, I can learn great lessons from the more experienced filmmakers with whom I work. I find that I am progressing at a smooth and even pace upwards to the greater responsibility and potential for artistic expression which I seek.

"In personal relationships, I find it so easy and pleasurable to communicate with people, to like them and see what is best in them. My perceptions seem to become deeper and more positive all the time. There just are not any problems any more in relating to other people. When I go home and meditate now I have the energy to enjoy the evenings with my family, to read, think or otherwise to grow in my chosen directions.

"Nothing is really hard any more. At work or at home, when something comes up, I figure out what the desired results are, how to accomplish them, and then take the necessary action. The energy is there and I use it. No problem. I also can see that my actions are becoming more and more supported by nature, as my needs, desires and ambitions are fulfilled at a smoothly, easily flowing pace. I now sleep better and have stopped smoking. My physical problems are all clearing up slowly but surely. My relations with my wife and child are very honest and usually blissfully happy, productive and loving.

"From the continued practice of TM I expect the fruition, intensification and fulfillment of all the good results I have already experienced. I expect to achieve my ambitions as an artist and also as a person desirous of helping humanity by becoming an Initiator [a teacher of TM]. I expect a happy family life with my children naturally getting on to meditation and growing to realization at a very early age.

"With things as good as they are and improving as fast as they are, I have little doubt but that the rest of my life is going to be an extremely enjoyable experience for myself and my loved ones."

This is a beautiful example of what Maharishi means by "the balanced development of all aspects of life." Among meditators experiences like these are not extraordinary.

Tommy, age seventeen, has just—to everyone's surprise—finished high school. He gives TM credit for this and for some other radical changes in his life. "When I started transcendental meditation," he said, "I was living at home and going to *high* school. (Before I started meditating, I was taking a lot of drugs.) While I was going to school I felt very confined and somewhat confused. The rest of the time I felt rather loaded and didn't care much about anything.

"Since I started this practice I have found myself much more interested in things happening around me. I feel much more love, concern, and understanding for my people. My abilities in art and music have increased, I'm happier, more energetic. I think that the meditation let me cut a pathway through my jungle of egotistical confusion to my self, my real self, me!

"Having been meditating for only this short period [four months], I see that I am much healthier. I am able to cope with my environment much more than I could before. I have stopped taking drugs almost entirely, I've graduated from high school, which I was going to drop out of. I am now going to go to college. I've got a direction in life. I'm happier than I've ever been before. I'm calmer, yet more alert, more productive. I get along much better with my family. I rarely become angered about anything. To sum it all up, it's good."

One question often asked at campus lectures on TM is, "Will my grades go up?" Although teachers are cautious about making promises, practical experience shows that the answer is usually yes. A typical example: "I just got test and term paper results back and my grades have improved 1.5 grade points: B pluses and A's with less effort than used to result in C's."

"Before I began meditation I was into a very heavy drug scene," wrote a recent graduate who has meditated 18 months. "As a result I had seemed to have lost contact with people. I could not communicate. I was barely getting by in school. Today things are unbelievably better. I just graduated and had my choice of graduate schools. I got straight A's last term."

Another student, explaining the benefits she has gained

from TM, said: "Usually at the end of a term I fall apart under the stress of papers and exams, and work continually and inefficiently, without sleep—turning in papers late and always feeling guilty about the work I haven't done. This past term I had more courses than ever before. I did not realize until it was over that I had made it without any crises, had written three papers I didn't even have to write in addition to the others (and got A's, which I don't usually get)."

Results II: What the Teachers Say

"For the past year and a half," said Bob E., a science teacher at a large private school in New Jersey, "I have witnessed the growth of transcendental meditation among the students. It started with only a few of the kids, but now there are over 60 meditators in an upper-school population of 350. In some cases the results have been dramatic, in others more subtle changes have taken place. Most students who practice TM find that they can cope with the pressures of school and grades more effectively. They are relaxed and more open with the faculty and their fellow students. Many find that their home situation has improved also; they no longer feel so hostile toward their parents.

"Students who had been using drugs previous to starting meditation find that TM gives them the impetus to stop. Those who continue to use drugs after starting soon find that they don't enjoy drugs as much and gradually stop.

"Three faculty members have started to meditate, and quite a few more are planning to start over the summer. The head of the Guidance Department, a meditator himself, can hardly wait until the entire school is meditating. Meditation, he claims, does his job for him."

A meditating college instructor told of some changes in her own abilities after beginning TM. "Before I started to meditate, I wasn't enjoying teaching that much; it wasn't a joy to me. But as your consciousness expands and you see more, you are able to empathize more with people. You're able to talk with them and understand them, open up to them, enter their world, and in teaching this is a tremendous asset. Students in college realize that most of the time the teachers don't open themselves up to their students: they don't have the time, they just can't be bothered, or whatever. After I started to meditate, I found that I could talk to my students, listen to them, open up to their whole world and help them create in their own ways. People were amazed at my classes, because my students were all energetic, working very hard, and loving it—and growing tremendously."

An elementary-school teacher expressed a similar discovery. "As a teacher I find that my students are a very real reflection of me. When I am enthusiastic, buoyant and energetic my students can feel this and respond positively. . . . I believe that understanding my Self has given me the basis I need to understand the individual problems of the children in my class. Most of the discipline problems stem from a lack of love and understanding in the first place. Transcendental meditation has given me a love of other people and an ability to understand their needs."

A young woman working as a teacher in the children's centers of the Los Angeles Board of Education told me, "I used to find it necessary to take a leave of absence every couple months because that was about the length of time I could tolerate the other teachers. The kids were fine but the teachers were unbelievable! . . . From the first day after beginning meditation, I enjoyed work more because all tension was relieved and I used less energy. The relationship between the children and myself is beautiful, complete harmony; and luckily, the deeper and broader perception has been accompanied by greater tolerance and understanding, especially toward the other teachers I work with. Every day is completely enjoyable!"

A high-school teacher told me, "Teachers ought to be the most patient, loving, understanding people; they have to set

an example for their students. But with the discipline problems, the pressures from the administration and the parents,
most teachers I know are exhausted or on the edge of being
nervous wrecks. TM is exactly what they need. The difference
I feel in myself is incredible. I hope this NIMH program is
the beginning of something very big." *

"As an educator who has been in the field of higher education for almost 20 years," said a professor at the University of Michigan, "I consider the movement for spiritual regeneration extremely valuable for our society and especially
for our youth, which is so desperately looking for ways to
improve our mode of living and thinking.

"The question the young people of today are really concerned with is not just, 'What can I do?' but 'Who am I?' . . .
and ultimately 'What is Man, and what is his destiny on this
earth?' Our educational system treats these fundamental is-
sues only superficially and provides no satisfactory solutions.
Such disciplines as sociology, economics, political science and
anthropology all deal with the Phenomenon of Man, yet each
from its limited point of view. . . .

"I believe that the question of what constitutes the source
of our thinking, which leads to all our 'rational' actions and
makes us distinctly 'human,' is indeed crucial and not purely
speculative and academic. The science of creative intelligence
as developed by Maharishi Mahesh Yogi . . . provides an-

----

* In the summer of 1972 the National Institute of Mental Health
(an agency of the U.S. Department of Health, Education and
Welfare) provided funding and scholarships for 150 secondary-
school teachers and administrators to attend a one-month SCI
training course at Humboldt State College. The 150, chosen from
over 400 applicants, coming to California from as far as New
York, New Jersey and Massachusetts, learned to teach the principles of SCI and returned to their home schools enthusiastically
armed with new and useful knowledge. Indications are that this
pilot program is the beginning of a trend that will see wide-scale
government support of TM and SCI on the federal, state and
local levels.

swers to these questions on both theoretical and practical levels. It shows how to utilize our human potential to the fullest, making it possible for our intellectual capacities to develop on a firm basis and in the process enabling all the other faculties to unfold and improve. Both the mind and the heart develop. This is the ultimate goal of all true education."

CHAPTER 5

Self-Actualization

Let each become all that
he was created capable of being:
expand, if possible, to his full growth;
and show himself at length
in his own shape and stature.

—THOMAS CARLYLE

A New Model of Man

"Every age but ours has had its model, its ideal," wrote Abraham Maslow in the introduction to his book *Toward a Psychology of Being.* "All of these have been given up by our culture; the saint, the hero, the gentleman, the knight, the mystic." Elsewhere, he noted that "all these myths failed, and are now giving way to a new one that is slowly developing in the minds of the most advanced thinkers and researchers on the subject." [1]

This new ideal is the self-realized individual: one who uses his powers fully and creatively, who acts with spontaneity and freedom, who radiates love and goodness, accepts himself and others, and is self-expressive and fully alive.

In the last chapter we found that the only real and proper goal of education is full development of man, or, as Erich Fromm put it in *The Art of Loving,* "Education is identical with helping the child realize his potentialities." [2] Full development of man means development of both the inner and the outer aspects of life; it means that all man's capacities for action in the world should be unfolded along with his potential for enjoying and appreciating the multifarious forms and phenomena of creation, and that the goal of his deepest spiritual longings should also be fulfilled. It means that man should enjoy full utilization of his mental, physical, emotional and spiritual capacities.

The quest for self-realization, we have seen, is a dominant theme of our age. Is there anyone today who does not want to *be* more, to develop his capabilities and live a fuller life? Not only have individuals felt the need for a greater measure of personal achievement and satisfaction, but, as Maslow said, "the most advanced thinkers and researchers" interested in human development, those who want to create conditions more conducive to a truly human way of life, are coming to the inevitable conclusion that if we want to make any lasting and profound change in the world we must turn to man himself. "States are not made out of stone or wood, but out of the characters of their citizens." Man must become more than he is: more intelligent, more creative, more perceptive and broad-minded, more compassionate and loving, more productive and effective. "Quite clearly the two great things for which we aim," Aldous Huxley said, "are the improvement of intelligence and the deepening and the extension of the feeling of friendliness and love." [3] Yet, there is no need to *give* man these qualities, to impose them from without. He holds them, potentially, within himself. What he needs is a way to bring them out and become what he really *is*.

For centuries man has suffered from an inability to be fully himself, to realize fully all that he inwardly knows he can be. As the German dramatist Hebbel expressed it, "The man I am greets mournfully the man I might have been." This is one of the most tragic statements any man can make about himself. And yet who among us has not had that thought? Who has not sometimes felt that life seems to be passing by, yet we are not full, not really alive, not producing what we could, enjoying as we could, giving as we would wish? Have we not all felt, at some time or another, that we have not made all that we could of our lives?

"The first point to agree upon in this enterprise," wrote the great early psychologist William James,

> is that as a rule men habitually use a small part of the powers which they actually possess and which they might use under appropriate conditions.
>
> Everyone is familiar with the phenomenon of feeling more or less alive on different days. Everyone knows on any given day that there are energies slumbering in him which the incitements of the day do not call forth, but which he might display if these were greater. Most of us feel as if a sort of cloud weighed upon us, keeping us below our highest notch of clearness in discernment, sureness in reasoning, or firmness in deciding. Compared with what we ought to be, we are only half awake. . . . We are making use of only a small part of our possible mental and physical resources.
>
> Stating the thing broadly, the human individual thus lives usually far within his limits; he possesses powers of various sorts which he habitually fails to use. He energizes below his maximum, and he behaves below his optimum. . . . We are all to some degree oppressed, unfree. We don't come to our own. It is there, but we don't get at it.[4]

The Lesson of Peak Experiences

This is true for most of us. And yet we sometimes have moments of feeling supremely alive, joyful, bursting with radiance and life. As Wordsworth expressed it, "Meadow, grove and stream,/The earth, and every common sight,/To me did seem/Apparell'd in celestial light."[5] We have all had such moments, when the glory of life, the beauty, perfection and unity of the cosmos are revealed to us, making all of life worthwhile. In these rare moments life becomes suddenly vivid and real. We function most creatively and efficiently, and we feel full of love and energy, truly free.

Today psychologists term these moments "peak experiences." What brings on these rare experiences? Sometimes love for someone else, sometimes art, sometimes nature. A face, a song, the ocean, a job well done—everyone has his own memories of these moments. Sometimes it seems as if nothing at all brings it about: it just happens of its own accord. But whatever causes peak experiences, there is one highly significant lesson to be learned from them. The joy, depth of understanding, creativity and reverence for life that we feel *all come from within us. They are our own.* Whether or not someone or something calls out these qualities, they come out of *us.**

These experiences give a vital insight into what we are and can be. It is nothing more than our own self that we experience at these times—but a deeper aspect of ourselves, ordinarily dormant, asleep, unused. The lesson to be learned, then, is that somewhere in us we all have the capability to function on a much higher (or deeper) level than we ordinarily do, and that self-realization means just that: realizing what we already are. As we have seen, this entails more than intellectual recognition. It necessitates direct experience.

The Impulse to Growth

Modern psychology is coming to recognize that we all have within us a tremendous, untapped source of creativity, energy and happiness, and that we are all moving toward the goal of tapping that source and living a fulfilled, joyful life. In *Toward a Psychology of Being* and other works Abraham Maslow demonstrated, from his own research and the findings of many others, that man *is* moving toward this state of ful-

---

* For a thorough understanding of the characteristics of peak experiences, see Abraham Maslow's works, particularly *Toward a Psychology of Being*.

fillment. "All the evidence that we have," he writes, "(mostly clinical evidence, but already some other kinds of research evidence) indicates that it is reasonable to assume in practically every human being . . . that there is an active will toward health, an impulse toward growth, or toward the actualization of human potentialities." [6] Along with such other writers as Erich Fromm, C. G. Jung, Kurt Goldstein, Carl Rogers, Gordon Allport and others, Maslow has described the " 'will to health,' the urge to grow, the pressure to self-actualization, the quest for one's identity," [7] which is essentially the same as the tendency toward growth evidenced by any normal biological organism. Maslow suggests that man's higher capabilities, such as "creativeness, spontaneity, . . . being able to love, yearning for truth are embryonic potentialities belonging to his species-membership just as much as are his arms and legs and brain and eyes," [8] and that these potentialities "press to function and to express themselves and to be used and exercised . . . and cease their clamor only when they *are* well used." [9] In short, man has within himself "a tendency toward, or need for, growing in a direction that can be summarized . . . as self-actualization or psychological health." [10]

Though telling us that "self-actualization is a relatively achieved 'state of affairs' in a few people," Maslow warns us that "in most people, however, it is rather a hope, a yearning, a drive, a 'something' wished for but not yet achieved." Indeed, he tells us that "we are confronted with the sad fact that so few people achieve this goal, perhaps only one in a hundred, or two hundred. We can be hopeful for mankind because in principle anyone *could* become a good and healthy man. But we must also feel sad because so few actually *do* become good men." [11]

This would be cause for sadness if we were left with the same conclusion Dr. Maslow reaches: "Self-knowledge and self-improvement are very difficult for most people. They usually need great courage and long struggle." [12] This has been true because the methods hitherto available have been crude, only partially successful, expensive and, to put it bluntly, insufficient: for if they were sufficient, we would not be witnessing today such constant research and experimentation in the field of human development.

In his work Dr. Maslow was able to be only descriptive. He demonstrated convincingly that human beings strive naturally toward fulfillment and that we can function more fully and perfectly, but he could not tell us how to accomplish this ourselves. This is a little like reading a hungry man a list of the world's tastiest dishes and then telling him we have nothing for him to eat.

Nevertheless, what Maslow has done is of very great interest to us. He has studied the lives of saints and creative geniuses and also of living individuals who are, to a greater degree than most, self-actualized; that is, people who are living up to their potential more fully than most, who are happier, more creative, "fully functioning and healthy human beings." He concluded that, by studying such individuals, "perhaps we shall soon be able to use as our guide and model the fully growing and self-fulfilling human being, the one in whom all his potentialities are coming to full development, the one whose inner nature expresses itself freely, rather than being warped, suppressed, or denied." [13]

From this study he has drawn a good many conclusions about the qualities of such individuals. These conclusions represent Western psychology's nearest approach to defining an ideal, a goal for man's development; it is the closest we have come to a model of normal, healthy, fully functioning humanity.

TM and the "Characteristics of the Healthy Human Specimen"

Let's look at some of the characteristics Maslow lists as "among the objectively describable and measurable characteristics of the healthy human specimen" [14]:

1. Clearer, more efficient perception of reality.
2. More openness to experience, greater freshness of appreciation.
3. Increased integration, wholeness, unity of the person.
4. Increased spontaneity, expressiveness, aliveness.
5. A real self; firm identity; autonomy; uniqueness.
5A. Resistance to enculturation.
6. Increased objectivity; detachment; transcendence of self.
7. Greatly increased creativeness.
8. Ability to fuse concreteness and abstractness.
9. Democratic character structure.
10. Ability to love.
11. Improved interpersonal relationships.

1. *Clearer, more efficient perception of reality.* This concept is self-explanatory. It implies not only sharper, but also a more *truthful* perception of things as they are. Meditators report:

"I am definitely aware of a greatly increased depth of understanding of things around me and of myself."

"I can more clearly and effortlessly understand and appreciate both myself and my environment."

"Mental perception and cognition have sharpened and increased. I feel able to think more clearly as well as see more deeply into many aspects of nature—color, objects, etc."

"I seem able to very easily grasp the whole of anything that is presented to me. That which I observe or experience seems immediately clear, instantly understandable. Often, honestly, I am baffled at this new state of mind."

2. *More openness to experience, greater freshness of appreciation.* This is also self-defining. Meditators report significant gains in this area:

"I am not afraid of experimentation in my life, not 'hung-up' on conformity."

"I . . . am in a constant state of discovery as to the simple beauty all about me."

"It seems to me that everything I see is more vivid, sharper, and colors brighter."

"I now study creative dancing and am generally more open to new experiences."

"There has been a startling change in my perception of beauty in nature—more prone to appreciate the glory of life."

"I appreciate just living each moment. Day-to-day living now holds a special fascination for me."

3. *Increased integration, wholeness, unity of the person.* This concept is a bit more difficult. What does it mean for an individual to be "integrated"? Let us follow Maslow here. He declares that a self-actualizing person is more harmonious, does not struggle against himself. "The Freudian 'instincts' and the defenses are less sharply set off against each other. The impulses are more expressed and less controlled." [15] We have already discussed this in Chapter 3. "I am more able to feel what I am feeling, rather than what I think I should feel," said one student, and another carried it a step further, to action: "I am better able to act on my feelings, thus making use of them." Or, as one girl said, "I have more control over my emotions, yet feel freer to express them." Naturally, this freedom of expression, this lack of repression, leads to the spontaneity that is Maslow's fourth point.

Maslow makes another point concerning integration. He states that "healthy people are more integrated in another way. In them the conative, the cognitive, the affective and the motor are less separated from each other, and are more synergic, i.e., working collaboratively without conflict. . . . What such a person wants and enjoys is apt to be just what is good for him." [16] In other words, as one student meditator phrased it, "There seems to be much more of a centeredness to what I am doing . . . more single-mindedness of purpose and less ambivalence in my life." Or, as we see again and again, "I don't decide—things just happen. Like I just stopped smoking." The entire organism begins to be harmonious and to desire and act on only what is life-supporting and beneficial. Many individuals state that they just naturally and effort-lessly begin to act in better ways. "I simply noticed I was a more perceptive and loving human being," one said.

Meditators themselves use such words as "whole" and "in-tegrated" in describing how they feel. "I feel more whole and healthy as a personality," one remarked. A girl said, "I have become more effective as a human being, more integrated and ready to act on every situation that arises."

Maharishi Mahesh Yogi uses the word "integration" in a different way, but in a way that only adds to this concept, without conflicting with it. He uses "integration" to mean the inclusion of the field of Being in an individual's conscious-ness, the integration, then, of the Absolute realm of life with the more familiar, ever-changing relative aspect. In this sense, "integration" means "bringing into harmony the inner crea-tive silence and the outer activity of life." [17] The more that the Absolute, Being, is integrated with the individual life, the more its qualities—unlimited energy, intelligence, happiness, peace and creativity—are expressed by that individual's every thought, word and act. Full integration means that at all times, in all situations, the direct awareness of Being is not lost, but is maintained along with whatever else is being ex-perienced, providing a stable basis for all of life's activity. This goal of a fully integrated state of consciousness is the primary goal of the science of creative intelligence. It is accomplished through the regular alternation of meditation and activity.

4. *Increased spontaneity, expressiveness, aliveness.* These natural qualities of a healthy life need no explanation. Medi-tators remarked:

"I'm better able to act on my feelings."

"I'm more open, less afraid of relating to people."

"My pattern of response ceased to be a game-like, *set* pat-tern—and became spontaneous."

"I am not afraid of being illogical."

"On the emotional level, I react more honestly to a given situation."

"Sometimes I just feel so good and full and alive. Always I felt life could be like it is, but I didn't know how to live it until I was initiated a year ago."

5. *A real self; firm identity; autonomy; uniqueness.* A growing sense of self is a topic discussed throughout this book, particularly in the chapter on freedom. One of the major results of transcendental meditation appears to be a greatly increased self-knowledge and inner harmony, a clarifying of one's own identity and direction.

"There is a harmony which is developing within me, which makes me really glad to be alive. Over the past 14 months [since beginning meditation] I've found myself; and I'm beginning to know who I am and what I'm doing now and will do in the future."

"I think that the meditation let me cut a pathway through my jungle of egotistical confusion to my self, my real self, me!"

"I no longer argue with my parents during my weekly visits with them; because I have established my own 'inner independence,' I no longer have to fight for it or prove it."

5A. *Resistance to enculturation.* Because they have a firmer grasp on their own identity and a stronger sense of autonomy, meditators find that they are more inner-directed, freer to find their own values and directions in life, less influenced by the opinions and values of others.

"I feel much more clearly defined and therefore stronger in character and intention—much less easily influenced by my environment. I have the security and self-assurance now to enjoy doing things independently and feel whole, rather than being dependent on others."

"I'm slowly becoming aware of the values that are real to me and the importance of respecting them rather than superimposing some value that I may have heard or read."

"I feel more of an internal core, less dependent on others."

6. *Increased objectivity; detachment; transcendence of self.* Increased objectivity means that we can see reality more clearly (as discussed under point 1) and also that we can see

ourselves more clearly. Meditators show this ability to view themselves objectively. They report growth with exuberance, but also note what remains: "There has been a little broadening, but I have a long way to go. I still grasp at people and things," said one. Another wrote that "although I still fall very short of my personal values, meditation has given me a path and a means to live up to a world of love, harmony, and openness."

"I can look at things (problems) more objectively and I don't worry about things but just start doing something to change the situation, if it seems to need it."

"I can stand back and gain perspective on myself and see myself working, studying and living."

"I've become much more aware of my capabilities and my limitations. It has helped me to realize that if I want to do something, I'll have to go ahead and do it myself, or at least supply the initiative."

"The most significant effect of meditation for me has been the increase in awareness of Self, during activity. This increased self-awareness has permitted me to see my actions more clearly and objectively, to be more deeply aware of my thoughts, to relate to my surroundings more intimately, and to people more empathetically."

In regard to objectivity, Maslow points out that "to the extent that perception is desire-less and fear-less, to that extent it is more veridical, in the sense of perceiving the true, or essential or intrinsic whole nature of the object. . . . Thus the goal of objective and true description of any reality is fostered by psychological health." [18]

Maharishi, too, has discussed this idea at length. In what state of consciousness, he asks, can man have a clear, unbiased, objective vision? In what state can the object be cognized for its full value, without the state of the subject influencing the perception? A truly scientific, objective vision would demand that the subject be uninvolved, a neutral witness to the object.

The deep-sleep state certainly cannot produce this vision,

for there is no awareness either of subject or object. Neither can the illusory dreaming state, in which, as Maharishi so delightfully expresses it, "the body, which in actuality can hardly jump 20 feet, is found flying!" [19] But is the ordinary waking state a valid basis for objective vision? We see that our perceptions are often as *we* are: sometimes those close to us appear lovely and wonderful, but not at other times. The same piece of music, the same sunny sky sometimes is most beautiful and sometimes hardly noticed. Our perception is influenced by our moods, by how we feel, by what else is on our mind, etc. Knowledge, as we have seen, is structured in consciousness. This certainly does not give us an objective, never-changing platform from which to discern the truth. It is as if we alternately put on green glasses, blue glasses, yellow glasses; we always see through whatever glasses we are wearing, and the true nature of the object is overshadowed by our subjective moods.

Therefore, deep, dreamless sleep, dreaming and waking states are ruled out as the basis of objective evaluation of reality. What about transcendental consciousness, the fourth state? In this state of awareness the object of experience is increasingly refined, until it becomes nil and the pure consciousness, or pure subjectivity, or Being, stable and unchanging, is all that remains. There *is* no object to perceive. There is only the subject, the Self, alone. So this state, too, is eliminated.

But if a state could be produced wherein this pure, unchanging awareness could coexist with the ever-changing, if there could be pure consciousness or Being *along with* the activity of relative life, then this could serve as a basis for a truthful, objective vision. Seen from the platform of unchanging, eternal nonactivity of the mind, full appreciation could be given to the object, without the unstable moods of the individual standing in the way and clouding the "doors of perception."

This integrated state Maharishi calls "cosmic consciousness" ("cosmic" in the sense of all-inclusive, including both the unstable outer and the eternally changeless inner, the relative and Absolute phases of life). It is fascinating and almost ironic that complete objectivity, completely scientific vision, can be brought about only by complete development and unfoldment of the *subject*. Only full expression of the subject's deepest value can allow for full appreciation of the *object's* full value. In this state the Self, established in its fullness, can stand alone, and one is an uninvolved witness to all relative experience. In this state alone can full justice be done to the object.

The science of creative intelligence, by doing justice to the subjective phase of life—unfolding the full potential—thus also does justice to the objective phase. Life grows nearer to truth.

7. *Greatly increased creativeness.* A number of comments from transcendental meditators concern creativity in various areas of life, both within the borders of the creative arts and outside them, in all the aspects of daily life. It is interesting, as we read these comments, to keep in mind a discovery of Maslow's, i.e., "I found it necessary to distinguish 'special talent creativeness' from 'self-actualizing creativeness' which sprang much more directly from the personality, and which showed itself widely in the ordinary affairs of life. . . . It looked like a tendency to do *anything* creatively: e.g., housekeeping, teaching, etc." [20]

"Always had talent. Lost fear of failure in creative side of my nature: Write a lot. Do wood sculpture."

"Quality of the products of my hobbies has gone up. (Photography and singing.)"

"Lately, I have had more of a chance to enjoy using the source of creative intelligence located within. It's really an interesting experience for me. All of a sudden I get an urge to do something—like decorating the house for Christmas—and end up getting marvelous compliments from all who see them. Before, I used to want to create pretty things but didn't quite know how to do it. Now it is a joy to come up with something looking very pleasant and nice with absolutely no effort involved."

"In my drawing and painting I am now able to express what I had previously been in search of. Trying isn't necessary—it just comes out naturally."

"Since I have begun the practice of transcendental meditation I have become more creative in all that I do. In the past I was creative within certain areas. I painted, worked in ceramics and danced but now I find that creativity is a way of life. When I work, cook, study or make gifts for my friends, I feel that I am creating."

8. *Ability to fuse concreteness and abstractness.* By this, Maslow seems to indicate the ability to deal with reality abstractly, understanding the categories of things so that we can move efficiently and freely through life, while still maintaining freshness, directness of perception, and the ability to live here and now. For instance, when we walk down the street, does our mind lazily relegate that object over there to "a tree with a bird in it," or, do we see this particular birch tree, with its many thin layers of peeling white bark, its delicate, lacelike drooping branches, patterns of sunlight and shadow playing on the trunk, and this particular bluejay sitting on a high branch, nodding its crowned head right and left and squawking?

"This means," says Carl Rogers, "that instead of perceiving in predetermined categories (trees are green; college education is good; modern art is silly), the individual is aware of this existential moment as *it* is, thus being alive to many experiences which fall outside the usual categories (*this* tree is lavender; *this* college education is damaging; *this* modern sculpture has a powerful effect on me)." [21]

Of course, it is also important to be able to perceive in categories—when we are driving we have only enough time to see that a *car* is heading in our direction. Whether it is blue or green, a Ford or a Chevrolet is irrelevant to our immediate concern. It is efficient to see the category. Both modes of perception, in their appropriate places, are valid to life.

Obviously, meditators experience increased ability to see reality more fully and clearly. Yet at the same time, they experience increased effectiveness and success in all they do. This would indicate that they are able to "fuse concreteness and abstractness."

9. *Democratic character structure.* By this Maslow means the capacity to respect an individual for what he is, to accept someone regardless of his race or religion, his social status, ideas or values. It implies respect to *any* human being just because he is a human individual. We have seen examples of this attitude in Chapter 3. A few meditators' remarks follow:

"I don't think I've ever really understood what love, compassion or brotherhood meant, before, but now, every day, I learn a little more."

"I maintain a higher degree of confidence in and respect for my fellowman."

"I noticed right away that I could tolerate people I wouldn't have talked to before. A few weeks later I actually liked them and felt no hostility."

"I find that everywhere I meet or run into people, I just naturally seem to look for the 'good' in them. It's a beautiful thing. Before, I used to pretend that I loved people, after all, it was the 'happy' thing to love everyone. But it was so insincere."

"I am surprised at how much better I get along with people, especially people who have different values, philosophies of life and religions. It is much easier to accept each person as he is."

10. *Ability to love.* Growth of love is one of the main and most significant results of transcendental meditation. This growth was touched on in Chapter 3 and is further discussed in Chapter 8.

11. *Improved interpersonal relationships.* The entire content of Chapter 3 is a confirmation of growth in this area.

Besides these categories describing the self-actualizing individual, Maslow includes a number of other qualities reported by such individuals. Let us look at about half a dozen of these, comparing them with statements by transcendental meditators.

Zest in living: "My life has become richer and more meaningful since I began to meditate. I am enjoying living more."

"I am truly able to love just about everyone I meet, and I am frequently bubbling over with joy. I am quite pleased with life."

"I have a great love and desire for life now. I want many children who will begin to meditate! I know that I will have a beautiful life."

Happiness: "My personal values have been: live well and happily and expansively and I have been able to do this more since meditation."

"One problem I'm having is that I grin a lot and some of the people in the dorm think I'm a little weird. (My cousin used to call me the great stone face.)"

Confidence in one's ability to handle stresses and problems: "Instead of being in a state of hyperconcern with everyday problems, I have great confidence in my abilities to handle any problem as it comes."

"I feel very capable of going on to get a Ph.D. while before I always felt I wasn't smart enough or capable of it."

"The big change in my attitude was the confidence I had in the future—because instead of looking forward to the same old drag of school, I knew that everything would become more easy and enjoyable as my experience of energy, intelligence, and happiness increased."

Transcendence of selfish and personal motivations: "From rather ego-centered values (money, big house, nice things) I have changed to other-people-centered values. I now have a real concern for those about me, and am no longer as much concerned with satisfying my own ego impulses."

"I am less selfish and self-centered, more giving, tolerant and understanding of others."

Decrease of hostility, cruelty and increase of kindness, etc.: "I seem to have a new sense of tenderness and compassion and am able to withstand attack with little or no pain. Where before I enjoyed a good fight, now I enjoy a good laugh."

"I don't seem to feel anger, nor to be suppressing anger. It just isn't there."

"My capacity to tolerate negativity with sincere compassion and love has grown to a level of unflinching and natural gentleness. This is how I have always wanted to be but in the past, whenever my temper was tested or I found myself in a situation of conflict, I always gave way to the emotion of anger and reaction. Now this is past. My capacity to love seems as high as it could possibly be."

In addition to these, throughout his writing Maslow has sprinkled other characteristics of the self-actualizing individual. Do they sound familiar?

"The ability to concentrate to a degree not usual for ordinary men." (See Chapter 7.)

"These individuals are strongly ethical, they have definite moral standards, they do right and do not do wrong." (See Chapter 8.)

I could continue to pull these quotations out; there are a great number that would be applicable to our material. However, my point in drawing this comparison has surely been made. It is a highly significant point and deserves to be spelled out: *Individuals practicing transcendental meditation exhibit to an exceptionally high degree the qualities Maslow has singled out as representative of the psychologically healthy, self-realized individual.*

TM and Psychological Tests

Slowly but surely objective reports, in the form of psychological studies of behavioral changes, have begun to give objective confirmation to these subjective reports of meditators. At the University of Cincinnati, Nidich, Seeman and Banta administered a widely used test,[22] based on Maslow's categories of self-actualization, to a group of 35 individuals. Half began TM two days later. After two months the groups were tested again.

On the first test the experimental (meditating) group and the control (nonmeditating) group did not differ on any of the scales. But after two months, following regular meditation sessions by the experimental group, there were statistically significant differences. The meditators scored higher on six of the 12 categories, in the direction of self-actualization. The control group's scores did not change.

Self-actualization was found in terms of increased "self-regard," greater "acceptance of aggression" and higher "capacity for intimate contact." "Spontaneity" was found to increase. There was a clear tendency toward "inner-directedness" rather than other-directedness.[23]

A larger study is underway at the University of Kansas, being conducted by Maynard Shelly, a professor of psychology, and Garland Landrith. Final analysis of all their data is not yet available, but preliminary findings are significant. Shelly and Landrith tested about 160 transcendental meditators and 145 nonmeditators. Their principal concern was: are meditators happier than nonmeditators, and if so, why? Their findings to date indicate that individuals practicing TM are happier; more relaxed; less sad; experience feelings of enjoyment more often; seek social contacts as often as nonmeditators (are not withdrawn) in spite of the fact that they tend to spend more time alone; seem to develop deeper personal relationships; and have more of what Shelly terms "personal resources"—they depend less on their external surroundings for happiness. A follow-up study, with an entirely new group of individuals, substantiated these first findings. A thorough discussion of these results will appear in Shelly's forthcoming book *Sources of Satisfaction,* a large portion of which is devoted to the value of transcendental meditation in allowing an individual to enjoy greater, more long-lasting happiness.[24]

These findings are supplemented by a small study at Pennsylvania State University's Hershey Medical Center. This study, sponsored by the Behavioral Science Department and a U.S. Department of Health, Education and Welfare grant, involved the administration of various psychological tests to a group of 13 subjects. The individuals were tested before beginning TM and then six weeks later. (The authors state that they would have preferred to retest after three to six months, to allow meditation to take effect more fully, but due to time limitations this was impossible.)

Several significant changes were noted, particularly "a significant decrease in verbalized hostility and anxiety." The subjects responded more positively, after six weeks of meditation, to these statements: "I feel as though I have a great deal of energy"; "I feel healthy"; "My mind feels fresh and creative"; "I am enjoying life"; and "I find it easy to get along with people." Also, there was a statistically significant decrease in the category that measured pessimism and a large improvement in the category that measured hostility in human relations. One of the tests assessed changes in the type and number of problems that an individual is concerned with. Results showed "a very significant reduction in the number of life experiences subjectively felt to be problems." [25]

These studies, even though small and still few, unanimously point to a strong correlation between what Maslow found to be the traits of self-actualized people (and what appear to be healthy and strong personality traits) and the experience of transcendental meditators. This strongly suggests that TM might be a highly useful supplement to psychotherapy (as suggested by a communication from Dr. A. James Morgan, director of Adult Treatment Services at the Community Mental Health Center of Pennsylvania Hospital: "The possible uses of the technique as an adjunct to psychotherapy are exciting indeed. . . . The general reduction in tension and increased alertness should complement any psychotherapeutic procedure" [26]), or, more radically, that TM might be a *replacement* for much of what is currently used by the psychotherapeutic profession in attempting to help individuals gain stability and happiness. There have been numerous subjective reports supporting this latter contention (a Brooklyn, New York, meditator told me, "I didn't tell my therapist that I had started meditating for almost two months—until one day he suggested that we stop the therapy or reduce to a once-a-month basis, due to the progress I had been making in the last couple of months!"). Wallace reported that 22 individuals (of a total 394, but an undetermined number involved in therapy) were able to discontinue various forms of therapy after beginning TM.[27]

Margaretta Bowers, an eminent New York psychoanalyst and author, has reported that her patients, after beginning TM, progress much more quickly in their therapy. "All who have persevered with TM have shown a much faster rate of improvement," she declares. "With several this improvement has been dramatic, even spectacular. Some have been relieved of symptoms that had never been helped by psychotherapy. With two such patients this relief and general improvement, increase in ego-strength, general productivity at work and happiness in living have continued with greatly decreased hours of psychotherapy. With every patient who has been faithful in TM the improvement has been at least twice the expected rate (as judged by previous experience with the patient). Sometimes it seems to be at least 10 times the expected rate. Sometimes when a patient complains about not moving at a satisfactory rate I find that the patient has stopped TM. When TM is again undertaken, movement picks up again. With TM, patients need fewer hours of psychotherapy and the sessions are more meaningful and useful. Sometimes TM becomes the principal therapy. Psychotherapy sessions become secondary and . . . can be understood as just talking things over with an old friend." [28]

It is a well-accepted fact of life for workers in the psychotherapeutic field that most of the available methods leave much to be desired. Some observers, witnessing the repeated failure of conventional techniques to free individuals from their suffering, and noting the dramatic rise of mental patients in their teens and twenties, speak of "an epidemic of mental illness" against which physicians and therapists are virtually helpless.

Maharishi is well aware of the state of contemporary psychology. He says, "When we consider the immense possibilities in the field of psychology and review the achievements made so far by that science, we find them discouraging. . . . The inner discontent felt by the great majority of people who are neither neurotic nor psychotic certainly indicates the need of a technique for achieving inner happiness. If modern psychology could satisfy this need then the study of the mind on modern lines could be considered useful and worthwhile. But what is the use of a study of the mind which fails both to unfold latent mental faculties and to quench the thirst for happiness?" [29]

Normal and Subnormal

I recently flew to central Pennsylvania to give a lecture on TM at Penn State University. One of the people who picked me up at the airport was a girl who had been meditating only three months. Driving through the serene landscape was a pleasure, and I enjoyed listening to her talk of the changes she was experiencing. "School seems a lot easier," she said, "and I don't even believe how enjoyable it's become. I even like writing papers! I seem to have a lot more friends, to be learning more in class—everything seems so much more fun. Is this normal?"

Being accustomed to hearing such stories every day (one of the occupational hazards of teaching TM is that one is constantly barraged by good news), I simply said, "Yes, it's very normal. Just keep on—it gets better all the time." She replied with a delighted laugh.

Later on, before the lecture, as I was walking across the campus, I reflected on that brief interchange and saw a great deal more depth in the implications of our discussion. I realized that it was indeed "normal" for a person to be creative, energetic, happy. It is *not* normal to be unhappy, to suffer, to be unfulfilled. When we see a suffering man, we don't smile and say, "That is normal life." Our heart goes out to him; we want to do what we can to restore him to "normal."

And we ourselves don't enjoy sickness or loss; we don't want to suffer. If we are ill, we don't say, "Oh, good, here's my winter cold, life would be a bore without it." Suffering is opposed to life. An efficient, healthy, creative, lively person is normal—and a *fully* normal person would be one who used his full potential of mind and heart.

So all the changes we have been documenting in this and other chapters are only progress toward becoming normal—progress away from the limitations of stress and strain, restricted understanding, narrow vision, which cripple a man's life and keep him from the fulfillment that is rightfully his. "Normality," Maslow states, "is the highest excellence of which we are capable. But this ideal is not an unattainable goal set out far ahead of us; rather it is actually within us, existent but hidden." [30] Self-actualization is not a super-normal state; it is the normal state of life which should be achieved by everyone.

Maharishi concurs with this definition. "When a man does not live a normal life," he says, "or *a life using his full potential,* he feels miserable and tense and suffers in many ways. . . . But when one naturally uses all the resources of mind, body and Being . . . then life can be said to be normal." [31]

One speaker at the 1971 Symposium on the Science of Creative Intelligence asserted that modern psychology knows a lot more about abnormality than about normality—that, in fact, "there isn't yet even a satisfactory definition of what is normal." [32] Maharishi replied, "What are accepted as normal human values by the world today are, in fact, subnormal in comparison with the possibility that is available to everyone through transcendental meditation. Only when we are enjoying the 200% value of life in daily living—100% inner value and 100% outer value—are we living up to normal human potential. Only living the full potential of life can be said to be normal." [33]

In the 1970's psychology is finally beginning to take seriously that most important human question: what is man's full, highest potential? What can he ultimately become? The science of creative intelligence offers not only a systematic exposition of man's possible evolution, but a systematic technique, transcendental meditation, which seems to be a profoundly effective method for enabling man to reach the high but realistic and deeply meaningful goal of becoming all that he can be.

CHAPTER 6

Without Chemical Crutches

> My search for happiness through drugs has
> ended and in its place I have found, through
> meditation, a long-lasting, even peace and happi-
> ness which has just begun to blossom.
>
> —STUDENT MEDITATOR

A Subjective Approach

"When I used drugs, I was looking for something from life
that I didn't have," wrote one student now practicing transcendental meditation. A twenty-four-year-old girl revealed,
"I took many different kinds of drugs for the experience of
subtler perceptions—but in my heart I always hoped that a
door would open to the true reality of life."

These words reflect the experiences of many people who
have believed that drugs could help to make their lives more
full and rewarding, or less tense and depressed. Such experiences demonstrate that the underlying motivation for drug
use is the same basic desire which leads to any choice in life:
the all-powerful drive toward more happiness, more energy,
more understanding of life, more ease in relating to others.
However, the experiences of literally thousands of transcendental meditators have shown that when life is naturally
happy and fulfilling, naturally satisfying and rich, the desire
for drugs is lost. "I have not taken drugs since meditation

because I feel better now than I ever did with drugs," said one student. "Life after meditation finally became satisfying."

Many young meditators have revealed that their search for happiness and fulfillment led them to experiment with drugs, but that drugs failed to provide the depth of satisfaction that they felt they could somehow, somewhere achieve. As one man expressed it, "I deeply felt that a better life was to be had, but I didn't know where or how to get it. I searched to fulfill my need for the 'something' in many different ways, never finding a lasting form of satisfaction for my heart or mind." An artist wrote that prior to starting TM his life was like "a leaf in the breeze, being blown wherever the breeze wished to blow me. My life seemed to have little purpose and my painting seemed to be going nowhere. For many years I knew inside that there was a better way of life but I could never find it."

"Before TM," a New England student wrote, "I was attempting to find something that I could use to help me evolve and become free of the confusion which confronted me. Through experiences with drugs, I was made aware of possibilities of consciousness I couldn't comprehend before. I discovered great frustration, however, in attempting to make any spiritual progress in this way. TM was the only logical step for me to take. Since learning the technique, all progress has been greatly accelerated and a factor of stability has been introduced. Things that seemed desirable yet unattainable in personal development previously have become easy, and my life takes increasing shape and direction."

When this begins to happen, when an individual feels that "TM gets me subtly and progressively higher, more relaxed, more 'in tune,' more energized," it is not surprising that drugs drop out of his life, without any effort on his part. "Drugs have naturally fallen by," one young person wrote. "I didn't try to stop—after a while I just found myself not taking them any more." Or, as another said, "I now feel I am totally free of any serious inclinations to take drugs again, and I feel meditation has made this possible."

Personal before-and-after stories abound. Teachers of TM love to tell each other of dramatic changes in their students, and meditators themselves take a real delight in relating their own stories. I could fill a whole volume just with those I have collected.

When I first began this study several years ago, I was a student, with little notion of writing a book. Beginning a research project on TM, I passed out several questionnaires one evening at a meditators' meeting at UCLA. Here is one of the first replies I received: "When I began transcendental meditation," Mary wrote, "I was attending high school. At the end of that summer I had been arrested for leading a supposedly desolate and immoral life, and for the use of dangerous drugs and narcotics. At that time I was sixteen. I was put on probation for a year. I was not especially depressed, but I was definitely looking for something that would add something tangible and constructive to my life; that would help me do better in high school, etc.

"What's happening now is fantastic! No drugs, nothing. Great grades for the first time in four years. I will go to Los Angeles City College for some credits in math and try to get into the University of California in the next two years. I have been offered a teaching scholarship by the head of the English Department. I have time to help 3rd and 4th graders in reading after school, belong to a modern dance repertoire, and attend classes Monday nights in serigraphy. If my life continues in this manner, there will be no question of my happiness and satisfaction.

"The new sensitivity I feel and understanding continue to strengthen every day of my life. My ability to communicate my thoughts and feelings to others is a source of satisfaction to myself, my friends, my teachers, and my mother. My ability to concentrate in school is greatly increased, as well as the quality of my work and what I receive from my studies.

"The decisions were mine; the energy, the clearness of thought, the self-confidence and self-knowledge are the products of meditation. I might have dropped out of school if I had not found something useful."

For many people who begin meditation and who have been using drugs, the inclination to use drugs disappears almost immediately. For others, however, it is a somewhat longer, more gradual process. Some have reported a sense of conflict between drugs, which had been a source of some pleasure or relief, and meditation. But for those who are fortunate enough to continue with regular meditation, a fulfilled, drugfree life seems to be the inevitable result.

Greg is a twenty-one-year-old student who had been meditating for about 18 months. He said that before starting TM he had "recently flunked out of college because of spending all my time with student government. I had just completed an acceptable semester at a new school, but had just squeezed through. I was doing a lot of drugs regularly.

"I started TM and continued to do drugs. I was convinced that the two could be combined. For nine months I meditated and used drugs. My efficiency in school increased, and I reached the point where I was able to do just about anything while under the influence of drugs. I was doing more and doing it better. However, I then began thinking that maybe drugs were unnecessary. I would stop using them off and on for three or four days. I noticed a marked difference in my meditation and finally stopped altogether about six months ago. Since then I have felt great. Not only more efficiency but much less worry. I have lost a great deal of my former self-consciousness and get along better with all people and life in general. For the first time I feel comfortable with the direction my life is headed."

Steve, a twenty-four-year-old California social worker who had been meditating about one year, summed up his premeditation woes in one sentence: "I was suffering from insomnia, had been taking almost daily doses of marijuana, occasional LSD and other assorted trips, was in the process of dropping out of my third graduate program in two years, was desperately searching for meaning and identity and could not make a decision about any aspect of my life." But, he wrote, "After a year of meditating, my creativity, energy and stability have increased to the point where my major problem is not having enough time to devote to all the meaningful activities I am engaged in. I have not taken drugs in many months. I am calm, productive, and the recipient of joy and beauty that were always there but unable to be experienced."

The one basic pattern that can be discerned in all the hundreds of reports concerning drug usage is that for whatever reason drugs were taken, whether in a conscious attempt to achieve a higher level of life, for "kicks" or for no particular reason, once TM was begun, fulfillment and happiness were experienced to such a degree that there was no desire to continue using drugs. As one girl mentioned, "Drugs no longer interest me; instead, they strike me as rather a waste of energy."

A dramatic lesson emerges from this material: campaigning against drug abuse is like fighting the smoke instead of the fire. Happy, creative, productive people do not even think of using drugs. Therefore the answer to the "epidemic" of drug use lies in strengthening individual lives, in strengthening the personality of individuals so that drugs have no allure. A contented mind and heart would have no use for drugs. Rather than campaigning *against* drug use, we need to campaign *for* more whole, integrated personalities, for broadened awareness, for improved health and more relaxed, spontaneously loving, harmonious relationships. Then the question of drugs will never arise. This is the real story that these meditators tell us.

An Objective Approach

To date there have been two objective, statistical studies assessing the effect of TM on drug usage.

In the first study, done by W. Thomas Winquist at UCLA, 484 meditators, of whom about 90 percent were between the

ages of fifteen and thirty, were asked to report on their use
of drugs prior to beginning TM and afterward.

Each of the 484 questionnaires was evaluated to determine if the subject was a regular user of marijuana,
hallucinogenics other than marijuana, or hard drugs immediately before beginning the practice of TM. . . .
The category of hallucinogenic drugs (other than marijuana) includes DMT, STP, LSD, hashish, peyote, psi-
locybin, morning glory seeds and woodrose seeds. The
hard drug category includes heroin, opium, methedrine,
amphetamines and barbiturates, etc.

Of the 484 S's [subjects], 143 (30%) were found to
be regular users of drugs for at least three consecutive
months immediately prior to beginning TM.[1]

These regular drug users were separated into the following
categories:

1. The S has completely stopped the use of all drugs for
   a minimum of three months.
2. The S's usage of all drugs has decreased and remained
   decreased to at least 50% of prior usage for a minimum of three consecutive months.
3. The S has increased the use of one or more of the
   drugs.

Of the 143 individuals who regularly used marijuana 84
percent stopped, 14.5 percent decreased, 1.5 percent increased. Of the 111 individuals who regularly used hallucinogenics other than marijuana 86 percent stopped, 14 percent
decreased, 0 percent increased. Of the 42 individuals who
regularly used hard drugs 86 percent stopped, 14 percent decreased, 0 percent increased.

49% of the regular drugs users stated that their use
of drugs changed after TM because life became more
fulfilling. 24% of the regular drug users stated their use
of drugs changed after TM because the drug experience
became less pleasurable. [Typical comments here were:
"Now I think dope makes me frazzled and passive."

"Three recent experiences by way of experiment proved temporarily dulling and moody. The continuance of drug use would be absurd." And finally, most succinctly: "Drugs bring me down."]

The Winquist study could be seen as a preliminary to a larger study, undertaken at Harvard Medical School in 1970 by Herbert Benson, M.D., and R. Keith Wallace, Ph.D. Their paper was presented to the International Symposium on Drug Abuse for Physicians in August 1970 and also before a House Select Committee the following year.[2] Dr. Benson, a cardiologist, had reported in *The New England Journal of Medicine* that he had been

measuring blood-pressure changes during "transcendental meditation," a yoga-like practice being taught in several centers in the United States. The results of these studies may be reported elsewhere.

The purpose of the present communication is to note that the practitioners of transcendental meditation claim to have stopped abusing drugs. The volunteers have been 20 men 21 to 38 years of age. Nineteen had previously abused drugs: marijuana, barbiturates, lysergic acid diethylamide, amphetamines and, in several, heroin. All reported that they no longer took these drugs because drug-induced feelings became extremely distasteful as compared to those experienced during the practice of transcendental meditation. Perhaps transcendental meditation should be explored prospectively by others who are primarily interested in the alleviation of drug abuse.[3]

Apparently these findings stimulated Benson to become one of those interested in the drug problem. He and Wallace distributed a questionnaire to about 1,950 individuals who had been practicing TM for at least three months. Of these, 1,862 individuals between the ages of fourteen and seventy-eight (approximately half between nineteen and twenty-three, however) completed the questionnaire. They had been practicing TM for an average of 20 months. The amount of their drug use was assessed for five time periods: (*a*) 6 months before starting TM; (*b*) 0–3 months after starting; (*c*) 4–9 months; (*d*) 10–21 months; and (*e*) 22 months or more after starting. The results are graphically shown on the following page.

Clearly, a marked decrease in the use of all drugs followed the onset of TM, and as the amount of time practicing TM increased, the amount of drug use progressively decreased. Of those who had been meditating 21 months or more, almost all had completely stopped using all drugs. For example, in the six-month period before starting TM, about 80 percent used marijuana, about 28 percent heavily (once a day or more). After six months, 37 percent used marijuana, 6.5 percent heavily, and after 21 months, 12 percent used marijuana, and *only one person* heavily.

With LSD, 48 percent were users before TM; within three months, only 11 percent were using it, and after 21 months, only three percent. Nonusers of the other drugs increased similarly: "Nonusers of the other hallucinogens after 21 months of the practice rose from 61% to 96%; for the narcotics from 83% to 99%; for the amphetamines from 70% to 99%; and for the barbiturates from 83% to 99%." [4]

These figures are remarkable in view of the rising problem of drug abuse ("It is to be expected that the use of all sorts of drugs in the next 10 years will increase a hundredfold," the director of the National Institute of Mental Health optimistically predicted in 1969 [5]) and the widespread knowledge that "few programs or treatments have been reported which alleviate drug abuse." [6] "As kooky as this sounds to many people," Benson was quoted as saying in a *Time* story, "it has just got to be investigated." [7]

Encouraged by these findings, innovative government leaders and leaders in the field of drug-abuse prevention are putting TM to practical use. For instance, the Governor's Office of Drug Abuse for the State of Michigan has issued a statement that it "supports the efforts of the Students International Meditation Society (Transcendental Meditation) as a positive and fruitful alternative to drug use and abuse. . . . We consider the Transcendental Meditation program a neces-

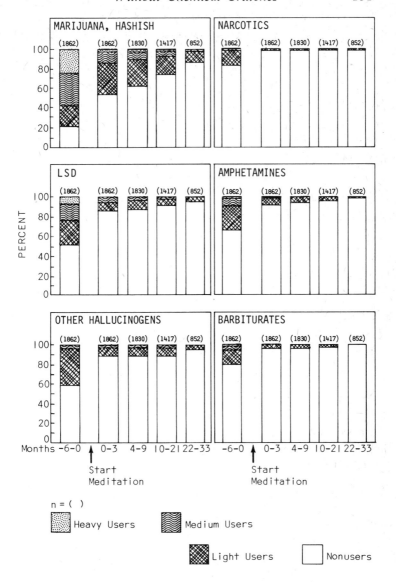

sary ingredient in every drug abuse education effort seriously concerned with providing strong and useful alternative life styles for its participants." [8]

The mention of TM as an "alternative" to drug use requires some clarification. Wallace and Benson noted in their report, "Student drug users are, as a group, knowledgeable about the undesirable effects of drug abuse. In general, it is not difficult for most student drug abusers to stop. The issue is to get them to *want* to stop. For a drug abuse program to be effective, it must provide a nonchemical alternative which can at least fulfill some of the basic motivations behind student drug abuse." [9] We have seen examples of how effective TM can be in bringing a greater measure of fulfillment to life, thereby eliminating the basic cause of drug use.* TM should not be thought of as an alternative type of "high"—it is an alternative to drug use in the same way that happiness is an alternative to suffering or that freedom is an alternative to bondage. As Benson and Wallace point out, the science of creative intelligence "is offered as a program for personal development and is not specifically intended to be a treatment for drug abuse: the alleviation of the problems of drug abuse is merely a side effect." [10]

"As former chairman of the House Special Committee on Narcotics," wrote Dale Warner, member of the Michigan House of Representatives, "my respect for the practice of transcendental meditation was tremendously increased when I began to realize that it operated directly, measurably and significantly in opposition to drug abuse. This overwhelming problem can be met head on by the practice of transcendental

---

* In calling unhappiness or lack of fulfillment the basic factor leading to drug abuse, I am fully aware of such other factors as social pressure, desire for "kicks," rebellion against authority, escape from social and personal problems, etc. These factors, however, would not and do not override a strong personality; a contented mind and heart would not succumb to them. The basic problem is, then, *weakness.* TM provides increased strength, rendering other pressures on the individual insignificant.

meditation, which should be carefully considered whenever drug abuse preventive and rehabilitative measures are implemented." [11] This remark, incidentally, was made before the publication of the Harvard study.

A Broader Perspective

Now let us look at the question of drug abuse from a different angle. Most of the publicity on drug use and abuse continues to center around young people, but it is only the uninformed who believe that the drug problem is exclusively or even predominantly a problem of youth. It is a major problem of our entire society, a major problem in the armed forces, and "one of the big problems being encountered by the financial community in particular, and by business in general. . . . More and more young executives and employees of all classifications are using drugs and advice from experts on how to handle the problem is weak at best and is for the most part non-existent." [12]

In addition, many physicians and public-health experts feel that the drug-abuse problem is not restricted to the use of illegal drugs such as marijuana and LSD. The Department of Health, Education and Welfare, in fact, considers alcoholism the major drug problem in the country. HEW's National Institute on Alcohol Abuse and Alcoholism issued a 121-page study in February, 1972, placing over 15 million Americans in the "problem drinker" category. *Newsweek* reported on the study, remarking that "the increasing use of heroin, LSD and marijuana in the United States is being viewed with alarm by some public figure or other almost every day. But, according to a newly issued government report, none of these relatively newfangled vices is as damaging to society as a weakness as old as Noah. The nation's No. 1 'drug problem,' the Department of Health, Education and Welfare asserted last week, continues to be alcohol." The study pointed out that "these 'alcohol abusers' cost the nation some $15 billion a year in lost work time, property damage and health and welfare costs.

They also shorten their own lives by an average of ten to twelve years. In addition, alcohol is blamed for about 28,000 traffic deaths a year." [13]

Further, there is no doubt that the major consumption of such drugs as amphetamines and barbiturates is *by prescription*. The use of "pep pills" and tranquilizers of all varieties abounds, along with a growing feeling throughout society that dependence upon these chemical formulations is unnatural and unhealthy. It is only simple common sense that the profound rest of TM and the attendant reduction of stress and strain can normalize the functioning of mind and body and allow an individual to rid himself of the need for chemical stimulants and relaxants.

Such practices as smoking and drinking—and dependence upon tranquilizers and such minor mind- and chemistry-altering agents as coffee, diet pills and various nonprescription formulations for nerves and headaches—are habits many people struggle with unsuccessfully as long as their lives remain stressful and tense. But after beginning to enjoy the profound relaxation of TM and the resultant increase of energy, clarity of mind and feelings of well-being, many find their undesired habits disappearing effortlessly. I have heard more than one businessman say that his lifelong habit of walking in the door after a day's work and having a drink or two to "unwind" has disappeared, in favor of a 20-minute meditation period which relaxed and refreshed him and prepared him for a lively and enjoyable evening. Others find that they simply "forget" to smoke or to drink, never feeling the need or the desire.

Smoking and Drinking

"In the past, I had had trouble breaking my smoking habit," said a woman meditating only three months. "Ever since meditation, it has been easy. I feel clean, pure, and exceptionally happy." "I used to smoke two packs a day," said a New Yorker. "After beginning meditation I noticed myself smoking less and less; finally I just didn't feel like it anymore."

A twenty-four-year-old engineering student wrote that before beginning TM "I had been smoking marijuana and drinking eight to ten cups of coffee a day with what you might call 'coffee nerves.' Since starting meditation I of course stopped smoking pot and I quickly decreased my coffee consumption to an average of a cup a day. My coffee nerves have all but disappeared."

"Before I started meditating I smoked fairly heavily," a thirty-six-year-old housewife wrote. "Now I don't smoke at all. I quit easily, without any effort, and without even realizing I was doing so at first, gradually over a year's time. I also drank alcohol at parties. Now I never do. . . . After meditating a year I found I could easily enjoy myself in any social situation without such crutches."

A Midwesterner wrote, "Before beginning TM I smoked pot and cigarettes frequently, awoke incessantly, drank to drunkenness often. . . . Now I don't smoke drugs or cigarettes, don't drink. . . . I am extremely more relaxed in my everyday activities and I enjoy life manifold more." "Drugs have completely dropped out of my life," said another person. "I have stopped both smoking and drinking, activities which I really hardly ever enjoyed but which I held on to for social and tension-release reasons."

The use of the phrase "dropped out of my life" indicates how naturally and effortlessly the changes occurred. It is important to reiterate here that the TM movement does *not* give out rules of behavior; individuals are not told to stop smoking, drinking or using drugs (although Maharishi *has* been heard to say, "If we know something is poison, it's only common sense not to take it"). These changes are the results of deeper changes within the person.

Once again, Benson and Wallace's study affirms the subjective reports. They found a marked decrease in the use of alcohol and tobacco, as well as nonprescription drugs. In the six-month period before starting TM 60 percent of the individuals studied had used hard liquor; 18 percent were medium or heavy users. After 21 months only 25 percent continued to use hard liquor, and only three percent were medium or heavy users. Cigarette smokers? Forty-eight percent smoked before TM, 27 percent heavily. After 21 months only 16 percent smoked, 5.8 percent heavily.[14]

An Ounce of Prevention

One objection that could arise in an observer's mind is, "Who knows whether these people would have stopped using these things—drugs, tobacco, alcohol—anyhow, without TM?" How can we be sure that TM is the decisive factor in the elimination of these various items? We cannot, of course, be absolutely sure. But we can certainly take seriously the meditators' evaluation. Benson and Wallace found that "most subjects felt that transcendental meditation was instrumental in their decreasing or stopping abuse of drugs: 61.1% stated that it was extremely important; 22.8% that it was very important; 12% somewhat important, and 3.6% not important." [15] That is, 95.9 percent felt that TM was at least somewhat important in the change in their behavior.

Very significantly, of those individuals who continued to use drugs after beginning TM, "55.9% had been irregular in meditation and 24.8% had stopped for a week or more." [16] This shows that it is not merely a mood of abstinence from drugs that meditators create; it is the actual *practice* that brings about the results. If the practice is not done according to instructions, benefits are less. When it *is* done properly (twice a day for 15–20 minutes), the results, as we have seen, are dramatic and highly beneficial physiologically and psychologically.

Obviously all those who are concerned with the problem of drug use and abuse in society, in all its many expressions, should know that this practice is available. It is inexpensive, easily learned and universally applicable. It could have incalculable benefit as the basis of drug rehabilitation programs.

A paper in *The Kentucky Law Journal* in mid-1972 examined the possible use of TM in combating drug abuse and concluded that "in our drug oriented and dependent society transcendental meditation appears to be one of the few effective tools available to prevent or stop drug abuse. Experts agree that most people could stop drug use if a sufficiently desirable and simple alternative were offered to make them want to stop. Transcendental meditation is available as such an alternative." [17] The author noted:

> Moreover, it is possible that the benefits of criminal rehabilitation through T.M. are by no means confined to the field of drug abuse. For example, it is clear that a decrease in the use of drugs will be followed by a decrease in related crimes such as prostitution, petty theft and muggings. In addition, proponents of T.M. claim that the technique may be effective in the total rehabilitation of persons charged with all forms of deviant behavior resulting from stress, emotional instability and a nervous system not in balance and harmony with its environment. [18]

This idea is explained in some detail by Maharishi in *The Science of Being and Art of Living:*

> Crime is a short-cut to satisfy a craving—a short-cut which goes beyond normal and legal means. Crime, delinquency and the different patterns of anti-social behavior express the tensions which arise from a deep discontent of mind, from a weak mind and from unbalanced emotions. A weak mind is one which lacks balance and a sense of proportion.
> No approach to the problem of delinquency and crime can be truly effective unless the basic weakness of mind is remedied. The solution lies in enlarging the conscious capacity of the mind and strengthening it. [19]

This expansion can be brought about through the practice of transcendental meditation, Maharishi concludes. *The Kentucky Law Journal* states, "Such a presumption seems credible when viewed in light of other claims made by advocates of T.M. which have been scientifically verified by western observers. If so, transcendental meditation warrants our attention as an easily instituted program for criminal rehabilitation." [20]

Of course, as we have pointed out, crime, drug abuse and other symptoms of weakness in life would disappear if every individual were given the opportunity to develop full creative intelligence. Drug and criminal rehabilitation programs would become unnecessary and obsolete. "An ounce of prevention," the old saying goes, "is worth a pound of cure."

CHAPTER 7

The Philosophy of Action

His beauty is within, but
it gives freedom to his limbs
and expresses itself in his works.
——I CHING

"My job requires that I travel a lot, keep long and irregular hours, and have dealings with literally hundreds of people in the course of a week: enough, you might think, to put me on the ulcer list, somewhere near the top—at least I would have thought so a couple of years ago," said Bill, a middle-management executive for a large international firm. "But meditation sustains me through even the most intense aspects of the job. Before I started meditation, my energy level left something to be desired, and I used to get very tense under a lot of pressure. But TM gives me a balanced, poised inner state that never seems to get overshadowed no matter what goes on around me. I see other people getting completely exhausted by their work, resorting to drugs or alcohol in order to relax, and they're still high-strung and barely coping. I don't mean to sound like I'm bragging, but as the responsibility and pressure of the job increase, I seem to enjoy it all the more.

"If all this had happened to me before I started TM, it would have been too much, I couldn't have handled it.

"It's not that I *feel* more creative now, or more intelligent; but when I look at what I'm doing with some objectivity, it's obvious that I'm seeing a broader perspective, I'm incredibly clear-headed and efficient, I'm coming up with the right decisions, I'm able to be relaxed and say the right thing to avert an argument, and so on. It's fantastic. And I give TM a lot of the credit. Morning meditation clears my mind and sets me in tune for the day, and no matter how hard the day has been, no matter what I've done or not done, those 20 minutes in the afternoon never fail to relax and refresh me. Sometimes the thought comes up, 'I'm too *busy* to meditate,' but now I see that nothing is so important it can't wait 20 minutes—in fact, the *more* important something is, the more certain I am that I want to meet it with maximum clarity and freshness.

"Without that evening meditation, I'd probably be really tired or tense, too knocked out to enjoy the evening—which is probably how most people feel. I can understand why so many meditators want to become teachers of TM: because all this tiredness and tension that we all take for granted is really unnecessary. I see all these people—they work so hard that they don't have the time or energy left to enjoy themselves, their accomplishments, their families. What are they working for? As time goes by they'll have to work even harder, the way things are going. I may work hard, too, but I'm enjoying all the way!"

"Yoga Is Skill in Action"

"The Art of Action" is one of the longest chapters in *The Science of Being and Art of Living*. In it Maharishi analyzes the components of successful action (including such factors as proper planning, performing action in minimum time and with minimum expense of energy, fixity of purpose and others). The chapter abounds in valuable, practical suggestions.

Throughout the chapter, however, Maharishi returns to a theme introduced on its first page. "More effective action requires more effective thinking, and more effective thinking requires more Being in the nature of the mind. So the basis of the art of action is the art of being." [1]

The "art of being" can also be called the "science of creative intelligence." Both terms mean the systematized knowledge of how to contact the inner field of Being or pure creative intelligence. This contact, accomplished by the technique of transcendental meditation, spontaneously expands the mind and brings more creative intelligence into the fields of thought and action. This strengthens the doer, who is the basis of all action. When the actor is strong, action will automatically be powerful.

This key to success in any enterprise is epitomized by Lord Krishna's advice to Arjuna in the Bhagavad Gita: "Established in Yoga, perform action," for "Yoga is skill in action." [2] In Chapter 1 we saw that the word "Yoga" means "union," the union of the outer, ever-changing, seeking nature of the mind with the inner source of thought, Being, defined as a field of bliss-consciousness or creative intelligence. *Established* in Yoga means that this state of union is permanent, that the mind is permanently attuned to that inner richness, never out of touch with its own essential nature.

Why is this called "skill in action"? Maharishi likens the practice of TM to pulling an arrow back on a bow—a process that, with a minimum expense of energy, sends the arrow flying forward with maximum force. TM, by bringing the mind to the state of restful alertness, allows the individual to live life most efficiently and skillfully, utilizing his maximum potential. He finds that he can do less, expend less energy and yet accomplish more.

As the arrow flies ahead, gravity and friction from the air gradually reduce its momentum, just as a man may become tired or may meet obstacles in his environment which drain his energies. Being *established* in Yoga means that a man would never lose access to that innermost storehouse of intelligence and energy. It is as if the arrow, while flying forward, could somehow maintain contact with the bow, and therefore lose none of its momentum. It could continue to fly forward indefinitely. This is the highest level of skill in action.

"I find," one student said, "that true to Maharishi's philosophy of action, I am far more efficient than I used to be. Each day is so full; I am doing so much more and wasting less time. I am more active, and my activities are better than they used to be . . . more useful. I feel a greater sense of accomplishment in school and out. My ability to concentrate on my studies—or any task—has increased greatly. Consequently, I can do less, but accomplish more. Mental perception and cognition have sharpened and increased also. I feel able to think more clearly as well as see more deeply into many aspects of nature."

This is clearly not the typical philosophy of renunciation and withdrawal from life often associated with the East. Maharishi (who often speaks of TM as a "technique of action") points out the simple fact that if we *begin* with an expansion of capability on the subjective level, objective results will naturally reflect that expansion. His teachings are aimed at the active man, whose responsibilities and aspirations require expanded abilities. In this increasingly complex, rapidly changing world, with its incessant pressure for decisions and creative response to ever-new situations, our energies and abilities must keep pace. If we want to expand our sphere of influence, we must expand our capabilities.

TM expands the conscious capacity of the mind, offering a man broadened awareness, greater creativity and more clear, powerful thought. At the same time, the deep rest and relaxation afforded by the practice refresh and rejuvenate the meditator. With increased energy yet greater calm, any activity becomes more dynamic and effective.

"I meditate before I go to court mainly because I find that I'm very intensely thinking about what I'm going to talk about, and TM is a way of putting my mind at ease and being more relaxed," said Ron, a welfare-rights attorney whose work has brought forth more humane legislation and hundreds of thousands of dollars to help the nation's poor. "The court-room is a very intense situation. TM helps me collect my thoughts and walk in much calmer. I normally didn't get nervous once the argument had begun, but I used to be fairly nervous at the beginning, just hoping, being very intensely involved in it: what is the judge going to be like, is he going to be sympathetic or not, what is it that I have to say, how can I convince the judge, all these questions would fill my mind. I find that TM very much helps me to be relaxed; I really am relaxed when I go into the courtroom. Many of my colleagues have commented that I seem much more calm than other lawyers.

"Also, in the office I work in there's been a long history of feuding, people with intense feelings about certain things and very frequently much of our energy was expended upon intra-office squabbles. I find that happening much less now; I found that I handled several incidents much better.

"I'm also better able to put things into perspective now. Very frequently I would get so engrossed in something that it would dominate all my thoughts and absorb my energy, and I would wind up getting very upset over something which now I consider very minor.

"I very definitely feel that I have a happier disposition. I look forward to meditation in the morning. It makes me feel much better. I leave the house happier."

"I Get a Lot Done These Days"

In his introductory lectures on TM, SIMS-IMS Director Jerry Jarvis often used to say, "Transcendental meditation brings fulfillment to an individual in his own terms," empha-sizing that growth through TM is an individual affair, not proceeding according to any set mold or code of standards. Meditators from a wide diversity of professions, students and nonstudents, are finding this an accurate assertion.

"I feel that my effectiveness in business has improved," a fifty-four-year-old aerospace executive said, "and has been reflected in increased responsibility and higher pay. The ability to concentrate has improved, and intelligent perception has increased for solution of problems in less time."

"I have gone from a period of three years of unemployment to having established my own business as a leather tailor," said one young man. "I have overcome a great deal of my Gemini procrastination since meditating. I get a lot done these days."

"In playing the piano I am much more precise, much more able to work out little subtle things for a long period of time and enjoy it," a musician said. "Meditation has tremendously improved my 'ear,' my ability to accurately hear and play notes."

"My success in my occupation (writer-musician-singer) is a 'mind-blower,' " another young man commented. "I must employ others to keep up with certain phases of it . . . attorney, producer, manager, etc. etc. I have found more ease in completing started projects; more return, both inner and outer, with far less physical effort. 'Work' has become a joy."

A young man told this story: "Recently I have been finding a definitely marked increase in efficiency and success in action. In my job I find my duties much easier and as I take on more responsibility the job gets easier. It really seems that I'm doing less and accomplishing more, and what I do is done with greater ease. And it isn't just me that notices it. I told my boss that I must quit in order to go to a one-week [meditators' residence] course, and he said, 'Oh no . . . don't quit, take the week off and we'll give you full pay!' "

New Directions

The evidence is convincing that TM increases a person's effectiveness in his chosen field of work. Often, however, in spite of all the options and opportunities available in our society, young people simply do not know what they want to do, what direction they want their lives to take. It is an understatement to say that this lack of definite direction is a major cause of confusion and anxiety among the youth of today. Anything that could put a person more in touch with himself and thereby give him a deeper, more personal, meaningful basis for choice would be invaluable. Many young meditators report this benefit from TM.

"When I started meditating," one student wrote, "I was confusedly going about changing majors, trying biochemistry, physiology, anthropology, art, etc., and my grade point average was 3.0. When all along my ability was in math, where I have a lot of talent. Now I have a double major in math and computer science. I have a 3.8 grade point average."

One man who had been working as an engineer for a number of years said that after beginning meditation "my dissatisfaction with the engineering profession, which I had knowingly harbored for some time, showed itself forcibly, and I left engineering to become a social worker. This work provides immeasurably more fulfillment than engineering."

A student wrote, "Before TM I was fed up with school, useless in practical matters, and over-zealous in 'mystical' matters. I was ready to emigrate to Canada and had little direction. Now I have become more practical and plan on finishing school, having a career and devoting time to helping others start meditating. I understand better what place practical matters have and also school is much easier. My mind is sharper and I am much more satisfied with the real, harmless pleasures of life like a nice day, pleasant friends, etc. and have little desire for too many frivolities or harmful pleasures like drugs."

Not all the changes are of the "back-to-school" variety. A girl told me that shortly after beginning meditation, "I decided to go to graduate school, although I was still not certain in my mind that it was what I wanted. I started last fall and in two quarters have become quite convinced that graduate school was *not* what I wanted. Therefore I am not going to finish out this year. Now it may seem on the surface that this has been a bad trend in my life, giving up grad school, but I consider it quite the opposite. I see it as not wasting further time pursuing a goal which is not true."

Her experience is quite different, outwardly, from the following: "When I began meditating, I was goofing off, flunking out of school, and taking drugs. I felt far out and my only interest was in getting further out. . . . I am now preparing to begin teaching junior high school this fall. I am a respected, responsible member of society. Meditation has transformed virtually every area of my life. Grades rose from academic probation to honors at UCLA—one small indication of the transformation."

"When I started meditating," another said, "I was working for a large corporation and was rather dissatisfied with what I was doing and where I was going (nowhere). As a result of meditation, I quit my job and returned to school.

"Meditation has given me a direction in life. It has helped me set goals for myself. I feel better mentally and physically. From being almost totally dependent on drugs, I now no longer have much, if any, use for them. The world around me has been brought into clearer perspective in interpersonal relationships. Meditation has evoked the necessary stimuli to find a direction in life."

These stories—and even a casual relationship with a group of meditators—demonstrate that meditation does not produce a certain "type" of person. It does seem to facilitate each individual's becoming more himself, living his own life and achieving success "in his own terms." Contact with the universal field of creative intelligence strengthens the unique, individual personality from within, and whatever a person sets out to do, he finds himself doing it better.

*The Steady Intellect: Concentration,
Contentment, Clarity*

One of the more specific areas of improvement most frequently mentioned by meditators is improved concentration.

"I could concentrate on and absorb material in large gulps," said one student. "Ability to concentrate without so much tension is one aspect of improvement I've enjoyed," said another. "My concentration is so much improved that at special times I almost forget what I am doing, I am so involved." A secretary said that "I am doing three times more than I was before meditation and am not becoming strained and am enjoying it. When I was going to school, I noticed that I could study for six or seven hours with never a stray thought and that what I learned was retained."

This improvement in the power of concentration is vital for success in any area. Ordinarily the mind wanders; much time and energy are lost in random and irrelevant thoughts, or the mind is strained by efforts to force it to concentrate. Many potentially very capable students find that "I was doing poorly in school because I could not sit down and concentrate on my studies." The mind is restless, and constantly reaching here and there in search of some greater object of happiness.

As we have seen, this thirst of the mind is an essential part of being human and is the basis of all growth and progress in life. But we have also seen that due to meditation the mind's incessant quest for greater happiness and satisfaction becomes increasingly fulfilled. Contacting the field of Being, which Maharishi sometimes describes as a field of "bliss-consciousness," the mind returns to activity infused with great happiness. This inner contentment provides a stable basis for all activity. "I have been less plagued by swirling torrents of unwanted images," a student reported. "I have had less trouble studying for longer periods of time."

"Once the mind becomes rooted in bliss-consciousness," Maharishi writes in *The Science of Being and Art of Living,* "eternal contentment becomes its very nature and it remains steady, even when it is associated with outer experiences and activity." [3] In the Bhagavad Gita this is called the state of steady intellect. "Just as a millionaire who has great wealth remains unaffected by the rise and fall of the market, so the mind which has gained the state of bliss-consciousness through transcendental meditation remains naturally contented on coming out from the transcendental state to the field of activity. This contentment, being grounded in the very nature of the mind, does not allow the mind to waver and be affected in pleasure or pain, nor allow it to become affected by attachment or fear in the world. This natural equanimity of the mind, even while it is actively engaged, is the state of steady intellect." [4] (It is also the state of freedom, for no matter what comes and goes in the ever-changing sphere of a man's experience, the mind remains established in "eternal contentment." This is the state of a mind "established in Yoga.")

"All last year," a student remarked, "I was constantly surprised at how long I could sit patiently and easily while reading and studying for school. This year I'm not spending nearly the amount of time studying, for there are many other activities which have become important to engage in, and yet when I do study things come much faster and results are the same or better than when I studied all the time."

"It has become so much easier to study," a girl said, "because I only have to read the material once in order to understand it. For a while—at the beginning of this last quarter, I was getting pretty upset . . . feeling guilty . . . because I knew I wasn't studying as much as I used to, and felt that I was neglecting my studies. However, the realization struck me that I wasn't behind in any class, and even more fantastic—my grades were better!"

The Van Gogh Syndrome

At twenty-eight Susan H. is quite a successful woman. An artist, she taught art for a while at the University of California in Berkeley, and her paintings have appeared in numerous one-man shows, including a recent show at the Whitney Museum in New York. She has a great deal to say about transcendental meditation.

"Before I started to meditate, I was teaching at the university and I was also a professional artist. I found myself extremely cynical and overworked. I never had time enough to do what I wanted to do, and my work was going rather slowly. I was extremely nervous, I drank continually and I found that my contacts with other people were superficial and extremely neurotic because I didn't have enough energy or spontaneity to cope with everything around me. I'll have to say I was also extremely cynical about any kind of meditation.

"Then I noticed a student of mine whose work was developing very fast. It would have taken me a long time to accomplish the kind of changes he would make in a few days. He was practicing TM, and everything, his work, his personal life, was getting better all the time. So in spite of my skepticism I started to meditate, and the minute I was instructed I started to laugh, because it was like a huge blockage being removed from my mind. I stopped drinking right on the spot. I didn't take any more cigarettes or smoking of any sort; drugs were completely out of the question. The effects were felt immediately in my teaching and have progressed all the way along.

"In terms of painting the amount of energy I am accumulating is astronomical. I have a tremendous ability to work long hours without feeling any tiredness at all. You'll notice if you work for a long period of time that you'll feel exhausted and have to sit down and that sort of thing; I don't feel that any more. The working just becomes better all the time. Ideas just come automatically, there's no trying, no struggle getting ideas any more. They just come, they happen.

"My paintings have become much more complex visually. Before, people would come upon my work and get the whole idea in a few minutes; now they come into a room of my work and they sit and they look at it, and it grows on them. Yesterday a museum curator came down to my studio to look at my work, and as she was sitting talking to me, she kept looking around the room. The work was growing on her and she was excited about it. This wouldn't have happened before TM; the images were much shallower, partly because I didn't have the energy to get involved that deeply. In terms of technical ability, my skills have just automatically increased. As my perceptions about life become greater, my ability to get them across is greater.

"We're all familiar with the idea that artists have to suffer, and I was into that pretty heavily before. You know, the Van Gogh image. But I see it as a lot of nonsense now. Do you know that very few artists live beyond the age of fifty-five or sixty? It's simply because they destroy themselves through drugs or drinking or whatever. Every day I feel better and healthier. I look at people my own age who aren't meditating and they're depressed all the time, they're in a rut all the time and I'm going up."

CHAPTER 8

Values

> For I have seen the truth; I have seen and I
> know that people can be beautiful and happy
> without losing the power of living on earth. I will
> not and cannot believe that evil is the normal con-
> dition of mankind.
>
> . . . .
>
> How simple it is: in one day, *in one hour*
> everything could be arranged at once! The chief
> thing is to love others like yourself, that's the
> great thing, and that's everything; nothing else is
> wanted. . . . And yet it's an old truth which has
> been told and retold a billion times—but it has
> not formed part of our lives! . . . If only every-
> one wants it, it can all be arranged at once.
>
> —DOSTOEVSKY, "The Dream of a
> Ridiculous Man"

There are those who say that this is a generation without
values. Many analysts of current American society conclude
that because we live in an age of "transition" between the
more traditional cultures of the past and an unknown post-
industrial "global village," our values are hopelessly up in the

air. Other observers, noting the broad and confusing, often contradictory diversity of life-styles existing in our society, each with its unique set of standards, conclude that we are "a society that has lost its consensus . . . a society that cannot agree on standards of conduct, language and manners, on what can be seen and heard." [1] And certainly, while earlier cultures did operate upon a solid foundation of commonly shared values, contemporary life exhibits a fragmentation of values that baffles the individual and causes him to pick up and discard sets of values in the same way he experiments with toothpastes or hairstyles. [2]

But on a deeper level a very large number of us share some very simple, basic and yet all-encompassing and important ideals. We want to be fully human and enjoy all aspects of life. We want to cultivate our mental, physical and emotional faculties and achieve real spiritual growth. We have a vital concern in world peace and the welfare of all men. We are determined to preserve nature from further waste and pollution. We realize that we are out of tune with ourselves and with all of nature, and we want to get back in.

Life and Non-Life: Revolution by Consciousness

Says Charles A. Reich in his widely acclaimed book *The Greening of America:*

> There is a revolution coming. It will not be like revolutions of the past. It will originate with the individual and with culture, and it will change the political structure only as its final act. . . . It is now spreading with amazing rapidity, and already our laws, institutions and social structure are changing in consequence. It promises a higher reason, a more human community, and a new and liberated individual. Its ultimate creation will be a new and enduring wholeness and beauty—a renewed relationship of man to himself, to other men, to society, to nature, and to the land. [3]

Erich Fromm, an astute observer of mankind, had pointed to this change several years before. "There is a growing polarization occurring in the United States and in the whole world," he wrote in *The Revolution of Hope,* and he went on:

> There are those who are attracted to force, "law and order," bureaucratic methods, and eventually to non-life, and those with a deep longing for life, for new attitudes rather than for ready-made schemes and blueprints. This new front is a movement which combines the wish for profound changes in our economic and social practices with changes in our psychic and spiritual approach to life. In its most general form, its aim is the activation of the individual, the restoration of man's control over the social system, the humanization of technology. It is a movement in the name of life.[4]

Accordingly, many people today, particularly in the younger generations, refuse to accept the divorce between what life could be, what anyone would deem good, and what society is. This generation has, to use Arthur Schlesinger, Jr.'s phrase, "the determination to make reality live up to rhetoric." But other generations have had high ideals, too. The ideals of freedom, of love, of achieving peace on earth, are as old as man. And yet we see that they have not been attained for centuries.

A clue to why success has not been achieved can be found in Fromm's statement. This movement, which is "in the name of life," has not succeeded because it is based on "a deep *longing* for life"—a *longing* rather than a realization, a desire for life rather than full experience of living. What we are really searching for is *life*—and with the experience of fullness of life these values are automatically and naturally lived.

"At the heart of everything," says Reich, "is what we shall call a change of consciousness. This means a 'new head'—a new way of living—a new man. This is what the new generation has been searching for. . . . Today's emerging consciousness seeks a new knowledge of what it means to be human. . . . in order that man once more can become a creative force, renewing and creating his own life and thus giving life back to the society." ⁵

A View from the Top Rung

Ed M. is a high-ranking executive of one of the world's largest, multinational corporations. At forty-six, with his stylishly long hair beginning to gray, he is a strikingly good-looking man, tall and strong-featured, with bright, steady eyes. We spoke one evening about his interest in transcendental meditation.

"The reason I began TM goes back over a long period of time and is due to things that have been going on inside of me. I think that most people who take up TM do so because they acknowledge certain needs within themselves. With me, these needs had been recognized for some time. It came to a head when I realized that I had reached the point where I had all the material things I needed.

"There was just nothing I couldn't have in a material sense. And it was a great shock (though I hate to admit it) to realize that this was not going to give me anything at all, literally nothing; I was no happier today than when I started, you know, 'up the ladder,' seeking something out of life that turns out to be far too material, I'm afraid; and it's a rather disquieting thing, at forty-six, to realize that if you haven't found it now, maybe you're on the wrong path.

"So I think already before I started TM I realized that somehow the answer was to be found within myself, and not outside myself, that I couldn't look into the store window and say, I want this, this and this and then find instant happiness. Instead of looking in the store window I had to look within myself and that's really what TM is all about: looking inward to find the answers to our own being, our own identity.

"On that point I want to make a comment about TM. Peo-

ple talk of it sometimes as if it were mystical because what
has happened to them is so extraordinary that they can't quite
believe it. But last night I was reading once again the preface to Maharishi's book *The Science of Being and Art of
Living,* where he points out that the search for Being, the
search for man's identity, for his Self, this thing that we're
all looking for, whether it's Being or God or what have you,
has always been looked at as essentially religious or mystical.
Up until now, it's never been recognized that in fact the
search for Being is a *science.* When you read his book you
realize that TM is grounded in physical science; this is not
mysticism at all. Everything that you learn is based on physics.

"But back to the main question. In the business world I
have always known anxiety, I've always known certain fears,
apprehensions, in part generated by a constant sense of com-
petition, a need to acquire something, whether status within
an organization, material position in the world or whatever.
There is always that fear and anxiety that somehow you are
not going to make it, or that when you do get one more rung
up the ladder somehow it doesn't have any reward. When I
started TM I found that the anxieties and fears began to dis-
sipate.

"War, racial prejudice, all the problems of our everyday
life stem from man's anxiety, man's apprehensions, things
that man doesn't understand. TM deals directly with this because it helps man to overcome his fears and anxieties by dissolving them, and by leading him to something far more important, which is love, love of himself, and love of things
around him, and a far greater realization of what life is. It
in a sense leads us to reexplore all the values that we have
learned in our lives.

"I think that through this inward search man will come to
a feeling of love for himself and for mankind beyond anything that has been known before in our civilizations. And
this of course is going to impinge upon war, violence and that
sort of thing because there won't be a need for it any more.
It will become obsolete."

As Plain as ABC: Values and Consciousness

"The values I have are the same good values that I had before meditating," one practitioner of transcendental meditation wrote, "but strengthened—as is my ability and will to live by them now facilitated and strengthened." Others find that not only are their values lived up to more easily, but that the values themselves have become considerably higher. "Religious, philosophical and personal values have developed in a way I couldn't even conceive of before I began meditating," one said. "Things just start coming out from the inside and life becomes less a matter of trying to live according to certain values. I simply noticed I was a more perceptive and loving human being."

"An increased maturity has given my ideals greater depth and greater purity," a student said. "Hitherto, my goals had been limited by a small consciousness and even smaller feelings of love and compassion. As Being is infused into the nature of my mind, I find previous rationalizations, jealousies, envies, etc., disappearing and implementation of my ideals comes much easier."

The innocent nature of this development is especially interesting, because quite a few people said, "Actually, I had hoped for much less before beginning meditation—more on a superficial level. I really didn't know the depth and breadth of what was being offered to me." Stated in another way, "I had no hopes when I started meditating, it was an intuitive decision, a grasp in the dark. I have discarded a whole set of meaningless values, and am in a state of constant discovery as to the simple beauty all about me."

"I simply *noticed* I was a more perceptive and loving human being. . . ."

"A state of constant *discovery* . . ." Through TM, an effortless, organic process of growth occurs, natural and unselfconscious, which nourishes every branch of an individual's "tree of life," including the values which guide our actions. It isn't necessary to judge ourselves, condemn ourselves for not living up to what we hold to be right or good. It is only necessary to begin to grow, for as we grow, so do our values and our ability to live by them.

The essential thing is that the level of consciousness must be raised; the individual must grow to a state of greater awareness and greater purity. For "throughout history, learned men have set out before mankind the rewards of virtue, the beauties of goodness," writes Maslow. "It's all as plain as ABC, and yet most people perversely refuse to step into the happiness and self-respect that is offered them. Nothing is left to the teachers but irritation, impatience, disillusionment, alternations between scolding, exhortation, and hopelessness. A good many have thrown up their hands altogether and talked about original sin or intrinsic evil and concluded that man could be saved only by extrahuman forces." [6] But the knowledge we are gaining of human nature, he says, gives us "the insight that human evil is largely human weakness" and that it is "forgivable, understandable and also, in principle, curable." [7]

Maharishi, too, emphasizes that wrongdoing stems from weakness and that right action is spontaneous from a higher level of consciousness. "Many people talk of inner feelings," he writes. "They say: I feel like doing this, so I do it. But *my* feelings and *my* doing can only be right or wrong according to the standard of *my* consciousness, and who knows whether *my* consciousness is absolutely pure or not?" [8]

A study of chickens in which they were allowed to choose their own food showed a difference in ability to choose what was good for them. Some became stronger, larger, healthier and more dominant than others. When the diet selected by the "good choosers" was forced upon the "bad choosers," the bad choosers became healthier and stronger. Thus, the good choosers were able to choose better than the bad choosers what was good for the bad choosers themselves! The implications of this for human values and human behavior are enormous.[9]

"In healthy people only," Maslow continues, "is there a good correlation between subjective delight in the experience, impulse to the experience, or wish for it, and 'basic need' for

the experience. . . . Only such people uniformly yearn for what is good for them and for others, and then are able whole-heartedly to enjoy it, and approve of it. For such people virtue is its own reward. . . . They spontaneously tend to do right because that is what they *want* to do." [10] The solution obviously lies in providing a means whereby the level of consciousness can be raised and awareness broadened, so that "bad choosers" can become "good choosers" and unhealthy personalities can become whole.

Unscrambling Values: Innocence and the Good Life

"Some people feel guilt because they cannot do the right thing," one man said. "They think they are not trying hard enough, or they may condemn themselves and think of themselves in their secret thoughts as 'bad people.' This is a great tragedy in many lives. Fortunately, it is every man's ultimate destiny to stand up strong and happy, to be able to give sincere thanks to his creator by everything he does, without having to think about right and wrong. Only this innocent state of life will fulfill the purpose of life for man and God. Transcendental meditation has put me on the road to such a way of life."

A young woman meditating for two and a half years wrote: "When I started meditation, I did not much consider my personal and religious values. There has been a complete change in this area. Meditation has given me an understanding of the nature of morality and what it means to be religious. I have become a truly moral and religious person. My religious concepts could be found in the scriptures of my religion, for meditation has made following the traditionally proven ethics of right behavior an easy and desirable matter.* My under-

---

* "If the various extant religions may be taken as expressions of human aspirations," says Maslow, "i.e., what people would *like* to become if only they could, then we can see here too a validation of the affirmation that all people yearn toward self-

standing of the laws of nature has developed so much (I don't think I had much understanding before I began meditating) that I just naturally do not perform any action which I know would go against the laws of nature or would be life-damaging. I never dreamed that I was this good a person. My values have developed as beautifully as I could have ever hoped and I know they are still in a process of becoming."

"Before I started meditating," said a nineteen-year-old girl, "my values were pretty scrambled. I had a vague idea of how I 'should' act, but I never really had the strength or the courage to practice what I considered a moral life. So I found myself doing things that I didn't really want to do simply because other people seemed to find them pleasing. (Drinking, first, then later grass.) However, since meditating, I've stopped trying to figure out how to act, and have just begun to behave naturally. Suddenly I found myself living a life that before meditating I wanted, but never thought I could have. . . . I am leading a life that allows me to like myself."

It is important that these people do not claim that they now know the ultimate truth; there is no arrogance in their statements, no dogmatic attitude. As one of them said, "My values are in the process of becoming." Another said, "I have very high values which are almost impossible to live up to, but, since I have been meditating, I can foresee the day of all things becoming a reality." In other words, growth is a gradual process. This is a very sensible realization. Nevertheless, it is obvious that the growth of meditators is exceptionally rapid.

Right Action

We have seen that many people report a greater ability to know what is right and what is wrong for them, and a corre-

---

actualization or tend toward it. This is so because *our description of the actual characteristics of self-actualizing people parallels at many points the ideals urged by the religions.*" [11]

spondingly greater ability to act rightly, according to their own standards. This development is individual and entirely natural. No morals, no codes of "do's and don'ts," no standards of behavior are given to meditators. The teachers of the science of creative intelligence feel no need to instruct others in proper values. They feel confident that everyone, at his level of development, will act as well as he is able, and as he grows, his actions will become better and better. Along with Maharishi, the teachers of TM and SCI all seem to possess an unshakable confidence in man's inherent goodness and in his ability to grow and express more of the good within him. No wonder the editor of a college newspaper in Ohio recently referred to those responsible for teaching the science of creative intelligence as "the most optimistic people in an age of pessimism." As we read these statements, we can begin to understand why this is so.

"If I feel something is wrong, I can't compromise—I have to stand up for what is right," one person told me. Another, speaking for his family (all of whom are meditating), told me that "we've all felt a strengthening of what is right and wrong. We're stronger in right and weaker in wrong. Wrong thoughts or wrong actions less and less frequently come into my consciousness. Even slight wrongs are becoming more and more foreign. While I was working at the delicatessen one night, I thought of stealing a sandwich but I couldn't do it. The thought came up and then just went away."

We have been talking a lot about right and wrong. What *is* right, or good? Philosophers have been trying to define this concept for centuries, yet most people recognize—and always have recognized—that good action (or thought or speech) is that which produces beneficial, life-supporting influences on oneself and others. Whatever helps to maintain and evolve life, whatever is conducive to growth and harmonious progress is right and good. "Right is that which produces a good influence everywhere," writes Maharishi.[12]

A definition similar to this appeared in a recent *Saturday Review* article, "What Would a Scientific Religion Be Like?"

The author, a physicist, concluded that "it is possible to evolve a guide to what I *should* be doing, namely, those things that help to bring about the full development of other human spirits." [13] Action which fulfills this purpose, directly or indirectly, is good action.

Looked at from this angle, we might say that a practice such as TM is the best action anyone could perform, because it not only leads directly to "full development," but this development naturally influences all actions, making them stronger and more life-supporting. Any other action can be said to be relative in nature, that is, it has some good effect and some bad effect. An action may be good in one situation but in another may be totally inappropriate. No action can be said to be all good unless it leads to a higher level of life. Growth to a higher level can have only good effects, on both the individual and all those whose lives fall within the range of his influence. Growth of consciousness, deepening of the powers of understanding, perception and love, is the one way to establish ourselves on a platform from which all actions *must* be good actions.

The Big Questions—and Their Answers

"Before meditating, many questions regarding the purpose of life, the nature of man, religious doctrines and philosophies, etc., puzzled, bothered and annoyed me," a film student wrote. "I needed something strong to hold to, to reassert a feeling I had, yet wondered about, that strength and power and happiness are born into and can be developed by an individual. That everything that counts can come from within. Meditation has given me that strength and . . . I am now finding it more possible to live according to the ideals I value."

"What is the purpose of life, the nature of man?" These are questions which have troubled mankind for centuries and which must remain unanswered and unanswerable as long as direct experience of the ultimate reality of life is not possible, as long as man's conscious mind is not expanded to its full capacity. From direct experience the answers can be found. They can never be found by speculation. We know this; this is why science (which rests upon direct observation) has replaced philosophy as our guide to knowledge of the universe.

It is interesting to note that Maharishi Mahesh Yogi, who brought the science of creative intelligence to the world, graduated from Allahabad University as a physics major. In his first book, *The Science of Being and Art of Living,* he tells us:

> This book presents a practical thesis to satisfy man's search for truth through science, religion and metaphysical thought. . . . The science of being, like every other science, starts its investigation into the truth of existence from the gross, obvious level of life and enters into the subtle regions of experience. The science of being, however, eventually transcends these subtle regions and arrives at the direct experience of the transcendental field of eternal Being.[14]

"I had always been searching for a basic and ultimate understanding of life and the universe," a man wrote. "Although I considered these things on the intellectual level, I knew that any true development would also fulfill the emotional side of life. When I found transcendental meditation I knew it to be the extension and completion of what I had been seeking. As my understanding of it and the direct experience grow, this conviction gains strength. Now, with the portion I understand, I know that my personal values will be totally fulfilled.

"In my life, I find that day-to-day living is a simple and effortless expression of states I could only conceive of before. It gets better all the time. Clarity of intelligence, peace of mind, and spontaneous joy have become common."

Selfish and Unselfish

Maharishi is often confronted with this question: "Surely one must be a very selfish person if he sees suffering in others and is happy and contented."

Maharishi replies:

An unhappy man, even if he has a great desire to help others, what can he do? An unhappy man is himself worried and miserable. In his sympathy he will begin to weep; other than that he has no ability to help. The result will be that before only one man was weeping and now the second also begins to weep.

But if he gains the technique of meditation and begins to meditate, he becomes happy in himself. He becomes wiser, more able than before, and then he goes with a happy face, a great atmosphere of harmony to the suffering man. He changes his atmosphere, cheers him up by his presence. Therefore, even if we have a desire, as all of us humanly have the desire to help other suffering people, the only way to help others is to get the technique of being happy in ourselves. If a poor man wants to help another poor man, the first thing would be to earn something. Grow rich and, being rich, approach him, give him something for the time being and give him the technique of earning so that he may not be poor any more.

So it is extremely necessary for us to acquire the ability of maintaining our own standard of peace and happiness before we jump into the world of suffering. When a man becomes happy, his compassion grows. A happy man would be able to see the unhappiness of others much more than an unhappy man. An unhappy man is busy suffering himself, he has no time to see the suffering of others. Compassion is not awake in an unhappy, miserable mind. But compassion and kindness are wide awake in a man who is happy, who is peaceful.[15]

This is the experience of many meditators. "From rather ego-centered values (money, big house, nice things) I have changed to other-people-centered values," a woman from California wrote. "I now have a real concern for those about me, and am no longer as much concerned with satisfying my own ego impulses. . . . It makes me a lot happier to have values that encompass other people, because when I give, I really do receive."

"I am also a great deal more effective in helping people,"

said a student, "because, of course, there is TM to offer, because I am stronger, and because I can more readily see what it is they need and how to present it."

Numerous similar comments have been made: "I seem to have a new sense of tenderness and compassion." "I don't think I've ever really understood what love, compassion or brotherhood meant, before, but now, every day, I learn a little more."

"Before meditation," a girl at the University of Arizona wrote, "I was going through a religious and philosophical crisis. I couldn't understand why so much suffering and hate. Meditation has helped me alleviate my own weaknesses and in a small way help others. I have always believed in the goodness and potentiality of mankind and meditation has strengthened this belief. Although I still fall very short of my personal values, meditation has given me a path and a means to live up to a world of love, harmony and openness."

Devotion, Direction and Personal Progress

In our society today, dominated as it is by rapid change, most individuals experience a shifting of values, a shift from overt or tacit membership in one subgrouping within society (hippie, executive, intellectual, etc.) to another, a shift in admiration for and emulation of one charismatic "hero" or exemplar (the Beatles, the Kennedy brothers, Kate Millet or Joan Baez) to another. This constant shifting of values implies that most of us have not found an individual, faith or organization which we feel is worthy of our admiration and devotion. We have found no one worth emulating, no standards, values or traditions which fully satisfy our practical or psychological needs, and therefore most of us have concluded that we must derive our own values, formulate our own standards and make our own decisions.

At this point—in view of the well-discussed human tendency to *seek* a feeling of belonging by submerging oneself in allegiance to some ideology or segment of society—it is important to reiterate that neither Maharishi nor the organizations which teach the science of creative intelligence seek to develop "followers" nor do they prescribe to meditators how to behave, how to dress, what to eat, etc. Maharishi is often pressed for answers to such questions as "What are the best foods to eat?" or "Which is the best candidate for President?" "Some good, nourishing food," he might answer; or, to the latter question, "It would be good to ask the advice of the political experts, and then decide for yourself." He seeks to allow every individual to develop in his own way, without imposing a value system upon anyone.

When one student was asked if he felt a devotion to meditation, he replied, "A devotion towards meditation—that seems to be an odd way to say it. I do have a keen interest in the physiological changes that occur, and a rational interest in my own mental and physical health, so naturally I meditate regularly. The only one you begin to love is Maharishi, and the reason you love Maharishi is that he has brought you the opportunity to receive all these benefits of life, he's given you something so valuable." This is a widely shared feeling among meditators, particularly among those who have had the opportunity to spend some time near Maharishi. It is not uncommon to see scores of meditators lined up in the aisle ahead of Maharishi as he enters or leaves a lecture, waiting to give him a flower. This is a traditional Indian way of expressing one's love and gratitude to the Master.

Some observers have written of a "cult of worshipers" surrounding Maharishi, but this type of expression is a gross exaggeration of the reality. Naturally some few are carried away to extremes of enthusiasm and emotionalism; their behavior has already been classified as "mood-making," which more mature meditators know will be short-lived, to be replaced by a deeper, more substantial and less ostentatious devotion.

Maharishi himself certainly discourages any tinge of idolatry. A reporter once asked him, "How many followers do you have?" and Maharishi replied, "I don't have any follow-ers; each man follows his own progress." In India and else-where some wise men are to be found with followers around them, but the followers are rarely enjoying the state of prog-ress or enlightenment of the leaders. TM gives each man the ability to progress rapidly toward that fulfilled state. This is its strength, and because it is Maharishi's work that has made TM available, any love or devotion directed toward him is well deserved. But it is TM, and only TM, that he teaches.

In the foregoing statements on values we see that each one reflects different concerns, and, to a great extent, different experiences. Most people discuss values as being purely per-sonal, discovered in the course of living. Others say that "the Scriptures now make sense to me," or, "I have come to be-lieve in God again without trying or looking for that belief." It is interesting that the person who made the last comment also said: "I have also come to feel more value and good in humanity as a whole and myself in particular." This is very heartening at a time when many of us find ourselves *losing* faith in the goodness and value of humanity.

Whether an individual speaks in terms of God, the scrip-tures of his or another religion, or solely of "what is right and wrong for me," it is certainly noteworthy that all these people state or imply that "I'm slowly becoming aware of the values that are real to me and the importance of respect-ing them rather than superimposing some value that I may have heard or read." Or, as a student said, "I am far more aware of my own morality—what is right or wrong for me—and act according to this naturally."

What matters is that these values come from the heart, from the experience of living, and, as one person said, "It is a joy to live with what little purity I have been fortunate enough to attain and know there is ever more to come."

A young man meditating less than a year wrote: "Since beginning meditation, my religious, philosophical, spiritual and personal values have developed far, far beyond any of my most distant expectations. They have evolved to a deeply spiritual, tremendously powerful set of values. A belief has flowered that all creation is steadily evolving to one common goal. The essence of this goal is pure, eternal bliss, total eternal energy, complete harmony, supreme enlightenment, final union with God. The one steady component at the base of this goal is the glorious quality of love. Through transcendental meditation I have been able to become one who radiates love, compassion and harmony in all situations. I have attained the God-sent good of contentment in life. At last my philosophy, how I picture myself ideally being, has solidified into a day-to-day reality. This clearly is the result of regular meditation. I know with my full heart that my actions are in accordance with the purpose of creation."

"The purpose of creation," Maharishi writes, "is the expansion of happiness . . . and evolution is the process by which it is fulfilled. Life begins in a natural way, it evolves, and happiness expands. The expansion of happiness carries with it the growth of intelligence, power, creativity and everything that may be said to be of significance in life." [16]

Do you recall the quote from Dostoevsky with which we began this chapter?

> For I have seen the truth; I have seen and I know that people can be beautiful and happy without losing the power of living on earth.

. . . .

If only everyone wants it, it can all be arranged at once.

CHAPTER 9

Freedom

Inner and Outer Freedom

"Freedom" is one of the most frequently used words in our age. What does it mean? What is a free man, a free action?

First of all, we ought to distinguish between two kinds of freedom. These correspond to the two aspects of life which we have been discussing, inner and outer.

Outer freedom is freedom of action. Defined in its simplest terms, it means that a man can do what he pleases, that no individual or institution will stand between his desire and its fulfillment. It means the ability to express openly any opinion, to move from one place to another unhindered, etc. We might call these aspects political or social freedom. They are governed by the laws of a society. But even more, they are governed by the level of consciousness of that society. It is plain to anyone, without discussion, that the more enlightened a society is, the more its members are educated and live at a high level of individual fulfillment and happiness, the more there will be freedom in that society. The more narrow a society is, its members filled with suspicion, suffering, hatred, violence, intolerance, the less freedom exists and can exist in that society. Here again we see the same fundamental principle: as a man is within, so will his outward actions be; as individuals are, so will society be. "By their fruits ye shall know them."

Knowing this simple truth of life, Maharishi does not concern himself in his teaching with the external aspects of freedom. His energies are directed toward bringing each individual to a state of liberation from the bondage of ignorance, ignorance of his own nature and its immense potentialities. For as long as a person is bound by fear, hatred, suspicion or confusion, as long as he suffers, it matters little whether he goes north or south, wears red or blue, eats rice or potatoes—he is not free, for he carries with him the prison of his own shortcomings, which restrict his understanding, his emotions and his activities.

The situation in the world today, particularly in the more developed Western nations and most particularly in the United States, is that man's external freedom, of choice and action, is very great. It is not unlimited or perfect; it can certainly be extended and deepened. But by comparison with past generations, and with less developed nations of today, where men and women were and are engaged in virtually continuous struggles merely to survive, where most people were born, lived and died in the same town or village, surrounded by the same people, and where a large percentage of the choices open to our generation were never even *conceived of,* our freedom of choice is literally fantastic. Not only is it already very extensive, but as man moves out of the age of industrialism with its emphasis on uniformity and conformity, he will increasingly face the problem of "overchoice," in which a proliferation of products and diverse life-styles may overwhelm the individual with more choices and possibilities than he can handle. Already the alternatives of dress, diet, occupation, entertainment, friends are more than many people can cope with.[1]

As the choices of where and how to live steadily multiply, it becomes increasingly obvious that the major obstacles to freedom today lie within ourselves. For instance, students can choose to study almost anything—but do they know what they *want* to study? How many have an easy time choosing a major field? How many of us, students or not, have the inner unity and certainty truly to know who we are and what we want to do in life? It is *inwardly* that we are not free. We have no place to stand, no adequate means of evaluation. And not knowing ourselves, we cannot choose, or act, from conviction and inner harmony.

In *Escape from Freedom* Erich Fromm points out that to a very great extent modern man "has become free from the external bonds that would prevent him from doing and thinking as he sees fit. He would be free to act according to his own will, if he knew what he wanted, thought and felt. But he does not know. He conforms to anonymous authorities and adopts a self which is not his. The more he does this, the more powerless he feels." Fromm asserts that modern man "is overcome by a profound feeling of powerlessness. . . . If life loses its meaning because it is not lived, man becomes desperate." [2]

Freedom as Self-Realization

Many people today are victims of this feeling of helplessness, doubt and desperation. What is the answer? The opposite of despair, Kierkegaard once said, is "to will to be what one truly is." To will to be what we truly are is to will self-realization. Fromm's conclusion is the same: "We believe that there is a positive answer, and that man can be free. . . . This freedom man can attain by the realization of his self, by being himself." [3]

Freedom, then, is self-realization. But what does that mean? "The realization of the self," Fromm states, "is accomplished not only by an act of thinking, but also by the realization of man's total personality, by the active expression of his emotional and intellectual potentialities. These potentialities are present in everybody; they become real only to the extent to which they are expressed. In other words, positive freedom consists in the spontaneous activity of the total, integrated personality." [4] Or, as he puts it elsewhere, "Positive freedom . . . is identical with the full realization of the individual's potentialities, together with his ability to live actively and spontaneously." [5]

We can see how remarkably consistent these ideas are with Maharishi's. "As long as the mind does not function with its full potential and is not in a position to use all the faculties it has," Maharishi writes in *The Science of Being and Art of Living,* "its freedom is restricted. Therefore the first important step in making the mind really free is the full unfoldment of its potentialities." [6]

Such ideas are not new or foreign to most of us. But, as we discovered in our discussion of values, our difficulty comes in living up to what we know to be valid. We know the value of self-realization, but how do we realize the self?

"It is a curious and a distressing fact," Aldous Huxley points out, "particularly in our civilization, that we are apt to propound very high ideals and to issue deep moral injunctions without ever offering the means to implement the ideals or obey the injunctions. We have been saying 'Know thyself' for an enormously long time." [7] The thought of freedom (or of happiness, food, love), a book on freedom, the desire for freedom are not the *experience* of freedom. "A thought of freedom," Maharishi writes, "although it seems good, is only a thought and is not a state." [8] What is required is a means to bring about the state.

Comments of transcendental meditators suggest the utility of TM as such a means. "I feel that I am more my true self," wrote a twenty-four-year-old student, meditating for two years, "and from the progress I have made so far, I feel it will not be very long before I am completely me." Another said, "I think the meditation let me cut a pathway through my jungle of egotistical confusion to my self, my real self, me!"

What Is the Self?

What *is* the self? Is it the body, with all its limbs and organs? This is certainly part of what we are, but there must be something deeper, for the body changes, grows, is completely renewed (except, biologists say, for brain and bone cells, which are not replaced) every seven years, yet some continuity remains to maintain our identity. Is the self our thoughts, our feelings, our memories, desires, likes and dislikes? Yes, surely; but these things, too, change. What we like or value today, tomorrow may seem foolish or unimportant. Our moods and values change, our perceptions change. Is the self no more than this ever-changing, unstable, limited mind and body, full of undeveloped capabilities and unresolved longings, this storehouse of memories and desires? If this were so, where would the freedom be in knowing this self? Where would be *freedom,* liberation, in actualizing a restricted, ever-changing self, bound by time, space and causation, bound by the ephemeral nature of life with its constant vicissitudes? It would certainly be a very tenuous and limited freedom.

But suppose, as has been suggested above, that the true nature of the Self, in its deepest aspect, were eternal and unchanging, infinite in intelligence, energy and happiness? "He is never born, nor does he ever die," says the Bhagavad Gita of the true, essential Self,

> nor once having been does he cease to be. Unborn, eternal, everlasting, ancient, he is not slain when the body is slain. . . . These bodies are known to have an end; the dweller in the body is eternal, imperishable, infinite. . . . Weapons cannot cleave him, nor fire burn him; water cannot wet him, nor wind dry him away. He is uncleavable; he cannot be burned; he cannot be wetted, nor yet can he be dried. He is eternal, all-pervading, stable, immovable, ever the same. He is declared to be unmanifest, unthinkable, unchangeable.[9]

If this is the essential nature of the Self, deeper than the whole relative bundle of ever-changing thoughts, feelings and actions, then, if a man were to know and be himself, he would be grounded in a source of true stability and freedom. For if he knew himself to be eternal and unchanging, unshakable and strong, no matter what experiences came along in the ever-changing sphere of life, he would be free; that is, if this were his *experience*—knowledge in the most profound sense, far beyond mere intellectual cognition. If this were his direct perception and an awareness that he had at all times, then nothing could overthrow his freedom. At all times, in all circumstances, he would know himself to be free.

Cosmic Consciousness: Eternal Freedom

This is the highest level of freedom possible to man, says Maharishi, and establishing this state of eternal liberation is one of the principal goals of the science of creative intelligence.

We have seen that during transcendental meditation the conscious mind arrives at the transcendental field of absolute Being. . . . Here in this field the mind transcends all that is relative, and is to be found in the state of absolute Being. The mind has transcended all limits of the experience of thought and is left by itself in a state of pure consciousness. This state of pure consciousness, or the state of absolute, pure Being, is called self-consciousness.

When this self-consciousness is forever maintained, even when the mind emerges from the Transcendent and engages in the field of activity, then self-consciousness attains the status of cosmic consciousness. Self-consciousness is then established eternally in the nature of the mind. Even when the mind is awake, dreaming or in deep sleep, self-consciousness is maintained. . . .

Cosmic consciousness means that consciousness which includes the experience of the relative field together with the state of absolute Being. This state of cosmic consciousness is one where the mind lives in eternal freedom, remaining unbound by whatever it experiences during all activities in the relative world.[10]

The state of cosmic consciousness can be seen to be a fifth state of consciousness, developing naturally out of the regular alternation of the fourth state (transcendental consciousness) with the ordinary activity of life. Maharishi explains that just as a cloth can be permanently dyed by a process of alternately dipping it in the dye and then fading it, repeatedly, until it is color-fast, the inner field of Being becomes permanently infused into the nature of the mind by allowing the mind to experience the inner silence of Being and then coming out into full activity. Gradually the mind is able to sustain that unbounded awareness more and more fully, until Being, or the Self, is not lost from awareness at any time.

As we discussed above (in Chapter 2) physiological psychology has found that every state of consciousness has a corresponding physiology, a corresponding style of functioning of the nervous system. The waking, dreaming, sleeping and transcendental states have physiological correlates, found whenever those states of consciousness are experienced. The fifth state of consciousness also has its unique physiology.

We have seen that during transcendental meditation, as the mind experiences increasingly subtle states of thought, the body correspondingly gains a deep rest. In that state of rest, deep-rooted stresses and strains are allowed to be released from the system. After meditation one feels refreshed, more alert, more energetic. Over a period of time, Maharishi explains, repeatedly allowing the body to gain this deep rest permits *accumulated* stresses to be released. Eventually, a totally stress-free system gives rise to the fifth state of consciousness.

Maharishi defines stress as an overload on the physical machinery of experience (the senses and the nervous system) caused by experience that is "unduly weighty": a loud noise, a bright flash of light, a frightening event, some physical or emotional strain, etc. Such experiences, causing chemical and even structural changes in the nervous system, leave an impression upon the body, which is stored until deep rest allows the body to normalize itself by releasing the stress. Dreams serve this function. But the rest of TM being deeper than the rest of sleep, deeper stresses are removed.

It is obvious that these accumulated stresses can block the full expression of our creative intelligence. They do not permit the mind and body to function at their full potential. As the stresses are removed, full potential begins to be utilized and enjoyed. When all the stresses are gone, the full depth of the mind is open to our awareness. The field of Being, which has always existed at the deepest level of our individual existence, permanently opens to awareness. When the experience of Being is never lost, the state of cosmic consciousness is gained.

"This state," Maharishi says, "has been the object of man's great quest from time immemorial because it glorifies all aspects of life. The material life of man is enlightened by the light of the inner Self." [11]

Meditators are beginning to verify such statements by direct experience. "The most significant effect of meditation for me," said one man, "has been the increase in awareness of Self during activity. This increased Self-awareness has permitted me to see my actions more clearly and objectively, to be more deeply aware of my thoughts, to relate to my surroundings more intimately, and to people more empathetically." This is what Maharishi has called living 200 percent of life: inner spiritual fulfillment along with enjoyment of the glories of creation.

Practical Consequences

We have seen that the degree of an individual's freedom corresponds to how much he is "self-realized"; that is, the more fully a man utilizes his inner faculties, the more fully and freely he can function in life. The state of unbounded inner freedom implies realization of the deepest aspect of the self and hence full development of inner potential. Fully developed potential means maximum strength in life. Thus maximum inner freedom results in maximum freedom of thought and action.

Let us look at some experiences reported by meditators and see if they could be considered practical consequences of increasing self-realization. For example, many have reported that fears diminished or were eliminated after beginning TM. This comes as no surprise. "Even a slight practice of TM relieves a man of great fears," Maharishi has often said, recalling Lord Krishna's words to Arjuna in the Bhagavad Gita.[12] Freedom and fear cannot coexist. Fear eliminates choice, prevents realistic evaluation and spontaneous response. As fear diminishes, openness to the possibilities of the moment increases, and freedom grows. "Many of my fears have left me," said a young woman, "and it's easier for me in my associations with others. The area of social contacts has always been hard for me because I'm very shy by nature, but through meditation I find this situation getting better each day."

A student echoed this statement: "Generally speaking, I'm more open, less afraid of relating with people. I'm also more accepting, because I have fewer fears and am not threatened." A person who is strong within himself is not threatened by others. "I feel much more whole and healthy as a personality," a Yale student said. "Instead of being in a constant state of hyper-concern with everyday problems, I have great confidence in my ability to handle any problem as it comes. I'm able to face my problems and solve them more efficiently, rather than worry about them." This liberating confidence in oneself and one's abilities is certainly another facet of freedom.

"Mother Is at Home": Freedom to Grow and Create

"I feel that my life is improving in a steady, consistent manner," one woman remarked. "For the first time I feel that

I am really growing—mentally, physically and spiritually— every day."

It is a great relief to feel that one's life is flowing easily toward greater fulfillment. Such a feeling comes as a comfort to the mind and heart.

Many people today experience the opposite: a feeling of "searching." We may not know exactly what we are looking for, but as we move from one experience of life to another somewhere quietly inside we feel, "No, this is not it either." We may feel that there is *something* waiting for us, some destiny, some person, and we have to keep moving, keep looking until we find it. And until we find it, as long as we do not feel at home with life, we are not free.

"Man has been so carried away that his thirst for eternal happiness has sought fulfillment in the fleeting joys of the outside world," says Maharishi. "The thirsty man has concerned himself with drops of water deposited on green grass, just dewdrops, leaving behind the big pond, the ocean of water. . . . Nothing of the outside world is able to satisfy the mind, but all the time the mind is pushing on to this and pushing on to that, being kicked by this and kicked by that. . . .

"Man," Maharishi continues, "is born of bliss, of consciousness, of creativity, of wisdom. . . . It is only necessary to begin to enjoy. But not finding it anywhere, obviously missing it in day-to-day life, the majority begin to suffer. It is just a little ignorance which makes a man suffer, ignorance of his own potentiality. If a millionaire happens to forget his status, if he happens to forget that he is a millionaire, if he happens to lose the connection with the bank, or the key of his treasury is lost, then, that same moment he begins to behave as an ordinary man. When a man loses conscious awareness of his own blissful real nature, he loses the divine dignity that belongs to him. His life becomes a struggle." [13]

But when contact with that "treasury" is restored, life ceases to be a struggle and begins to be lived in freedom. The search is over, and instead of searching, one is free to begin enjoying. "From the first meditation," a woman said, "I just never doubted that I had finally found what I once had been looking for." Or as another person said, "I felt as though 2,000 pounds were taken off my shoulders. The burden was removed and I have emerged free."

Great confidence and security are born of contact with inner Being. Maharishi has described it as feeling that "mother is at home"—as a child feels safe and able to display maximum creative intelligence when he knows, as he is playing about, that his mother is at home in the next room, so a man who gains harmony with the unboundedness of his own Self feels increasingly peaceful and at home with all fields of knowledge and activity. Deep within, on a quiet level of the mind, a profound inner stability gives a basis of comfortable confidence to all his activities.

"Ever since I started meditating, there has been a constant, steady improvement in my life," a student said. "The big change in my attitude was the confidence I had for the future. . . . I wasn't any longer at the mercy of luck or fate because I knew that I could manipulate something to change my fate, and that one thing was meditate regularly morning and evening. I knew regular meditation was the one thing I could do because I had tried many things and this simple program was the only thing that really worked."

Taking It as It Comes: Freedom for Today

Ordinarily most of us reach out to the future, planning, dreaming, scheming. The present feels empty, dull or not sufficiently satisfying. We hope that tomorrow will be better, that our life may breathe and move with more energy, more happiness. But when we are fulfilled in the present, when we feel fully alive, fully real, and our accomplishments today give us intense and profound satisfaction, we are free of the future and free *for* the future. And for the present. Every moment is real and vital.

"I have before wondered," a young man said, "why I felt myself reaching out for things (woman, excitement, fulfillment, knowledge). I felt an anguish when completion was not found. Since starting transcendental meditation, I have found such inner happiness that it outshines relative joys, thus there is no tension connected with the things I desire. I do not fear losing anything any more. . . . Reaching out I've found is the result of lack of unity with the Self. Reaching out has changed into extending a hand and not expecting."

"I now take each day as it comes, without worrying about the future," a California girl wrote. "Everything just goes right." Not *worrying* about the future does not mean not *thinking* about the future. Maharishi emphasizes the importance of foresight and proper planning for maximum accomplishments in life. What is meant by these comments is that happiness today and a real confidence in one's capabilities to cope with and enjoy tomorrow free one from the useless anxiety that develops from uncertainty and overspeculation about what the future will bring. If we are able to live fully today, we won't be overly concerned about tomorrow.

"I'm pretty sure that life isn't setting any fewer or easier problems in my path," said a television producer, "but I find all problems much easier to cope with. All facets of life, work and play become more of one thing, a joy of being alive in a world that seems to get bigger, richer and better every day. Before, life seemed to be narrowing down like a funnel; now I'm looking out the other end, and the horizon expands and grows into possibilities I never dreamed existed. And wonder of wonders, I'm more and more capable of making use of all the increasing possibilities. Physically, I feel stronger, healthier, more alert and stimulated. Overall, I am more at peace with the world."

Aging in Freedom: New Horizons

This comfortable confidence—that as time goes by things will continue to improve—has profound implications for a complex problem of our culture, the problem of aging. Often, as an individual advances into the later years of life, rather than opening up, life narrows down; rather than becoming increasingly joyful, each day frequently brings new ills, more loneliness, new suffering. It is a curious fact that in our society old age usually brings with it not serenity and wisdom, but anxiety and a quiet despair. Is this situation really necessary?

"To a meditator, the aging process is different," a woman in her midfifties told me. "As we get older, we feel younger. There is a reversal of the concept of age. Those of us who meditate look forward to reaching advanced states of unfoldment. If we've been meditating one or two years we eagerly anticipate the time when we will have been meditating five or ten years, never once stopping to bemoan the fact that we will be that much older. We're not too much concerned with our numerical age because we're too occupied with enjoying life and finding new areas to explore."

A Provocative Proposal

Although we have not dealt at any length with political or social freedom, but have "confined" ourselves within the boundaries of the more internal, individual aspects of freedom, external liberty, which occupies most of our attention these days whenever freedom is discussed, certainly rests upon and is inseparable from internal freedom. To a man who doesn't know who he is or what he wants, freedom of choice can be a burden and a cause of great anxiety. As Erich Fromm put it, "The right to express our thoughts means something only if we are able to have thoughts of our own." [14] Increased inner freedom not only gives validity to external freedom, but also creates it.

If even a small percentage of people in society were enjoying the liberated, joyful, creative state of life we have seen expressed in these chapters, is it too idealistic to believe that political and social freedom would be an inevitable result? We explore this provocative possibility further in Chapter 11.

CHAPTER 10

A Short History
of the Movement

When suffering grows, the invincible force of nature moves to set man's vision right and establish a way of life which will again fulfill the high purpose of his existence. The long history of the world records many such periods in which the ideal pattern of life is first forgotten and then restored to man.

—MAHARISHI MAHESH YOGI

A Parable

There once was a village of farmers located on the east bank of a wide river. The land of the village was divided by this river. Each day some of the farmers would cross the river in boats to farm the land on the other side. The village was fortunate and had many, many prosperous years. A surplus of food was built up and put in storehouses in the village. Eventually the storehouses became full, and it was unnecessary to farm the land on the other side of the river. By using the food in the storehouses and farming the small amount of fertile land around the village, there was enough to eat.

For several years no one bothered to cross the river. The boats, not being used, decayed, and no new ones were built to replace them. No one in the village noticed, for all were happy

and contented. Eventually all those men who had the knowledge of boat building died or left the village. The people
farmed the small amount of land next to the village and
picked the fruits and berries in the woods. After many generations the land across the river was forgotten; all knowledge
of it was lost.

Meanwhile, the population of the village had started to
grow, and there were several years of drought. The food supply
began to run out. The people had to farm the land next to the
village to such an extent that it became overworked. It lost
its fertility and each year produced fewer crops. The people
of the village had to work harder each year with smaller yield.

Soon the whole village was in poverty, and it was a struggle
even to survive. This struggling caused stress and frustration in
the people, which led to the quality of life rapidly deteriorating
in the village. The villagers lived in misery and each succeed-
ing generation came to accept the misery as the normal way of
life, for they had never known anything better.

One day an adventurous young man of the village climbed
a very high and steep mountain, from which he could look
down upon the village and all the surrounding countryside.
To his surprise, he saw that just across the river, for as far as
he could see, was green and fertile land! He ran to the village
to tell the people of this knowledge.

But just the *knowledge* of abundant and available land could
not feed them. In fact, it only increased their suffering, for
now, in addition to their misery, they knew that just across
the river there was plenty of fertile land, but they had no way
of getting to it.

It happened that a very old and wise man passed through
the village. He possessed much knowledge. When he learned
the plight of the villagers, he told them of things called boats
in which they would be able to cross the river and make contact with and use all the land they needed. With his help the
villagers constructed the boats and crossed the river. Before
leaving, the wise man instructed several young men of the
village in the art of boat building and set up a school for boat

builders, so that the village would never again be without boats.

Now the village was once again prosperous. The people no longer had to struggle for survival. They all had more than they could use, and life to them was a joy.

As the villagers in this story suffered because of their lack of knowledge, so man is suffering today because of his lack of knowledge.[1]

The Rise and Fall of Knowledge

According to Maharishi, several revivals of the true understanding of life and the means to fulfillment have occurred within man's written memory. The first was about 5,000 years ago, when Lord Krishna, in the story recounted in the Bhagavad Gita, gave the teaching to Arjuna, the greatest warrior of the age. Within 2,000 years the teaching was lost. It was restored by Buddha. "Lord Buddha's message was complete," says Maharishi, "because He incorporated the fields of Being, thinking and doing in His theme of revival. But because His followers failed to correlate these different fields of life in a systematic manner . . . realization of Being as the basis of a good life became obscured."[2]

Why is it that the truth of life, once revealed, can be lost? What is responsible?

"It has been the misfortune of every teacher," Maharishi writes, "that, while he speaks from his level of consciousness, his followers can only receive his message on their level; and the gulf between the teaching and understanding grows wider with time."[3] "This is the tragedy of knowledge, the tragic fate that knowledge must meet at the hands of ignorance. It is inevitable, because the teaching comes from one level of consciousness and is received at quite a different level."[4]

Once again the teaching was revived in its purity, about 2,500 years ago, by Shankara. A great teacher and commentator on the Upanishads, Bhagavad Gita and Brahma Sutras, Shankara "not only revived the wisdom of integrated life and made it popular in his day, but also established four principal seats of learning in four corners of India to keep his teaching pure and to ensure that it would be propagated in its entirety generation after generation." [5] The teaching was given out correctly for several centuries, but despite Shankara's foresight, his message, too, was obscured with time.

Maharishi asserts that the reason life has been lived in suffering and unfulfillment for the last many hundreds of years is that man has lost both the understanding of Being as the basis of life and the technique for contacting Being and developing mind and heart to their fullness. "This age has, however, been fortunate," Maharishi writes. "It has witnessed the living example of a man inspired by Vedic wisdom in its wholeness and thus able to revive the philosophy of the integrated life in all its truth and fullness." [6]

Guru Dev

Maharishi is, of course, speaking of his teacher, Swami Brahmananda Saraswati, Jagadguru, Bhagwan Shankaracharya of Jyotir Math, Himalayas, often referred to as Guru Dev (Divine Teacher). Maharishi recounts that "at the tender age of nine, when the other children of the world were mostly busy in playgrounds," Guru Dev "left home and went to the Himalayas in search of God," in search of "the ideal happiness and bliss, that is not far from man but exists in his own heart." [7] After about five years of searching he found a master who came up to the ideal he had set for himself. He studied with this man (Swami Krishanand Saraswati) for a number of years, but spent most of his life in solitude and silence, first in the Himalayas and then, later, in the deepest forests of central India.

As the years passed, he came to be known as a great, enlightened saint. At this time the seat of Shankaracharya of the North (Jyotir Math, principal of the four seats of learning established by Shankara) had been vacant for over 150 years. No man was deemed worthy of holding that position as a guide to the spiritual lives of the people. It took 20 years to persuade Guru Dev to come out of seclusion and accept the seat of Shankaracharya, but in 1941, at the age of seventy-two, he accepted. Maharishi points out that the political freedom of India dawned while Guru Dev held this position. "He was worshipped by Dr. Rajendra Prasad, the first President of the Indian Union," and Dr. S. Radhakrishnan, the famous philosopher and India's second President, called Guru Dev "Vedanta Incarnate," or, the embodiment of truth.[8]

> He inspired all alike and gave a lift to everyone. . . .
> He was never a leader of any one party. . . .
> His entire personality exhaled always the serene perfume of spirituality. His face radiated that rare light which comprises love, authority, serenity and self-assuredness; the state that comes only by righteous living and Divine realization.[9]

> He expounded the Truth in its all-embracing nature. His quiet words, coming from the unbounded love of his heart, pierced the hearts of all who heard him and brought enlightenment to their minds. His message was the message of fullness of heart and mind.[10]

In speaking of the inspiration for his work in the world, Maharishi always brings out that "it was the concern of Guru Deva, His Divinity Swami Brahmananda Saraswati, to enlighten all men everywhere, that resulted in the foundation of the world-wide Spiritual Regeneration Movement in 1958, five years after his departure from us." [11]

Maharishi

One time someone asked Maharishi, "What were Guru Dev's accomplishments? Did he write books?" and Maharishi answered, bursting into laughter, "He made *me!*" This remark may seem presumptuous, but anyone who has met Maharishi for even a moment knows that it was uttered in complete humility, and that at the same time it speaks the truth: for the living presence of Maharishi is far more powerful than any book, or, as SIMS-IMS Director Jerry Jarvis expressed it once, it is "a new kind of book, a living book giving out the wisdom of life unfailingly on every page." No matter how exalted the language one chose to describe Maharishi, the picture would be gray compared to the reality. His love seems to know no bounds, his energy no limits, his creativity and intelligence no obstacle that cannot be overcome. His goal—to eliminate suffering from man's life—is the most elevated goal imaginable, and he moves forward toward its fulfillment with an unequaled singleness of purpose. Not a moment is wasted, not a possibility overlooked, in considering how to expand his worldwide movement, how to bring his message before greater numbers of the people. Yet with all this high seriousness, the seemingly omnipresent peals of his laughter are a constant reminder that for him every moment is "a wave of joy in the ocean of bliss."

In his book *Love and God* Maharishi describes the state of life of one who has risen to the highest peaks of human possibility. Because the words are written from the state of realization that they describe, they are a beautiful and precise self-portrait:

> Cosmic life gains expression in his activity. The thought of cosmic life is materialized in his process of thinking. His eyes behold the purpose of creation. His ears hear the music of cosmic life. His hands hold on to cosmic intentions. His feet set the cosmic life in motion. He walks on earth, yet walks in the destiny of heaven. Angels enjoy his being on earth. This is the glory of unity born of love.[12]

It is certainly true that an atmosphere of purity, goodness and love surrounds Maharishi at all times. Being near him, you begin to feel, as one person expressed it, that "he is your very best friend": when you have something to say or to ask, he is the perfect listener; you know that his mind is not straying, that he is right with you, and his answer shows that he knew—perhaps even better than you knew yourself—exactly what was on your mind and in your heart. It also becomes obvious, after some time of meditating, that what he has made possible in terms of your ultimate fulfillment in life is a gift far more precious than any other you could ever receive. When you begin to see that he is working unrelentingly, virtually around the clock (he seems to allow himself only a few hours' rest out of every 24) day after day, week after week, solely for your benefit, and that this is all he has been doing for the last 15 years, a tremendous respect and love begin to take shape within you. It is no exaggeration that every word, every action of his is for others.

It takes little imagination to see that what he has accomplished is all but incredible. Not only has he expressed a profound, eternal wisdom of life in terms understandable to any man and offered a practice by which any man can rise to the supreme fulfillment of life, but in 15 years he has established centers to propagate this teaching in over 60 countries of the world. He has personally trained over 4,000 teachers to carry on his work, written two books (with half a dozen more in various stages of completion), while supervising the organizational growth and operation of the movement in every country. He works efficiently, with extraordinary creativity and decisiveness, yet maintains a quiet dignity, a serene, graceful walk, a thoroughly noble, unhurried bearing.

Anger, impatience, annoyance are absolutely foreign to him. He will repeatedly explain a point to someone who has not grasped it, entirely patient when even the rest of the audience has become exasperated! His lectures are a unique combination of clarity, profundity, simplicity and apparently inexhaustible creativity. New images continually arise, and old ones *seem* new. His lectures have been known to last three hours or more, and although listening to his wisdom is fulfilling in itself, however long he speaks, the time always seems too short.

He is a great teacher, with a great wisdom to offer and the ability to convey it fully and clearly. He is a great leader, who sees the goal of life and knows how to lead others to it.

And as an example, he radiates a perfection toward which anyone would do well to aspire.

When Maharishi met Guru Dev he had been searching for a spiritual guide for a number of years, without success. As Maharishi tells us, one evening a friend brought him to a private home where Guru Dev was staying. They arrived at night, in the dark, and made their way up a long flight of stairs to the veranda of the house. They asked to see Guru Dev, and someone said, "Wait, just wait." They waited in the darkness; after some time a distant car turned on the road and as the headlights swung around the light illuminated the face of Guru Dev, who had been sitting on the veranda in the darkness. As soon as Maharishi saw him, he recognized Guru Dev as his Master.

When Maharishi started in Guru Dev's service as a young Brahmacharyi (disciple), he started by doing simple chores, taking care of things, in order to be around the Master, to "breathe his air." He asked the man who swept Guru Dev's room if he could help, just so that he could be near. After a while he had the opportunity to draft an answer to some of Guru Dev's correspondence and showed one letter to Guru Dev. The Master liked what he had done, and the young disciple soon became Guru Dev's private secretary. As time went on, he took on more and more responsibility and at the same time grew in the Master's love. It is said that Maharishi was the favorite disciple, and those who knew Maharishi at that time say that he spared nothing in Guru Dev's service. Brahmacharyi Sattyanand, once a pupil of Guru Dev and now a close follower of Maharishi, recalls that when Maharishi began a task for Guru Dev he would frequently neglect to eat or sleep, often for a period of several days, until the job was done, so great was his devotion.

Early Travels: Sowing the Seeds

Because he had chosen the way of life of a recluse, after Guru Dev passed away (in 1953) Maharishi withdrew to a cave in the Himalayas, in an area called Uttar Kashi or The Valley of the Saints. He lived there for two years in peaceful solitude. Then an idea occurred to him to visit a particular temple in South India. The idea recurred frequently, and when Maharishi consulted an older saint in the valley the older man suggested that he go. Maharishi soon decided to make the journey.

One day when he was in the South a man approached him and asked, "Would you bring some of the wisdom of the Himalayas to us?" Maharishi replied, "I don't lecture," but the man persisted and set up a series of seven talks for Maharishi to give. "Over all these years Maharishi's message has not changed," says Jerry Jarvis, who read a transcript of one of those lectures when he was in South India with Maharishi years later. "He began to speak, and out came the whole teaching, in all its purity."

He began to teach. The practical results in the lives of the people multiplied, and more and more lectures were set up for him to give. He traveled to many parts of India, lecturing and teaching transcendental meditation.

Then in December of 1958, at Madras, at a gathering called the "Congress of Spiritual Luminaries," assembled to celebrate Guru Dev's 89th birthday anniversary, Maharishi gave a talk reviewing what he had accomplished in his few years of teaching. He said, "With the results we have seen so far, we can envision the spiritual regeneration of all mankind." He received a five-minute ovation for expressing this thought, which prompted him, the next evening, to announce the formation of the Spiritual Regeneration Movement, dedicated to the accomplishment of that goal.

Soon after, he began the first of his more than 12 world tours. He taught in Kuala Lumpur, Singapore, Hong Kong, then in the early spring of 1959 he landed in Hawaii on his way to the United States mainland. He had no intention of remaining in Hawaii, but a man at the airport recognized that there was something special about him, asked him to stay and speak, and he ended up staying for two months. He finally arrived in San Francisco in April 1959.

At first, most of those who heard and responded to Maharishi's message were businessmen and professional people. Many were so taken by the perfect integration of practicality and spirituality in his message that they decided to make use of their skills to propagate the movement. As more and more people started to meditate and the activity around Maharishi increased, it became clear that Maharishi's time and energy could be most effectively utilized if he were freed from such chores as making travel and lecture arrangements, so that he could focus on teaching.

Getting Organized

By necessity, then, in midsummer of 1959 an organization was created in Los Angeles, under the name of the Spiritual Regeneration Movement (SRM), to make the necessary arrangements for his travel, to raise funds, procure halls and provide publicity materials. The first president of SRM was Dr. John Hislop, a businessman who had formerly been an English professor. Within a short time, however, Dr. Hislop's work took him from Los Angeles, where the organization was centered, and Charles Lutes, a top salesman for a construction firm, became president. Mr. Lutes, who still holds the presidency of SRM, has been a stronghold of practical guidance, helping the movement to grow in an organized way.

At first (from 1959 to 1965), SRM was the only organization teaching TM in the United States. In 1965, however, interest among the youth began to grow, and in order to meet that demand the Students International Meditation Society (SIMS) was formed to teach TM and the science of creative intelligence on high-school and college campuses throughout the world. Since that time other organizations have been founded to meet the demand for teachers of TM and SCI on all levels of society. The International Meditation Society

(IMS) was the first to follow SIMS, offering courses to the general public. When the business world became fascinated by the prospect of increasing creativity among both workers and administrators through TM, the American Foundation for the Science of Creative Intelligence (AFSCI) was formed.

Because the specific needs of different segments of society are different, different benefits of TM are emphasized by each of the four organizations. A student, for example, may not find increased energy and efficiency as relevant to his life as a businessman, although both would receive the same benefits from the practice. Similarly, an older person would undoubtedly be more intrigued by the prospect of deep rest and relaxation than a student would be, even though TM would bring that profound restfulness to both. Thus the presentation of each organization is geared to the segment of society which it serves, but the fundamental teaching remains the same.

The fifth and final branch of the organization, Maharishi International University (MIU), was founded in 1971 to train teachers and develop curricula and teaching materials for courses in the science of creative intelligence. As early as 1959 it became apparent that Maharishi alone could never instruct all the people who were interested in learning to meditate, and accordingly, he announced his intention to "multiply myself." In the spring of 1961 about 35 people attended the first International Teacher Training Course, under rather primitive conditions in India. Sixteen of that first group became teachers, among them one lady from the United States, Mrs. Beulah Smith of San Diego, California. From 1961 until 1966 Mrs. Smith was the only teacher of TM in the United States. During that time Maharishi continued to travel around the world, teaching and opening centers in Canada, England, Germany, Sweden, India, Burma, Ceylon, East and South Africa, Australia and other countries, and also returning to the U.S. once a year.

Devotion

At this point let us introduce a new—and, for the development of the TM movement, a very important—character in the story, Jerome W. Jarvis. A native Californian, Mr. Jarvis (or Jerry, as he is known to meditators of all ages) attended Shimer College in Illinois, where he majored in philosophy. After serving in the Army he graduated from California State Polytechnic College. He then went to Washington, D.C., and worked for three years as a research writer and reporter for a news service covering Congress and the Administration. After this he returned to California, and it was here that he met Maharishi and started to practice transcendental meditation in 1961; from that time onward his whole life has been devoted solely to teaching the principles and practice of transcendental meditation. In 1966 he became a teacher of TM and also was appointed by Maharishi as the director of SIMS and IMS when they were founded.

He has spoken to hundreds of thousands of students and adults throughout the country, and countless thousands of them have begun TM because they saw in him the embodiment of all that he said. He has personally instructed over 5,000 in TM and many of those who are today's teachers of TM were inspired to become teachers by Jerry's example. Since 1966 he has traveled extensively with Maharishi and has been at all the teacher training courses that Maharishi has conducted, helping with the training of new teachers. For him Maharishi's teachings are a living reality, and he represents Maharishi with purity, dignity and love. His full time and energies are devoted to making TM more readily available to others. I have seen him go through a day of lectures, media appearances and meetings after only a few hours' sleep—and this day after day—without ever losing his evenness, clarity of mind and ready wit.

For example, in early April of 1972 Jerry flew to Los Angeles from the course in Italy, spent a week there on administrative activities of the movement, and then went to Iowa, where he met with about 400 meditators who were gathered at a weekend Residence Course. He met with them for a few hours and then went to North Carolina, to inspect some land being considered as a possible site on which to build an academy to train teachers of TM and the science of creative intelligence. Late in the afternoon he took another plane to New York City, where he was met and driven to a hotel in the Catskills, where another Residence Course consisting of about 350 meditators and teachers was taking place. Arriving there at 10 P.M., he spoke with the entire group until 1 A.M., then met with the teachers till about 5 A.M., got back in the car, and was driven to Kennedy Airport where, at 8 A.M., he boarded a plane bound for Italy and Maharishi's Teacher Training Course there. It is this kind of energy, devotion and dedication that has allowed SIMS-IMS to develop as quickly and extensively as it has.

At that course in the Catskills, someone asked Jerry how he personally had met Maharishi and become involved with TM. A portion and paraphrase of his answer follows.

The Origins of Expansion

We [Jerry and his wife, Debby] saw an advertisement in the newspaper. (That was in September 1961.) It said that His Holiness Maharishi Mahesh Yogi was going to speak at a hall in Los Angeles. Above the information was a picture of him. I knew what the word "rishi" meant—holy sage or seer—and had often thought that if a man could fulfill that title it would be something great. I used to think that it would be wonderful and profoundly helpful to meet such a man, to hear what he spoke, to see how he walked, what he did. . . . I looked up "maha" in the dictionary and found that it meant "the great," so Maharishi was "the great holy sage." It sounded very good and we decided to go. We got to the door of the lecture hall and found that there was an admission charge of one dollar. We were disappointed, and turned around to leave, because I had the idea that money should not be charged for spiritual things.

But because we had driven so far to get there—over an hour—we started to rationalize. We thought maybe the hall was charging, and not Maharishi, that it must cost some money to rent a hall like this (which, of course, was the case).

So we paid the admission and waited for Maharishi to come in. After a few minutes he came in and sat down; I listened and was very impressed by him and what he said. I knew he had something great.

A few nights later we heard Maharishi give another public lecture. What he was saying was very beautiful, but I don't think we really grasped that he was talking about a technique that we could actually use to experience what he was telling us about—the inner bliss consciousness of Being, the profound rest, the harmonious unfoldment of mind and heart. However, we did begin TM, and of course we experienced everything that he said we would.

During that time Maharishi was lecturing every evening, week after week, to new meditators and we attended every meeting. After about a month it was announced that Maharishi would be conducting a three-week course for the training of Meditation Guides on Catalina Island off the coast of Southern California. It was really a joy to attend that course. Afterwards, Maharishi left to continue with his world tour and I started giving introductory lectures.

The next year, in 1962, Maharishi returned and gave another two-week course at Catalina Island. Following the course he called a few of us to come with him to Lake Arrowhead, California, where he made the tapes for *The Science of Being and Art of Living*. Each morning we transcribed the tapes and read them back to Maharishi in the afternoon. Like this, his first book was completed in only a few short months.

Meanwhile, when Maharishi was away from the U.S., we continued to give introductory lectures, using a series of seven lectures that he had written out as a guideline. (A person in those days had to hear seven lectures before he could start TM.)

For two and a half years I read those seven lectures word for word. I'll always remember the first public lecture given at the old Court House in Malibu, California. When it was time to begin there were only one man and one woman present (in addition to my wife and one other meditator). The written lecture started out, "Good evening, ladies and gentlemen," and I thought, "It's a good thing there are two people here and that one is a lady and one is a gentleman," as I didn't want to deviate even that much from Maharishi's lecture. I said, "Good evening, ladies and gentlemen," and then after a brief introduction asked them to sit for a minute with eyes closed as a silent beginning to a dynamic lecture; when we opened our eyes I was again supposed to say, "Good evening, ladies and gentlemen." Luckily, while we were sitting with our eyes closed, one more couple had walked into the room! Everything worked out so perfectly that I really delighted in following the lectures word for word.

Many more lecture courses were given in homes here and there. One night, in the spring of 1965, I was giving a course for about eight people in a friend's living room in Los Angeles. Two young men, college students, were there who asked if I could come give a lecture to a group of their friends. Of course I said I would be glad to. Sure enough, the following week there were about 20 eager boys and girls gathered to hear about transcendental meditation. It was really inspiring for me to have so many young people there at one time, and they were so eager to hear about TM and asked so many good questions that I ended up giving the material for the first three lectures all at once. It was such a thrilling evening with its great promise that I couldn't sleep all that night. At our next meeting they received the contents of the remaining four lectures. Afterwards, Beulah Smith, who was at that time the only Initiator in the United States, came and instructed these students. That was probably the origin of the two-part lecture [which is now the standard introductory presentation on TM throughout the world].

Following that first course more and more young people became interested in meditation, and in the autumn of 1965 SIMS was set up on the UCLA campus, and the first course in TM was offered on a university campus. About 40 came to the lecture. I remember starting by saying, "This is a truly great moment in the history of higher education," when this wisdom of the unfoldment of man's full potential is being offered on a college campus in the context of higher education.

There had been no other teacher-training courses since 1961, and then in January 1966 Maharishi held the first International Teacher Training Course at the new Academy of Meditation in the foothills of the Himalayas beside the Ganges. Debby and I went for about four months and came back as teachers. That summer we put posters up around UCLA announcing a six-week course on the principles and practice of TM. We gave two lectures a week for six weeks. About 60 responded, and we decided it was the right time to look for a center. A few blocks from campus we found a small but suitable suite of rooms; that was SIMS' first center. Many leaders of the movement today came from those courses given at UCLA during the summer and autumn of 1966.

In 1967 Maharishi himself gave lectures at UCLA, Berkeley, Harvard and Yale, and things began to grow very rapidly. New centers were opened throughout the country and more and more courses were held on campuses in every state.

In the fall of 1969 the Associated Students of Stanford University (ASSU) nominated me as the ASSU professor for that year. In this capacity we were able to present a course of our choice. Rather than call the course "The Principles and Practice of Transcendental Meditation," which didn't sound very academic, we called it "The Science of Creative Intelligence." The Admissions office gave us 25 enrollment cards, thinking that would be enough, but at the first meeting of the new course over 300 students came! It was one of the largest responses to a new course in Stanford's history. It was a great experience to teach the science of creative intelligence (SCI) in the context of an academically accredited course. This course in SCI is what really developed the interest of the academic community in Maharishi's teaching. Since then there have been more SCI courses established and Maharishi has been working to prepare comprehensive courses for teaching SCI at all levels of education.

Meanwhile the teacher-training courses in India continued to increase in size. By 1970 the facilities there could no longer accommodate the numbers applying for admission, so facilities at Estes Park, Colorado, were used, with 350 new teachers graduated in December 1970. The next year we moved to Mallorca, where 800 attended, and this year there are over 2,000 becoming teachers in Italy. Plans to establish Maharishi International University (MIU) have begun, and the preliminary steps toward receiving accreditation as a university have already been accomplished. We plan to have the major MIU campuses in the United States, India and Europe.

And now Maharishi has announced that 1972 is the "Year of the World Plan"—to open 3,600 SCI Teacher Training Centers throughout the world, one for each one million population. Each of the centers will train 1,000 teachers of SCI to give out the knowledge. In this way Maharishi hopes to have one teacher of the science of creative intelligence for every 1,000 population in the world in a very short time.

And all of this from just one man, mused Jerry.

Statistics, Scholars and Symposia: A World Plan

The remarkable growth of SIMS-IMS can be measured in many ways. Statistically the number of meditators has grown an average of over 250 percent every year since the creation of the organization in 1965. At the end of 1965 there were 220 meditators; by the end of 1968, 12,000; two years later, 33,000. By January of 1973 over 200,000 had been instructed in the practice. In SIMS' sixth year (1971) more people started TM—42,000—than in the entire first five.

As we have seen, there was only one teacher of TM in the United States until 1966; by the end of 1969 there were about 200, and by June of 1972, almost 2,400. When I studied with Maharishi in India in 1970, one auditorium, one kitchen and dining room, and one small meeting room next to Maharishi's bedroom were sufficient for all the activity of the course and its 175 participants. Exactly two years later nearly 2,000 future teachers from more than 35 countries filled 12 huge hotels and spilled into bungalows and apartments along the east coast of Mallorca. A staff of over 300 meditators ran the kitchens and worked on some of the myriad activities of the course: video tape crew, nursery, medical staff, etc.

"The nerve center for all this activity," wrote David Bolling in the *MIU International Newsletter* early in 1972, "is one half of the seventh floor of the Hotel Samoa. . . . Down this hallway of knowledge are 23 rooms, all quietly humming with activity." He went on:

> The first room . . . is the MIU office. Here is planned the detailed structure of Maharishi International University and the projection of its many divisions. . . .
> Down the hall, past Maharishi's kitchen and dining room is the Literary Room. Here major publications are planned and transcripts edited for release to the public. In addition to a condensed book of symposium excerpts and a full-length anthology of all the symposium proceedings of last summer, a book of essays by Maharishi is being prepared. . . .
> The Tape Library is next, a treasury of all Maharishi's lectures going back to the last course held in India. Over 1,100 hours of tape are stored here, the equivalent of something like 46 days round-the-clock listening. . . . Staff members work steadily cataloging and arranging tapes for release. . . .
> Across the hall is the SCI Room. . . . Frequently packed to the doorway, this room is the center of planning and development for both SCI curriculum and the international symposium program. From this room, Max Flisher, MIU International Director of Education, co-

ordinates SCI activities and plans major pieces of writing, including an SCI syllabus and an illustrated handbook for SCI teachers. . . .

The Vedic Studies Room exudes an air of sober scholarship. Bookshelves are lined with Vedic texts, translations of the Bhagavad Gita, the Brahma Sutras and the Upanishads. Two researchers in Vedic studies—one from India, the other from California—pore over both Eastern and Western studies of the Vedas and prepare the material for review and commentary by Maharishi. . . . Foremost among the Vedic studies being pursued is a unique commentary on the Rig Veda. . . . In addition . . . a commentary on the Brahma Sutras is 75% finished, and future plans include more commentary on the Bhagavad Gita. . . .

And finally, there is the Government Room. It is the most important room of all. On the walls hang charts and maps and graphs in many colors. One chart lists each country in the world, another shows each country's population, and yet another details the 3,600 major cities of the world. . . . Maharishi has long held the goal of providing one Initiator for each population of 1,000. With 3,600 teacher-training centers around the world, each dedicated to training at least 1,000 Initiators, that goal should become a reality. . . .

The boundlessness of Maharishi's vision is becoming clear. This is a World Plan. From room to room, down this hallway of knowledge, Maharishi goes each day. In each room there is a world globe and a portrait of Guru Dev.[13]

A Living Reality

While Maharishi and his staff work on these projects, the teacher-training course participants work on their own projects: developing into teachers of TM and the science of creative intelligence. This work consists of several hours each day of meditation for their own progress and development, plus three lectures daily (many conducted by Maharishi himself) on various aspects of the philosophy and practice of TM. Notes are taken and printed materials distributed for study. Visiting lecturers in the sciences, arts and humanities bring the latest knowledge of their fields to bear on the science of creative intelligence. There are always a few minutes to sit in the warm sun or to chat with course participants from one's own country or about 35 others, an opportunity to try out what is left of one's high-school or college French, Spanish, German, Dutch, Swedish, Hebrew, Japanese, Arabic, Italian, Greek, etc.

And there are the meals. "Napoleon, among others, once observed that an army travels on its stomach," Bolling writes. "He was thinking, no doubt, that the quality of one's food had something to do with the efficiency of one's achievements. Maharishi would agree." Although meals at the teacher-training courses are simple, Maharishi has been careful to insure that future teachers of TM should have fresh, wholesome, tasty food "as they prepare to do battle with ignorance." [14]

It is no wonder, with the intellectual stimulation, the loving atmosphere of community, the presence of Maharishi and the generally delightful and supportive atmosphere of these courses, that people stay on as long as they can, joining the staff whenever possible if their own funds run out. Most people feel that the time they spend with Maharishi is the most precious of their lives, but when they leave him, they carry in their hearts and minds his message, the promise of life in fulfillment, to all those back home. Then begins the unique joy of informing others of that fulfillment which alone is the goal of all human endeavor—and the privilege of teaching transcendental meditation, a simple technique to make the goal a living reality.

CHAPTER 11

The World We Can Create

> If you have built castles in the air, your work
> need not be lost; that is where they should be.
> Now put the foundations under them.
>
> —THOREAU

While the growth of SIMS-IMS continues at an astounding
rate, a wide gap still exists between what most of us experience as our everyday reality and the joyful, optimistic, fulfilled life apparently enjoyed by individuals practicing transcendental meditation. What is the cause of this discrepancy?

We have carefully analyzed the results of TM and ascertained the reasons for its beneficial effects. The reasons
are simple and logically intelligible; there is nothing mystical
about deep rest or unfolding mental and emotional faculties
which already exist within oneself. There is nothing strange
about dissolving deep-rooted stresses and becoming more loving, more intelligent and creative, more healthy, energetic and
alert. What begins to appear strange is why everyone is *not*
living a normal, fulfilled life.

And indeed, why is it? Why is it that in spite of the good
intentions of leaders and citizens of every country for hundreds of years the world continues to be burdened with suffering? It seems that if we really want to accomplish the

goals we have set for ourselves, individually, socially, nationally and internationally, if we really want to establish peace on earth and put an end to poverty, pollution, bigotry, injustice, all the myriad faces of human weakness and suffering which surround us everywhere, we must ask ourselves why even the most sincere efforts of countless individuals have failed to produce the desired results. We have tried every approach, political, legal, economic; revolutions in the name of freedom, justice and peace have been conceived in the minds and hearts of men, have been fought and have been won, yet we stand no closer to the realization of these ideals.

Our own nation was born of a great revolution in the name of life, liberty and the pursuit of happiness, for all men. These are very high ideals. "Those who won our independence," the Supreme Court Justice Louis Brandeis once wrote, "believed that the final end of the State was to make men free to develop their faculties." [1] What has happened to such men and to these values? *Something* is wrong, for in spite of all our achievements, in spite of "wealth and prosperity, technological advance, widespread education, democratic political forms, even honestly good intentions and avowals of good will," we still have not been able to "produce peace, brotherhood, serenity and happiness." [2] In fact, this century happens to be bloodier than all the preceding recorded centuries. [3]

Why? Certainly all of us recognize the necessity for changing the direction of the world away from violence, fear, hatred and all forms of suffering, toward love, harmony and fulfillment. And most of us realize that the responsibility for creating that change is ours; no one is going to do it for us. But not all of us have rejoiced at that responsibility or responded to its challenge with energy and enthusiasm. Even the youth of the world, usually the most vociferous and actively involved in the struggle for social betterment, seem to have become increasingly and disquietingly silent and resigned.

Recently New York's Mayor John Lindsay verbalized this,

expressing his concern over the number of young people who are "dropping out." Speaking of the many present leaders who should be replaced by better ones, Lindsay noted that "those younger ones who should ultimately replace these counselors of despair have begun to show a tendency to renege on their potential, to drop out, to disavow, to try to hide from the inequities and stupidities of society." Some go so far, he said, as to "cop-out altogether, having concluded that the world is run by fools and madmen." [4]

What is wrong? In our attempts to improve the world, have we been fighting the smoke instead of the fire?—the symptoms instead of the disease? Is an entirely different approach necessary? But what kind of approach? What haven't we tried?

A Radical Solution

The ideas we have been considering, along with the results reported in the foregoing chapters, suggest a new and radical solution. The word "radical" comes from the Latin *radix,* meaning "root." To be truly radical a solution has to deal directly with the root of a problem, not wasting time with the twigs and leaves. It has to meet the problem at its basis, at its source. Just as watering the root of a tree is the most efficient way to bring nourishment and life to all parts of the tree, the most effective way to deal with the innumerable problems which confront us would be a radical one.

If it could be found that all the problems before us have one common source, and if that source could be located and eliminated, the problems could be eradicated in one stroke, just as turning on the light puts an immediate end to the darkness of a room. Could this be the case? The problems seem so complex and diverse that a single source or solution seems highly unlikely.

Let us look at it more closely. We have already discussed the case of a gardener who finds a tree with drooping branches, drying leaves and small, undeveloped fruit. He knows the tree has the potential to flower and produce in abundance, but instead it is burdened with problems. What does he do? Discuss the situation with each individual leaf? Sprinkle water on each fruit? Hack off the weakest branches? Form an Inter-Branch Committee for Greener Leaves?

He waters the root. The problem of the leaves can never be solved on the level of the leaves. It is too complex and diverse a problem; there are hundreds of leaves. But if the tree can make and maintain contact with its source of nourishment in the soil (which is the source of its entire structure), then the basis of its life is strong, and the entire tree will flourish. If the flow of nourishment is cut off, all parts of the tree suffer and the tree ceases to grow.

Maharishi applies this analogy to man's life by pointing out that the three main aspects of the tree—outer branches, inner root and surrounding field of nourishment—correspond to the three basic fields of man's life—the body and its activities; the mind; and Being, the source of creative intelligence within. Just as the roots of the tree serve as a link connecting the outer, visible tree with its source of nourishment, man's mind serves as the link between the outer field of action and the inner reservoir of energy and intelligence. By expanding the conscious mind, taking it from the outer, gross fields of attention to increasingly subtle levels, we can locate, deeper than the deepest aspect of our individual nature, a universal field of life which gives rise to our individual characteristics as effortlessly and profusely as the universal field of the soil gives rise to oak and pine, roses and morning glories.

A field of permanence and of unity, it is the source of all change and multiplicity. It is a field of Being as distinct from becoming, a field of Absolute life, a fullness, an inexhaustible and unlimited reservoir of life energy, creative intelligence, happiness and peace. It has been called by many names, in different ages, by great seers of the truth of reality. Buddha called it Nirvana; Jesus called it the Kingdom of Heaven within; Hindus call it Sat-Chit-Ananda (Absolute Bliss Consciousness); Confucius and Lao-tse called it Tao. For centuries, the profound vision of these men provided a goal for countless seekers of truth and fulfillment. The essence of Maharishi's teaching is that in transcendental meditation a systematic technique has been made available by which any-one can incorporate this infinitely rich field of Being within his conscious experience.

The innumerable problems of the world are, Maharishi asserts, due to lack of contact with this unbounded field of creative intelligence. The specific individual problems are only symptoms of a deeper disease, and it is time to stop treating the symptoms and begin to deal directly with the underlying ailment. "The sickness of American society," says Arthur Schlesinger, Jr., "does not reside in the existence of problems. Nor does it reside in the existence of discontent, ferment and rebelliousness. . . . Our sickness resides rather in our incapacity to deal effectively with our problems." [5]

This sickness, unfortunately, is worldwide. Its symptoms are violence, despair, alienation, restlessness, dissatisfaction—we know them all too well. It is essentially a deficiency disease: a lack of strength, an "incapacity to deal effectively with our problems." If the deficiency in our diet is iron or vitamin C, the prescription is more iron, more vitamin C.

Man today faces one macroproblem: an inability to cope with the increasing pace, complexity and responsibilities of life, an inability to be the master of his destiny and create the kind of world he knows, in his heart, that he *can* create. All other problems are due to this inability and can be subsumed under that heading.

The macrosolution? To unfold more of man's latent potential, so that he can display greater creative intelligence and energy in action. Weakness, then, lack of full use of our potential, is the root of suffering. The root of happiness and peace will be to improve the coordination of action, thinking and Being, putting individuals in touch with the resources they need—and already own—in order to function effectively and fulfill their lives.

First Things First

"I live badly," wrote Tolstoy, "because life is bad. Life is bad because people, we, live badly. If we, the people, lived well, life would be good and I should not live badly. I am included in the people. And if I cannot make all people live well, I can at least do so myself, and thus can improve, however little, the life of other people and my own. What confirms this reasoning is that if everyone adopted it—and this reasoning is irrefutably just—then life would be good for everyone." [6] Can there be any argument against this simple logic?

Many modern thinkers have realized this. "The evils of the world," Bertrand Russell said, "including the evils which formerly could not possibly have been prevented, can now be prevented. They continue to exist only because people have passions in their souls which are evil. I think the whole trouble in the modern world . . . lies in the individual psychology, in the individual person's bad passions." [7] If the world is to change, *man* must first change, for "whatever form our group life may take," writes D. T. Suzuki, world-famous writer on Zen Buddhism, "its constituents are individuals after all. . . . As long as man himself does not go through a transformation no amount of science and knowledge will improve the human situation." [8]

"The custom of our time," Lewis Mumford noted in *The Condition of Man,* "is to think no change worth even discussing unless it can be at once organized into a visible movement," yet "only in one place can an immediate renewal begin: that is, within the person; and a remolding of the self . . . is an inescapable preliminary to the great changes that must be made throughout every community, in every part of the world." [9]

When man *does* change, when enough people are able to live differently, changes in social, political, legal and economic institutions will follow naturally and easily, reflecting the growth of their creators. If enough individuals change, society will change, for "all culture begins with the individual, and radiates from him as a center. It is only through the efforts of people of broader views, who take an interest in the general good, and who are capable of entertaining the idea of a better condition of things in the future, that the gradual progress of human nature towards its goal is possible." [10] Or as the *I Ching* says, with typical succinctness, "He improves his era and does not boast about it. His character is influential and transforms men." [11]

Certainly any truly significant change in human life must begin with the minds and hearts of men. "Laws and institutions must go hand in hand with the progress of the human mind," Jefferson pointed out. "As that becomes more developed, more enlightened . . . institutions must advance also, and keep pace with the times." [12] And this is sure to happen. It cannot be helped. Changes will continue to be made, and they will continue to be based upon the level of consciousness of the people. What is called for today is not *just* change, but real growth, which will be reflected in an improved society and a better world. Our age demands more decisive, dynamic action, coming from a higher level of consciousness, a deeper insight, a clearer mind and a purer heart. We must have more intelligent, creative leadership and action that is all life-supporting, if we are to have a really *new* world, not just a replay of the same old songs.

Every individual, Lewis Mumford maintains, within his or her own sphere of influence—the home, school, church, factory, office—"must carry into his immediate day's work a changed attitude. . . . His collective work cannot rise to a higher level than his personal scale of values. Once a change is effected in the person, every group will record and respond to it. . . . Without that change, no great betterment will take place in the social order. Once that change begins, everything is possible." [13]

The results of our study (and of the numerous physiological and psychological investigations we have examined) indicate that we have entered a new age—an age in which mankind's fondest visions of an ideal world, creative, peaceful and just, can become a reality. Until recently, such a transformation as Russell, Mumford, even Suzuki advocate would have required stern self-discipline and practically heroic effort; it is more than most of us could ever accomplish. The science of creative intelligence, however, has brought self-realization within easy reach, allowing individuals of every age and background to find greater inner resources and *effortlessly* live richer, more meaningful lives. This is the only foundation upon which that ideal world can be built.

One vision of such a world occurs in Bertrand Russell's book *Human Society in Ethics and Politics*. In view of all we have learned about the development and realization of human potentiality, it is not an impossible or implausible vision.

> There is no reason why, in the ages to come, the sort of man who is now exceptional should not become usual, and if that were to happen, the exceptional man in that new world would rise as far above Shakespeare as Shakespeare now rises above the common man. . . . When I allow myself to hope that the world will emerge from its present troubles, and that it will someday learn to give the direction of its affairs, not to cruel mountebanks, but to men possessed of wisdom and courage, I see before me a shining vision: a world where work is pleasant and not excessive, where kindly feelings are common, and where minds released from fear create delight for eye and ear and heart. Do not say this is impossible. It is not impossible . . . if men would bend their minds to the achievement of the kind of happiness that should be distinctive of man. I say the kind of happiness distinctive of man, because the happiness of pigs, which the enemies of Epicurus accused him of seeking, is not possible for men. If you try to make yourself content with the happiness of the pig, your suppressed potentialities will make you miserable. *True happiness for human beings is possible only to those who develop their godlike potentialities to the utmost.*[14]

No Corner on the Market of Soul:
The Black/White Problem Disappears

We have already seen the effectiveness of the science of creative intelligence in dealing with a number of major problems of our day, such as drug abuse, ill health, poor interpersonal relationships and the confusion of values. What about racial tension (in our country, the conflict of whites and blacks, but a global problem of increasing size among all races)?

The following excerpts are from an interview I had with the two young black men, Bob K. and Stanley L., who are responsible for establishing a transcendental meditation center in the Watts area of Los Angeles. It was the first center serving a predominantly black community.

JF: Why did you go about starting a meditation center?
BK: Basically, the reason I got involved in establishing a center was my own personal experience after a very brief period of time meditating. I started meditating because I found myself not being fulfilled. Up until then I had been looking at my environment and asking it to show me how to become fulfilled. Within a month after I began meditating I found that my whole life actually had changed. I wasn't blaming society any more for my state, my level of activity.
JF: And you were before?
BK: Yes, before I was looking at it and I was saying, "Well, it's because of the slave thing," or "It's because I didn't have the chance to go to the best college," or just about any excuse, and there are all kinds of excuses that black people use to cover up for their own deficiencies, their own inability to completely do their thing, to do what they really think they should be doing—we use a lot of excuses. We have in the past; now the tide is changing. . . .
JF: It seems to me that you can't just say it's *only* the black man's personal deficiency; it works both ways.

Isn't it fair for the black man to blame the environment and the white man's attitude?

BK: You say you think it *is* fair?

JF: Yes, I think it is, to some extent. Doesn't change have to come from both sides?

BK: Here's the thing I discovered about that: no matter what kind of power or what stratum of institutions you're talking about, all of that can be gotten around once an individual begins to meditate. That's the most beautiful aspect of meditation and it's the most tremendous result that any man can experience: that no matter what you happen to be hung up on, whether it's economic position, social involvement, education, no matter what it is that's hanging you up as far as advancing or moving in society, as soon as you begin to meditate, you will find yourself overcoming those barriers, no matter what those barriers happen to be. And you find yourself adjusting to your environment to such an extent that no longer do you look upon the white man as an obstacle, as the holder of power, you look upon him as just another human being, and you discover that you can gain that power yourself. This has been my personal experience.

JF: Don't you think it also has to come from the other side? The white man also has to think of the black man as just another human being.

BK: Yes, but as far as I can see that's been a problematic area, because the black man has been saying, "You've got to do this, you've got to do that, you've got to do the other," and personally, I see that as a weakness. . . . If I accept the status of a second-class citizen, then this is the position that I actually will find myself in. The maintenance of that particular attitude is only the result of stress and tension in the atmosphere. Now, I can't put the blame on the white man or the black man for the presence of that stress and tension, but it's there. I can't spend my time or waste my energy being concerned about what the white man is going to do about it, for myself, because in the final analysis—and this is the total reality that every man is confronted with whether he's a meditator or not—we

come into this life, most of us, we come in by ourselves; and when we go out of this life, we go out by
ourselves; and the portion that we measure in between
that we call living is something that, even though we
may join together in collective groups for different
activities, it's an individual trip, something we have to
do for ourselves. We can work together, but I still have
to put the food on my table and pay my rent. . . .
Every man has got to reckon with himself and discover where he's at and what he's going to do about
it, for himself.

It's just that cut and dried, and again this is where
TM really works, because once you know where you
are as an individual, once you know who you really
are and what you're doing, you can choose the area of
involvement that is most advantageous for your own
evolution and as an end result the evolution of the collective whole. . . . I can remember many times before I started meditating . . . I used to sit and watch
people and listen to people and ask all kinds of questions, and nobody was ever able to tell me who I was,
why I was here and where *here* really was, until I
started meditating. Now I know who I am, and I
know why I'm here, and I know what I'm supposed
to be doing. If something like that can be revealed to
me just through a simple technique of meditation, it
can be revealed to anybody. And it's regardless of
color, it doesn't matter whether you're white, black,
green or blue. So—does that answer your question?

JF: The original question was, "Why did you start a
center?"

BK: To make it available, so that someone else—whatever his particular status happens to be in life—can
discover that he doesn't have to suffer, that he doesn't
have to be hung up if he doesn't want to be.

SL: We started a center because our past experience
has been that we had a need, white people had a need,
black people had a need, everybody had a need. We
were looking for the solution to that problem, for our
own benefit, in our own lives. It just so happened that
the solution we found was a universal one, that any-

one could use to gain what we know we've gained from our own experience. Once we discovered that there was something valuable and truthful in life, something that could be used by any person to change his level of consciousness for the better, to change his everyday experience for the better, we decided that we couldn't do anything less than make it available to people.

JF: I'd like to talk a little bit more, if you can, about the relationship between black people and white people, and how that would be affected by meditation. It seems to be a very important problem. Or isn't it? Is it something that will just solve itself as each individual becomes more able to be himself and fulfill himself?

BK: When man *A,* whether he's white, black, yellow or purple, is in tune with himself, then he spreads harmony wherever he goes. The result is that rather than taking tension into his activity, into his daily life, he takes harmony with him. Everybody is affected by it. All he needs to do is be in harmony with himself, and he carries that atmosphere.

SL: Also, our experience is that desires are satisfied much more completely, much more quickly, and with far less energy since we've been meditating. . . . So here's the opportunity to gain not only the physical, material things that are desired, easily and simply, without effort, but also to gain what is really the important thing, what Bob mentioned at the very beginning: the spiritual satisfaction of knowing yourself, knowing where you are, what you are and what it's all about, having this communion with the deepest level of your existence. . . . So the black/white problem dissolves, it just doesn't exist any more.

BK: One of the most beautiful advantages of TM, whether you are consciously aware of it at first or not, is that you develop an awareness of the universality of yourself and of all men. You discover that you don't have a corner on the market of soul, that soul is everywhere. . . . You see everyone as part of the whole thing, and that we're all moving toward an objective, collectively and individually, and that's all that's really important.

This interview clearly indicates that to suggest that the science of creative intelligence is a solution to the problem of the relationship between races is not utopian fantasizing. If we add to the above the comments of meditators throughout the book, with their reports of an increased ability to love, growing compassion for others, greater acceptance, tolerance and understanding, the social ramifications of such changed attitudes and behavior begin to be obvious.

Good behavior between people, Maharishi repeatedly asserts, is based essentially on happiness. A. S. Neill, author of *Summerhill,* graphically affirms this truth of life: "No happy man ever disturbed a meeting, or preached a war, or lynched a Negro. No happy woman ever nagged her husband or her children. No happy man ever committed a murder or a theft. No happy employer ever frightened his employees. All crimes, all hatreds, all wars, can be reduced to unhappiness." [15]

In *The Science of Being and Art of Living* Maharishi emphasizes that really good behavior between people will only be possible

when their minds are broadened, when they are able to see the whole situation, to understand each other more thoroughly, to be aware of each other's need and attempt to fulfill that need. This naturally necessitates an expanded consciousness, a right sense of judgment and all the qualities that only a strong and clear mind possesses.

Small minds always fail to perceive the whole situation and in their narrow vision create imaginary obstacles and restrictions which are neither useful to themselves nor to anyone else. Then their behavior towards others only results in misunderstanding and increase of tension. Good social behavior is based on a strong, clear and contented mind. [16]

The science of creative intelligence is a natural way to expand our limited, restricted vision and become established in the unbounded awareness that perceives all men as brothers with a common goal and purpose. There are many who feel that such an expansion of vision would automatically set right the twisted relationships of individuals and races.

"Wars Start in the Minds of Men"

"Wars start in the minds of men," says the UNESCO charter. But peace also starts in the minds—and hearts—of men. A former president of the UN General Assembly, Vijaya Lakshmi Pandit, phrased the situation this way: "There is superficial order, but there is no inner tranquility and understanding. . . . Without a sound state of mind, diplomatic, economic and trade conferences can achieve nothing. The only true foundation for peaceful coexistence is the right state of mind." [17]

"Where there is no love of man, no love of life," said Thomas Merton, "then make all the laws you want, all the edicts and treaties, issue all the anathemas, set up all the safeguards and inspections, fill the air with spying satellites, and hang cameras on the moon. As long as you see your fellow-man as a being essentially to be feared, mistrusted, hated, and destroyed, there cannot be peace on earth." But, he added, "Where there is a deep, simple, all-embracing love of man, of the created world of living and inanimate things, then there will be respect for life, for freedom, for truth, for justice." [18]

Every man's outer life is the expression of what he is within. Every action we perform, every word we speak is an expression of our inner state and constitutes our contribution to our family, our friends, our society. Every expression of ourself, positive or negative, creative or useless, wise or foolish, influences those around us, and thereby influences the state of the world. A man who is peaceful and full of love contributes peacefulness and love to his environment. A man who is inwardly stressed, frustrated, full of tension and anger —no matter how vehemently he may wave the banner of peace—is contributing tension and anger to his surroundings and the world.

"An individual influences the entire cosmos by every thought, word and action," says Maharishi. "Therefore someone with peace in his heart naturally radiates peace and harmony and influences the whole universe. Those who are restless, worried or troubled and who have no experience of bliss-consciousness continually produce unfavourable influences in their surroundings. . . . When large numbers of people are unhappy, tense and unrighteous the atmosphere of the world is saturated with these tense influences. When tensions in the atmosphere increase beyond a certain limit the atmosphere breaks into collective calamities." [19]

Everyone has experienced walking into a room or a home where there has just been—or where there always is—some argument, some tension. We feel it. In the same way, a warm, loving home invites us, holds us; we hate to leave such places and such people. Their atmosphere is supportive and comfortable. Just as tension and stress can build up inside us, until finally it breaks out, the same thing can happen in a family. In Chapter 3 we saw how a burned piece of toast can become the focal point for a major family upheaval. The toast is not the real cause of the argument; accumulated stress and tension within the individual are the real cause; the toast is just a catalyst, an excuse, causing the pent-up feelings to erupt.

When individuals within a society are tense, strained and dissatisfied with life, the foundation is laid for conflict in its various forms: riots, demonstrations, strikes, individual and collective crimes, wars. But a society composed of happy, creative individuals could not give rise to such outbreaks of discord.

Microscopes and Macroscopes: A New Approach
to World Peace

Thus we can see that the problem of world peace is not insoluble. The solution lies in reducing the problem to its essential terms: individuals. It is the greenness of every tree that makes the whole forest green.

The problem seems immense when it has the magnitude of a world problem. But—the world is composed of nations; nations are made up of states and cities; states and cities, in turn, are composed of numerous neighborhoods and communities; each neighborhood is filled with families. Each family is composed of individual human beings. Individuals who are fulfilled and happy, who are able to work and live together without discord, form the basis of a harmonious family. Harmonious families spontaneously create a peaceful community—and so on. The vast and intricate structure of the world is made up of separate, individual people: you, me, our friends, and about three and one-half billion others!

Just as the branches of an individual's tree of life—his family, education, friendships, marriage, occupation, etc.—are all important aspects of life, the tree of the world is also composed of many branches: Russia, China, Vietnam, the Middle East, the United States of America. These different areas of the world should be centers of peace and development, offering an opportunity for free, mutually beneficial interchange among peoples. They should not be centers of war, destruction, violence and hatred, as they so often are. But the problem cannot be solved by dealing with each turbulent area in its own particular terms. For centuries statesmen the world over have dealt with the world's conflicts by turning from one trouble spot to another. It is clear that, in spite of all the energy, intelligence and sincere efforts expended in the name of peace, this method has not succeeded in creating a peaceful world.

"As long as statesmen remain ignorant of the possibility

of improving the lives of individuals from within and of thereby bringing them abundant peace, happiness and creative intelligence," Maharishi writes, "the problem of world peace will always be dealt with only on the surface, and the world will continue to suffer its cold and hot wars. . . . Any generation whose leaders sincerely try to apply this principle widely will succeed in creating lasting world peace. If present statesmen and public leaders do this, the credit will be theirs and they will have the satisfaction of leaving a better world for coming generations." [20]

Leadership for a New Age

Even if only a small percentage of all the individuals in the world were living a fulfilled life, their mere presence in society could begin to neutralize the tensions of those less fortunate than themselves. Maharishi has frequently expressed the view that a permanent state of world peace would be achieved if one person in ten were practicing transcendental meditation and therefore expressing a higher degree of intelligence and morality. This ten percent of the population would become centers of peaceful, creative, life-supporting influence and actions. They would be leaders—*real* leaders, worth emulating and listening to—who could help the rest of mankind develop in a more human way.

Maharishi has noted that such people do not have to hold political power in order to be constructively influential in the world. The mere fact that they exist is a factor in bettering world conditions. Everywhere they go, they bring harmony, they inspire love and respect, they help others to be free and spontaneous. Wherever they are, whatever they do, by being in tune with nature, by helping others live better, by living well themselves, they are exercising an important influence on their society and on the whole world.

In August 1968, in Squaw Valley, California, Maharishi conducted the first month-long Leadership Training Course,

TRANSCENDENTAL MEDITATION

the first phase in developing new teachers of transcendental meditation. On the first evening of the course he gave the 750 participants what, for most, was a new conception of leadership:

> In whatever area we may be, we want to give the art of living in happiness, so that those around us are not unhappy. The job of a leader is to see that the goal of the followers is achieved. All mankind has one common goal in infinite bliss-consciousness. The task of the leader of human life is to lead his followers to this ultimate goal in life. All other things are secondary. . . .
>
> The result of this course should be that wherever you may be, you'll be like a lighted lamp. The world is there to follow. What has been lacking is leadership. . . . The need of the time is to have enlightened leaders, to give a direction to society. All of you are in a position to lead society toward all good. You have the ability, only it has been underneath the water; during this time, we'll bring it out.
>
> Our goal is laudable—we want to bring the light of life to everyone.

A Vision of Possibilities

A quiet undercurrent of confidence filled the Sierra air that August evening. Although the 750 meditators assembled with Maharishi represented nearly one-tenth of the total number of meditators in the country at that time—all together just a tiny drop in the immense ocean of three billion faces—we somehow knew that this man's goal of bringing freedom from suffering to all humanity was going to succeed. Many of us had the strange, strong sense of living and witnessing history being made. I remember one person quietly musing, "Someday our great-grandchildren will read about this and say, 'They were actually *there!*'" Today, less than four and a half years later, the 10,000 meditators have become 200,000; the few dozen teachers in the U.S. have multiplied to 2,400.

The number is still tiny but by any standards the growth has been phenomenal.

As my good friend Joseph Clarke, SIMS-IMS Regional Coordinator for the East Coast, once said, "It is a great inspiration to realize that the broadest goal of mankind is becoming a reality. The key solution to the complex problems of society was cognized by one person a few years ago. By remaining one-pointed to his single purpose of relieving stress and suffering, Maharishi has seen our movement grow to support a World Plan. Scientific research has clearly established the unique value of TM; education is recognizing its fulfillment through the Science of Creative Intelligence. . . . It is an honor to participate in this revival of pure knowledge."

For those of us who have met Maharishi, who have felt and seen the effects of transcendental meditation and who have watched or participated, even for a few years, in the unfolding of this revival, there can no longer be any doubt that Maharishi's vision of a creative, harmonious world will one day be the reality of life on earth.

Of course, this vision is not new, nor uniquely Maharishi's. It belongs to all of us. But for centuries it has remained a vision. The results of this study indicate that we now have the means to breathe life into it, by fully developing our potential for experience and action.

"Transcendental meditation in its pure form will help people at all times to alleviate suffering and to remove shortcomings and ignorance," writes Maharishi, bringing *The Science of Being and Art of Living* to a close. "It will usher in a new humanity developed in all life's values—physical, mental, material and spiritual—and enable man to live a life of fulfillment. . . . The peace and prosperity of people everywhere will be secured. Higher consciousness will guide the destiny of man. All will be established in the true values of life. Accomplishments will be great in the family, the society, the nation and the world. And man will live naturally in fulfillment, generation after generation." [21]

APPENDIX A

Recent Events

I. The Government of the State of Illinois resolves to support Maharishi's World Plan:

STATE OF ILLINOIS
SEVENTY-SEVENTH GENERAL ASSEMBLY
HOUSE OF REPRESENTATIVES

HOUSE RESOLUTION NO. 677

Offered by Mr. Murphy

WHEREAS, Transcendental Meditation is a simple natural technique of gaining deep rest and relaxation which is easily learned by everyone; and

WHEREAS, School officials have noted a lessening of student unrest and an improvement in grades and student-parent-and-teacher relationships among practitioners of Transcendental Meditation; and

WHEREAS, Transcendental Meditation offers an alternative to drug abuse and studies indicate that it shows promise of being the most positive and effective drug prevention program being presented in the world today; and

WHEREAS, Physiological experiments provide evidence that through the regular practice of T.M. (twice daily for 15–20 minutes) the main causes of hypertension, anxiety, high blood pressure, cardiac arrest, and other psychosomatic illnesses are removed; and

WHEREAS, Through the efforts of the Students International Meditation Society, a non-profit educational organization, credit courses in the Science of Creative Intelligence, the practical aspect of which is T.M., have been offered at many of the largest universities throughout the United States; and

WHEREAS, Under a World Plan, 350 teaching centers of the Science of Creative Intelligence are being founded in the largest cities throughout the United States and the world, one of which is to be located in Chicago, Illinois; and

WHEREAS, The purpose of these centers is the training of teachers to accomplish the objectives of the Science of Creative Intelligence which are:

(1) to develop the full potential of the individual.

(2) to improve governmental achievements.

(3) to realize the highest ideal of education.

(4) to solve the problems of crime, drug abuse, and all behavior that brings unhappiness to the family of man.

(5) to maximize the intelligent use of the environment.

(6) to bring fulfillment to the economic aspirations of individuals and society.

(7) to achieve the spiritual goals of mankind in this generation; and

WHEREAS, The whole thrust of the programs of the Students International Meditation Society and the International Meditation Society is to aid in the practical development of happy and productive citizens through their teaching of Transcendental Meditation as taught by Maharishi Mahesh Yogi throughout the world; therefore, be it

RESOLVED, By the House of Representatives of the Seventy-seventh General Assembly of the State of Illinois, that all educational institutions, especially those under State of Illinois jurisdiction, be strongly encouraged to study the feasibility of courses in Transcendental Meditation and the Science of Creative Intelligence (SCI) on their campuses and in their facilities; and be it further

RESOLVED, That the Department of Mental Health of the State of Illinois, Drug Abuse Section, be encouraged to study the benefits of T.M. and insofar as the Drug Abuse Section deems it to be practical and medically wise, to incorporate the course in T.M. in the drug abuse programs; and be it further

RESOLVED, That the State of Illinois give all possible cooperation to the new Center for the teaching of the Science of Creative Intelligence to be founded in Chicago, Illinois; and be it further

RESOLVED, That a copy of this resolution be sent to: The Superintendent of Public Instruction: The Deans of all State Universities; The Department of Mental Health, State of Illinois to inform them of the great promise of the programs herein mentioned; and be it further

RESOLVED, That copies of this resolution also be sent to the Students International Meditation Society and to his Holiness, Maharishi Mahesh Yogi, founder of the Science of Creative Intelligence, and to William J. Murphy and John J. Murphy, students and teachers of Transcendental Meditation, trained by his Holiness, to encourage them in their endeavors, and advise them of our interest in their program.

Adopted by the House of Representatives May 24, 1972.

W. Robert Blair
Speaker of the House

Fredric B. Silcke
Clerk of the House

II. U.S. Government Grant to Train Teachers of the Science of Creative Intelligence.

In August 1972 over 100 secondary-school teachers attended a teacher-training course on the science of creative intelligence at Humboldt State College in California. More than half were supported by a $21,540 grant from the National Institute of Mental Health of the Department of Health, Education and Welfare. Over 400 had applied for the scholarship aid.

The participants in the course had the benefit of visits from prominent educators—a superintendent of schools, a Dean of Innovative Studies from a major state university, an educational consultant for the Department of Health, Education and Welfare, etc.—who, along with Maharishi, acted as consultants in the formulation of a syllabus for presenting SCI in the nation's high schools. A 33-part presentation on SCI by Maharishi on color video tapes was viewed by the group; smaller groups met to discuss the tapes and create teaching methods for most effective presentation of the material.

The majority of the teachers had been practicing transcendental meditation before applying for the course, but many had not been. By the end of the month, all were meditating and were enthusiastic and optimistic about the potential value, for themselves and their students, of the knowledge they had gained.

The teachers ranged in age from twenty-two to sixty-five, and represented private and public, inner-city, urban and suburban schools in 17 states.

A similar, though greatly expanded program is being planned for summer 1973; it is expected that several thousand teachers will be able to participate.

The results of the 1972 course are being evaluated by a year-long study, headed by Professor J. Kravitz of Howard University. The study will employ various measures of teacher capability to determine the effects on the teachers themselves, and study student gains by measuring grades, drug abuse patterns and various categories of social competence.

III. Further Studies on TM (unpublished as of January 1, 1973):

Superior Perceptual-Motor Performance
(Mirror Star-Tracing Test)

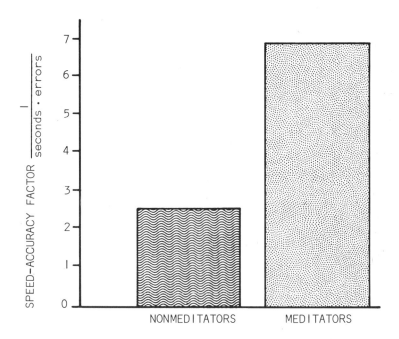

A. Superior perceptual-motor performance by meditators was found in a study by K. Blasdell of the UCLA Department of Kinesiology. Practitioners of TM performed faster and more accurately than a control group of non-meditators in a complex perceptual-motor test called the mirror star-tracing test. The group of meditators averaged 21.12 errors in 67.05 seconds; the non-meditating control group averaged 39.3 errors in 104.3 seconds. Good performance indicates greater coordination between mind and body, greater efficiency, increased perceptual awareness and neuromuscular integration.

B. Reduced use of tranquilizers, stimulants and other *prescribed* drugs was found in a study of 570 subjects conducted by Leon Otis of Stanford Research Institute, Menlo Park, California.

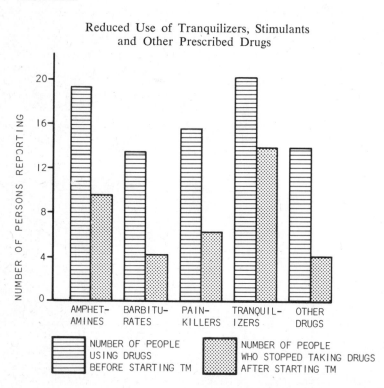

Reduced Use of Tranquilizers, Stimulants and Other Prescribed Drugs

C. Reduction in *non-prescribed* drug use was also found by Dr. Otis in the SRI study of 570 subjects.

Reduction in Non-Prescribed Drug Use

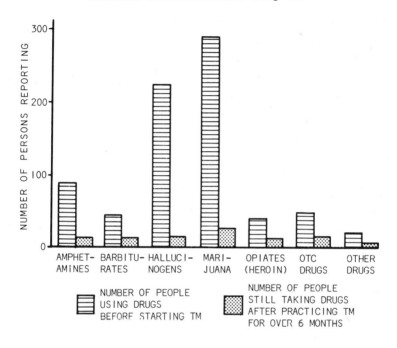

A Selected Bibliography on TM

Books

by Maharishi Mahesh Yogi
    The Science of Being and Art of Living (revised by the author; International SRM Publications, 1966). Available through SIMS-IMS.
    On the Bhagavad-Gita, A New Translation and Commentary (International SRM, 1967; Penguin edition, 1969).
    Love and God (SRM, 1965). Available through SIMS-IMS.

about TM
    Tranquility Without Pills by J. Robbins and D. Fisher (Peter Wyden, 1972).

Articles

General
    "Chief Guru of the Western World," B. Lefferts, *New York Times Magazine* (December 17, 1967).
    "Non-Drug Turn-On Hits Campus," William Hedgepeth, *Look* (February 6, 1968).
    "Mind Over Drugs," Behavior Section, *Time* (October 25, 1971).
    "Transcendental Meditation: Can It Fight Drug Abuse?," Gurney Williams, III, *Science Digest* (February 1972).
    "Consciousness 4: It Probes the Inner Core of Being,"

Ssg. Don Mallicoat, *Soldiers Magazine* (February 1972). "Meditation as a Drug Trip Detour," K. Goodall, *Psychology Today* (March 1972). "What Science Is Discovering about the Potential Benefits of Meditation," Terri Schultz, *Today's Health* (April 1972).

Scientific

"Yoga for Drug Abuse," H. Benson, M.D., *New England Journal of Medicine,* Vol. 281, No. 20 (November 1969), p. 1133.

"The Physiological Effects of Transcendental Meditation," R. K. Wallace, *Science,* Vol. 167 (March 27, 1970).

J. Allison, "Respiratory Changes During the Practice of the Technique of Transcendental Meditation," *The Lancet,* No. 7651 (April 18, 1970), pp. 833–834.

"Toward Pinning Down Meditation," Anthony Campbell, M.D., *Hospital Times* (London, May 1, 1970).

"A Wakeful Hypometabolic Physiologic State," R. K. Wallace, H. Benson and A. F. Wilson, *American Journal of Physiology,* Vol. 221, No. 3 (September 1971).

"The Physiology of Meditation," R. K. Wallace and H. Benson, *Scientific American,* Vol. 226, No. 2 (February 1972).

Anonymous, "Meditation May Find Use in Medical Practice," *JAMA* (Journal of the American Medical Association), Vol. 219, No. 3 (January 17, 1972), pp. 295–299.

"A Study of the Influence of Transcendental Meditation on a Measure of Self-Actualization," S. Nidich, W. Seeman and T. Banta, *Journal of Counseling Psychology,* Vol. 19, No. 3 (1972), pp. 184–187.

Education

"Transcendental Meditation and the Science of Creative Intelligence," Paul H. Levine, *Phi Delta Kappan,* Vol. LIV, No. 4 (December 1972), p. 231.

"Transcendental Meditation as a Secondary School Subject," Francis G. Driscoll, *Phi Delta Kappan,* Vol. LIV, No. 4 (December 1972), p. 236.

"Transcendental Meditation and Its Potential Uses for Schools," Al E. Rubottom, *Social Education* (December 1972), p. 851.

APPENDIX C

Where to Learn TM

There are 205 world plan centers
in the United States offering courses
in the Science of Creative Intelligence and
Transcendental Meditation.

MAJOR CENTERS

ATLANTA
1827 North Decatur Road
Atlanta, Georgia 30307
phone 404 373-8228

BERKELEY
2728 Channing Way
Berkeley, California 94704
phone 415 548-1144

CAMBRIDGE
33 Garden Street
Cambridge, Mass. 02138
phone 617 876-4581

CHICAGO
828 Davis Street
Evanston, Illinois 60201
phone 312 864-1986

COLUMBUS
1611 Summit
Columbus, Ohio 43201
phone 614 294-7467

DENVER
P.O. Box 6182
Denver, Colorado 80206
phone 303 893-3480

DETROIT
248 Adams South
Birmingham, Mich. 48008
phone 313 642-4444

HAWAII
2865 Manoa Road
Honolulu, Hawaii 96822
phone 808 988-3166

HOUSTON
1216 Hawthorne Street
Houston, Texas 77006
phone 713 526-2582

IOWA CITY
1606 Muscatine Avenue
Iowa City, Iowa 52240
phone 319 351-3779

KANSAS CITY
P. O. Box 16016
Kansas City, Mo. 64112
phone 816 523-5777

LOS ANGELES
1015 Gayley Avenue
Los Angeles, California 90024
phone 213 478-1569

MINNEAPOLIS
2323 N.E. Garfield
Minneapolis, Minn. 55418
phone 612 781-6946

NEW HAVEN
Box 1974 Yale Station
New Haven, Conn. 06520
phone 203 777-6259

NEW YORK
Wentworth Building
59 W. 46th Street
New York, N.Y. 10036
phone 212 586-3331

PHILADELPHIA
3905 Spruce Street
Philadelphia, Penn. 19104
phone 215 387-1733

PORTLAND
1246 S.E. 51st Avenue
Portland, Oregon 97215
phone 503 235-3624

SANTA BARBARA
131 Anacapa Street
Santa Barbara, California 93102
phone 805 968-9872

SEATTLE
P. O. Box 253
University Station
Seattle, Wash. 98105
phone 206 524-6464

WASHINGTON, D.C.
2127 Leroy Place
Washington, D.C. 20008
phone 202 387-5050

U.S. NATIONAL CENTER
SIMS-IMS
1015 Gayley Avenue
Los Angeles, California 90024
phone 213 477-4537

INTERNATIONAL WORLD PLAN CENTERS

ARGENTINA
SIMS
Gelly y Obes 2398
Buenos Aires, Argentina

AUSTRALIA
SIMS-IMS National Center
P. O. Box 259
Paddington, N.S.W.
Australia 2021

AUSTRIA
SRM
1040 Wien
Argentinierstrasse 20
Austria

BRAZIL
Sociedade Internacional de
Meditacao
Avenida Rio Branco 185
GR 2107
Rio de Janeiro, Brazil

BURMA
SIMS
206/210 Shwe Bontha Street
Rangoon, Burma

CANADA
Administrative Offices
65 Bank Street
Ottawa, Ontario

Alberta
Calgary World Plan Center
2315-22A Street N.W.
Calgary, T2M-3X6, Alberta

British Columbia
Victoria World Plan Center
1270 Pandora Avenue
Victoria, B.C.

Manitoba
Winnipeg World Plan Center
#4-300 Main Street
Winnipeg, Manitoba

Ontario
Ottawa World Plan Center
65 Bank Street
Ottawa, Ontario

Toronto World Plan Center
39 Mount View
Toronto, Ontario

Quebec
Quebec City World Plan
   Center
AIME C.P., 9693
Ste. Foy
Quebec, 10, Quebec

Montreal East World Plan
   Center
36 ESt. Beau Vien
Montreal, Quebec

CHILE
SIMS
Casilla 141, San Miguel
Santiago, Chile

COLOMBIA
SIMS
Carrerra 13-A #38-32
Bogota, Colombia

DENMARK
SIMS
c/o Trier
Vesterbrogade 65
1620 Copenhagen, Denmark

ECUADOR
SIMS
Casilla 3064
Quito, Ecuador

ENGLAND
SRM Foundation of
   Great Britain
32 Cranbourn Street
WC2H 7EY
London, England

EGYPT
35A Mohammed Mazher Street
Zamalek
Cairo, Egypt

ETHIOPIA
c/o Dawit
Yared Music School
P. O. Box 30097
Addis Ababa, Ethiopia

FINLAND
SIMS
Kylanevantie 2A3
00320 Helsinki 32, Finland

FRANCE
AIMT France
B.P. 164-09
13, rue de la Tour des Dames
F-75 422 Paris Cedex 09
France

GERMANY
SIMS-SRM
Akademie fuer
   Persoenlichkeitsentfaltung
Bremen-Blumenthal
Ringofenstrasse 58
West Germany

SIMS-IMS
Gerd Hegendorfer, Director
Dortmund
Hoestrasse 13
West Germany

SIMS-SRM
Deutsche Zentrale
Praesident Ritterstaedt
Duesseldorf 30
Luetzowstrasse 6
West Germany

SIMS
Muenchen
Harthauser Strasse 127
West Germany

GREECE
SRM-SIMS
4 Mitseon Street
Athens, 144, Greece

HOLLAND
Centrum voor Transcendente
    Meditatie
Valeriusplein 13
Amsterdam, Holland

INDIA
International Academy of
    Meditation
Shankaracharya Nagar
Rishikesh, U.P., India

IRAN
c/o Edwards
Faculty of Science
University of Meshed
Meshed, Iran

IRELAND
The Irish Meditation Society
125 Foxrock Park
Foxrock, C., Dublin, Ireland

ITALY
SIMS
c/o Romano
Via de San Pantaleo,
    Campano 27
00147 Roma
5230331 Italy

JAPAN
SIMS
c/o Masami Itoh
Shakujidai 3-17-12
Nerimaku, Tokyo, Japan

KENYA
SIMS
P. O. Box 5027
Subudla, Kenya

MEXICO
Sociedad Mexicana de
    Meditacion
Palacio de Versailles #225
Mexico 10 D.F., Mexico

MALAYSIA
SRM Foundation of Malaysia
M. P. Sellasamy
11, Jalan Tenggiri
Kuala Lumpur, Malaysia

NEW ZEALAND
National Transcendental
    Meditation Center
17 Horoeka Avenue,
    Mount Eden
Auckland 3, New Zealand

NIGERIA
SIMS
256 Herbert Macavley Street
Lagos, Nigeria

NORWAY
SIMS
Postboks 16, Blindern
N-Oslo 3, Norway

PAKISTAN
SIMS
509 Prince Sadrudin Building
Rehmatullah Street
Kaaradar
Karachi 2, Pakistan

PANAMA
SIMS
Box 1779 Panama
Republic of Panama

PUERTO RICO
Box 21609
University Station
San Juan, Puerto Rico, 00931

SCOTLAND
SIMS
10 Middleby Street
Edinburgh, Scotland

SIERRA LEONE
SRM
64 Wilkinson Road
Freetown, Sierra Leone,
    West Africa

SOUTH AFRICA
SIMS
3 Orchart Street
Newlands
Capetown, South Africa

IMS
3 Frere Road
Parktown West
Johannesburg, South Africa

SOUTH VIETNAM
SIMS
102 Tudo Street
Saigon, South Vietnam
(Brig. Gen. H. H. Hiestand)

SWEDEN
SRM Stockholm Meditation
    Center
Skeppargatan 6
11452 Stockholm, Sweden

SWITZERLAND
Administration Center
CH6446 Seelisberg,
    Switzerland

TURKEY
SRM Center
Ruhi Gelisme Derneigi
Kazanci Yokusu Sormagir
    Sokak
Kangy Apt Kat 1, Taksin
Istanbul, Turkey

VENEZUELA
SIMS
c/o Muellen
Apartado 2299
Caracas, Venezuela

WEST INDIES
SRM
8 Coblentz Gardens
St. Anns Port-of-Spain
Trinidad, West Indies

YUGOSLAVIA
c/o Rade Sibila
41000 Zagreb
Jagiceva 21, Yugoslavia

Notes

Introduction

1. Maharishi Mahesh Yogi, quoted in *International Symposium on the Science of Creative Intelligence* (Seelisberg [Switzerland]: MIU Press, 1971), p. 47.
2. Ben Gerson, "Maharishi Makes It in the Groves of Academe," *Boston After Dark*, August 17, 1971.
3. "Mind Over Drugs," *Time* (October 25, 1971), Behavior section.
4. Herbert Benson, M.D., and Robert Keith Wallace, Ph.D., "Decreased Drug Abuse with Transcendental Meditation," paper presented to the International Symposium on Drug Abuse for Physicians, University of Michigan, August 1970, and to the House Select Committee on Crime, printed in *Hearings Before the Select Committee on Crime of the House of Representatives,* Ninety-second Congress, first session, 1971.
5. R. K. Wallace and H. Benson, "The Physiology of Meditation," *Scientific American* (February 1972), p. 86.
6. Francis G. Driscoll, Superintendent of Schools, Eastchester, New York, in a letter to Dr. Roger Meredith, Assistant Superintendent for Instruction, Department of Education, British Columbia, Canada.
7. Open letter, "To Whom It May Concern," from Chris Merriam, Prevention Manager, Governor's Office of Drug Abuse, State of Michigan, June 29, 1971.

Chapter 1

1. Erich Fromm, *Escape from Freedom* (New York: Rinehart, 1941), p. 269.

2. Abraham Maslow, *Toward a Psychology of Being* (2nd Ed., New York: Van Nostrand Reinhold Co., 1968), p. 153.

3. *Ibid.*, p. 155.

4. *Ibid.*, p. 160.

5. Carl R. Rogers, "Toward a Theory of Creativity," in *Creativity and Its Cultivation* (New York: Harper, 1959), p. 72.

6. Julian Huxley, *Evolution in Action* (New York: Harper, 1953), p. 162.

7. William C. Schutz, *Joy, Expanding Human Awareness* (New York: Grove, 1967), p. 15.

8. Charles A. Reich, *The Greening of America* (New York: Random House, 1970), p. 351.

9. Rogers, *op. cit.*, pp. 69–70.

10. J. A. Comenius, "The Great Didactic," quoted in *Classics in Education*, Wade Baskin (ed.) (New York: Philosophical Library, 1966), p. 102.

11. Paul Tournier, *The Meaning of Persons* (New York: Harper, 1957), p. 223.

12. Psalms I, 3.

13. Maharishi Mahesh Yogi, *The Science of Being and Art of Living* (revised by the author; International SRM Publications, 1966), p. 54. (Hereinafter cited only by title.)

14. Verse 25, trans. Arthur Waley in *The Way and Its Power* (New York: Grove Press, 1958), p. 174.

15. Verse 4, trans. Lin Yutang, in *The Wisdom of China and India* (New York: Modern Library, 1942), p. 585.

16. Verse 6, Waley, *op. cit.*, p. 149.

17. Walt Whitman, "Passage to India," in *Leaves of Grass*.

18. Maharishi Mahesh Yogi, *On the Bhagavad-Gita*, p. 9.

19. Aldous Huxley, "Human Potentialities," in *Control of the Mind*, S. Farber and R. Wilson (eds.) (New York: McGraw-Hill, 1961), p. 71.

20. Maharishi Mahesh Yogi, transcribed from lecture notes.

21. Maharishi Mahesh Yogi, from a letter to Walter Koch, teacher of TM.

22. For studies on the effects of sounds on plants, see "Chant of the Plant," *Newsweek* (August 17, 1970), p. 82; "What Noise Does to Plants," *Science Digest* (December 1970), p. 60; "Ultrahigh-Frequency Electromagnetic Fields for Weed Control," *Science* (August 6, 1971), p. 535.

23. Maharishi Mahesh Yogi, *The Science of Being and Art of Living*, p. 56.

24. *Ibid.*, p. 57.

25. *Ibid.*, p. 58.

26. *Ibid.*, p. 81.

Chapter 2

1. Robert Keith Wallace, *The Physiological Effects of Transcendental Meditation, A Proposed Fourth Major State of Consciousness,* Ph.D. thesis (University of California at Los Angeles, Department of Physiology, 1970), p. 1.

2. W. Penfield, "The Physiological Basis of the Mind," in S. Farber and R. Wilson (eds.), *Control of the Mind* (New York: McGraw-Hill, 1961), p. 13.

3. *Cf.* E. Hartman, *The Biology of Dreaming* (Springfield, Ill.: C. C. Thomas, 1967) and others.

4. Demetri P. Kanellakos, "The Physiology of the Evolving Man," unpublished address given at Stanford University, 1970. Kanellakos is head of a research project at Stanford Research Institute to determine the physiological and psychological effects of TM.

5. R. K. Wallace, "The Physiological Effects of Transcendental Meditation," *Science,* V:167 (1970), p. 1751.

6. *Ibid.,* p. 1754.

7. Wallace and Benson, "The Physiology of Meditation," p. 86.

8. R. K. Wallace, "The Physiological Effects of Transcendental Meditation," p. 1753.

9. R. K. Wallace, H. Benson and A. F. Wilson, "A Wakeful Hypometabolic Physiologic State," *American Journal of Physiology,* 221:3 (September 1971), p. 797.

10. R. K. Wallace, *op. cit. supra,* note 1, p. 24.

11. R. K. Wallace, *op. cit. supra,* note 5, p. 1753.

12. R. K. Wallace, *op. cit. supra,* note 1, pp. 28, 56–59.

13. David Orme-Johnson, "Autonomic Stability and Transcendental Meditation," paper presented at Stanford Research Institute, August 5, 1971, and at the Second International Symposium on the Science of Creative Intelligence, Humboldt State College, August 22, 1971.

14. F. N. Pitts, "The Biochemistry of Anxiety," *Scientific American* (February 1969), pp. 69–75.

15. Wallace and Benson, "The Physiology of Meditation," p. 88.

16. *Ibid.*

17. R. K. Wallace, *op. cit. supra,* note 5, p. 1752; Wallace, Benson, and Wilson, *op. cit.,* p. 797.

18. A. Kasamatsu and T. Hirai, *Psychiatria et Neurologia Japonica,* 20, p. 315. Reported in R. K. Wallace, *op. cit. supra,* note 5, p. 1751.

19. Wallace and Benson, *op. cit.,* p. 89.

20. R. K. Wallace, *op. cit. supra,* note 5, p. 1753.

21. R. K. Wallace, *op. cit. supra,* note 1, p. 29.
22. N. Kleitman, *Sleep and Wakefulness* (Chicago: University of Chicago Press, 1963), pp. 329–330.
23. R. K. Wallace, *op. cit. supra,* note 1, p. 30. (My italics. J.F.)
24. Wallace and Benson, *op. cit.,* p. 798.
25. R. Shaw and D. Kolb, unpublished study, University of Texas, Austin, Texas.
26. D. P. Kanellakos, *op. cit.,* p. 2.
27. R. K. Wallace, *op. cit. supra,* note 1, p. 54.
28. D. P. Kanellakos, *op. cit.,* p. 3.
29. *The Science of Being,* p. 201.
30. Wallace and Benson, *op. cit.,* p. 89.
31. *The Science of Being,* p. 201.
32. *Ibid.,* pp. 195–196.
33. *Ibid.,* p. 196.
34. *Ibid.*
35. Sidney H. Scott, "Mind over Matter," *Mensa Journal* (December 1970), p. 9.
36. *The Science of Being,* pp. 189–190.
37. A. James Morgan, M.D., letter to Jerry Jarvis, April 20, 1972.
38. Scott, *op. cit.,* p. 9.
39. Anthony Campbell, M.D., "Toward Pinning Down Meditation," *Hospital Times* (London) (May 1, 1970).
40. Andy Palley, "Meditation May Be the Answer," *Albany Student Press,* October 8, 1971.
41. Alvin Toffler, *Future Shock* (New York: Random House, 1970), p. 3.
42. *Ibid.,* p. 13.
43. *Ibid.*
44. *Ibid.,* p. 290.
45. René Dubos, "Adaptation to the Environment and Man's Future," speech at the Nobel Conference, Gustavus Adolphus College, 1966.
46. Walter McQuade, "What Stress Can Do to Your Heart," *Fortune* (January 1972), pp. 102–107.
47. Opinion of Herbert Benson, M.D., cardiologist at Harvard Medical School, in *International Symposium on the Science of Creative Intelligence* (Seelisberg: MIU Press, 1971), p. 38. The context of Benson's remark was the following: "Well over 30 percent of our population in the United States today is hypertensive or has high blood pressure. This is an alarming number of people, close to 44 million, since hypertension in turn is related

to the possibility and probability that one will develop coronary heart disease."

48. Terri Schultz, "What Science Is Discovering About the Potential Benefits of Meditation," *Today's Health* (April 1972), p. 37.

49. Reply of Maharishi Mahesh Yogi to Harvey Brooks (president, American Academy of Arts and Sciences), First International Symposium on the Science of Creative Intelligence, University of Massachusetts, July 1971.

Chapter 3

1. Haim G. Ginott, *Group Psychotherapy with Children* (New York: McGraw-Hill, 1961), pp. 180–182.

2. Haim G. Ginott, *Between Parent and Child, New Solutions to Old Problems* (New York: Macmillan, 1965), p. 11.

3. *Ibid.,* pp. 49–50.

4. *The Science of Being,* p. 51.

5. *Ibid.,* pp. 182–183.

6. *Ibid.*

7. Maharishi Mahesh Yogi, *Love and God* (Norway: SRM, 1965), p. 19.

8. *Ibid.,* p. 21.

9. *Ibid.,* p. 20.

Chapter 4

1. Aldous Huxley, *The Perennial Philosophy* (London: Fontana, 1961), p. 186.

2. Ashley Montague, *The Direction of Human Development* (rev. ed.; New York: Hawthorn Books, 1970), p. 300.

3. Immanuel Kant, quoted in Wade Baskin (ed.), *Classics in Education* (New York: Philosophical Library, 1966), p. 327.

4. *The Science of Being,* p. 210.

5. *Ibid.*

6. Erich Fromm, *Escape from Freedom* (New York: Rinehart, 1941), p. 274.

7. Confucius, quoted in Wade Baskin (ed.), *op. cit.,* p. 164.

8. Robert M. Hutchins, *The Conflict in Education in a Democratic Society* (New York: Harper, 1953).

9. John Dewey, "My Pedagogic Creed," quoted in Wade Baskin (ed.), *op. cit.,* pp. 186 and 189.

10. Analysis of the dilemma of higher education adapted from Dr. Paul Levine's introduction to his proposal to the University of

California at Los Angeles to establish the Science of Creative Intelligence as an accredited course, January 15, 1971.

11. Montague, *op. cit.*, p. 317.

12. Albert Einstein, *Out of My Later Years* (New York: Philosophical Library, 1960).

13. *Critique of a College,* Swarthmore's self-critique (November 1968).

14. Franklin Patterson, quoted in Harris Wofford, "In Search of Liberal Education," *Saturday Review* (July 20, 1968), p. 50.

15. *The Student in Higher Education* (Hazen Foundation, 1968).

16. R. A. Millikan, *Science and Life* (Boston: Pilgrim Press, 1924), p. 88.

17. Maharishi Mahesh Yogi, comment at the First International Symposium on the Science of Creative Intelligence, University of Massachusetts, July 1971.

18. David Starr Jordan, *The Relation of Evolution and Religion* (Boston: American Unitarian Association, 1926), p. 10.

19. Albert Einstein, *Cosmic Religion* (New York: Covici Friede, 1931), p. 52.

20. Edmund Sinnott, "The Creativeness of Life," in *Creativity and Its Cultivation* (New York: Harper, 1959), p. 16.

21. *Ibid.,* pp. 16–17.

22. *Ibid.,* pp. 17–18, 27–28.

23. Maharishi Mahesh Yogi, opening address to the First Science of Creative Intelligence Symposium, University of Massachusetts, July 18, 1971.

24. Albert Einstein, *Cosmic Religion,* p. 52.

25. "Perspectives on SCI," unpublished SIMS pamphlet (1971), p. 3.

26. *Ibid.*

27. Buckminster Fuller, transcript of Fuller-Maharishi press conference, Science of Creative Intelligence Symposium, University of Massachusetts, July 22, 1971.

28. Melvin Calvin, in *International Symposium on the Science of Creative Intelligence* (Seelisberg: MIU Press, 1971), p. 31.

29. Maharishi Mahesh Yogi, in *ibid.,* p. 31.

30. Frank Barron–Maharishi exchange in *ibid.,* p. 50.

31. Schutz, *op. cit.,* p. 15.

Chapter 5

1. Abraham Maslow, *Motivation and Personality* (New York: Harper, 1954), p. 340.

2. Erich Fromm, *The Art of Loving* (New York: Harper, 1956), p. 125.

3. Aldous Huxley, "Human Potentialities," in S. Farber and R. Wilson (eds.), *op. cit.,* p. 65.

4. William James, "The Energies of Men," *Memories and Studies* (New York: Greenwood Press, 1968), p. 237.

5. William Wordsworth, "Ode: Intimations of Immortality," in *Wordsworth, Poetry & Prose* (Cambridge: Harvard University Press, 1970), p. 576.

6. Abraham Maslow, "Neurosis as a Failure of Personal Growth," in *The Farther Reaches of Human Nature* (New York: Viking, 1971), p. 25.

7. Maslow, *Toward a Psychology of Being,* p. 193.

8. *Ibid.,* pp. 160–161.

9. *Ibid.,* p. 201.

10. *Ibid.,* p. 155.

11. *Ibid.,* p. 163.

12. *Ibid.,* p. 166.

13. *Ibid.,* p. 5.

14. These characteristics are listed on pp. 26 and 157 of *ibid.*

15. *Ibid.,* p. 207.

16. *Ibid.,* p. 208.

17. *On the Bhagavad-Gita,* p. 136.

18. Maslow, *Toward a Psychology of Being,* p. 203.

19. Maharishi Mahesh Yogi; my lecture notes. J.F.

20. Maslow, *Toward a Psychology of Being,* p. 137.

21. Rogers, *op. cit.,* p. 75.

22. Shostram's Personal Orientation Inventory (POI). When the study was written up (May 1971) the bibliography of research with the POI consisted of 53 published and 58 unpublished (M.A. and doctoral) items.

23. S. Nidich, W. Seeman and T. Banta, "A Study of the Influence of Transcendental Meditation on a Measure of Self-Actualization," *Journal of Counseling Psychology,* Vol. 19, No. 3 (1972).

24. Research data by personal communication from Garland Landrith and Maynard Shelly. Dr. Shelly's book, *Sources of Satisfaction,* will be published by Addison Wesley.

25. E. Boese and K. Berger, "In Search of a Fourth State of Consciousness: Psychological and Physiological Correlates of Meditation," unpublished study, Milton S. Hershey Medical Center, Pennsylvania State University, Hershey, Pa.

26. A. James Morgan, M.D., Director, Adult Treatment Services, Community Mental Health Center, Pennsylvania Hospital,

in a letter to Jerry Jarvis, Director, Students International Meditation Society, April 20, 1972.

27. R. K. Wallace, *The Physiological Effects of Transcendental Meditation*, p. 54.

28. Personal communication from Dr. Bowers.

29. *The Science of Being*, pp. 264 and 218.

30. Maslow, *Motivation and Personality*, p. 352.

31. *The Science of Being*, pp. 78–79.

32. Robert Kantor, Clinical Psychologist at Stanford Research Institute, quoted in *International Symposium on the Science of Creative Intelligence* (Seelisberg: MIU Press, 1972), p. 48.

33. Maharishi's reply in *ibid.*, p. 48.

Chapter 6

1. W. Thomas Winquist, "The Effect of Regular Practice of Transcendental Meditation on the Regular Use of Hallucinogenic and Hard Drugs," unpublished study, University of California at Los Angeles, Department of Sociology, August 1969.

2. Herbert Benson, M.D., and R. Keith Wallace, Ph.D., "Decreased Drug Abuse with Transcendental Meditation," paper presented to the International Symposium on Drug Abuse for Physicians, University of Michigan, August 1970, and printed in *Hearings Before the Select Committee on Crime of the House of Representatives,* Ninety-second Congress, first session (1971), p. 681. (Hereinafter cited as *Hearings.*)

3. Herbert Benson, M.D., "Yoga for Drug Abuse," *New England Journal of Medicine,* Vol. 281 (November 13, 1969).

4. *Hearings,* pp. 683–684.

5. S. F. Yolles, Director, National Institute of Mental Health, statement before the Subcommittee on Public Health and Welfare of the Interstate and Foreign Commerce Committee, on H.R. 11701 and H.R. 13743, 1969.

6. *Hearings,* p. 682.

7. "Mind Over Drugs," *Time* (October 25, 1971), Behavior section.

8. Open letter, "To Whom It May Concern," from Chris Merriam, *op. cit.*

9. *Hearings,* p. 684.

10. *Ibid.,* p. 684.

11. Open letter, "To Whom It May Concern," from Dale Warner, Member, Michigan House of Representatives, 56th District.

12. John Gage, "Pillar to Post," *California Business* (January 4, 1971).

13. "The No. 1 Drug Problem," *Newsweek* (February 28, 1972), p. 54.

14. *Hearings,* p. 684.

15. *Ibid.*

16. *Ibid.*

17. Stephen B. Cox, "Transcendental Meditation and the Criminal Justice System," *Kentucky Law Journal,* Vol. 60 (1972), p. 416.

18. *Ibid.,* p. 418.

19. *The Science of Being,* p. 221.

20. Cox, *op. cit.,* p. 418.

Chapter 7

1. *The Science of Being,* p. 156.

2. *On the Bhagavad-Gita,* verses 48–50.

3. *The Science of Being,* p. 166.

4. *On the Bhagavad-Gita,* p. 154.

Chapter 8

1. Paul D. Zimmerman, "Anything Goes: Taboos in Twilight," *Newsweek* (November 13, 1967), p. 74.

2. See Toffler, *op. cit.,* Chapter 14, "A Diversity of Life Styles."

3. Reich, *op. cit.,* p. 2.

4. Erich Fromm, *The Revolution of Hope* (New York: Harper, 1968), p. 5.

5. Reich, *op. cit.,* pp. 3–4.

6. Abraham Maslow, "Psychological Data and Value Theory," in A. Maslow (ed.), *New Knowledge in Human Values* (New York: Harper, 1959), p. 134.

7. *Ibid.*

8. *The Science of Being,* p. 226.

9. Maslow, *Toward a Psychology of Being,* p. 151.

10. Maslow, "Psychological Data and Value Theory," p. 129.

11. *Ibid.,* p. 128. (My italics. J.F.)

12. *The Science of Being,* p. 224.

13. H. G. MacPherson, "What Would a Scientific Religion Be Like?," *Saturday Review* (August 2, 1969), pp. 44–47.

14. *The Science of Being,* p. 19.

15. Maharishi Mahesh Yogi, transcription of lecture notes.

16. *The Science of Being,* p. 80.

Chapter 9

1. See Toffler, *op. cit.*, Part Four, "Diversity."
2. Fromm, *Escape from Freedom*, pp. 255–256.
3. *Ibid.*, p. 257.
4. *Ibid.*, p. 258.
5. *Ibid.*, p. 270.
6. *The Science of Being*, pp. 234–235.
7. Aldous Huxley, "Human Potentialities," in S. Farber and R. Wilson (eds.), *op. cit.*, p. 71.
8. *The Science of Being*, p. 237.
9. *Bhagavad Gita*, II:18–25, translated by Maharishi Mahesh Yogi.
10. *The Science of Being*, pp. 249–250.
11. *Ibid.*, p. 240.
12. *Bhagavad Gita*, II:40.
13. Maharishi Mahesh Yogi, transcription of lecture.
14. Fromm, *Escape from Freedom*, p. 241.

Chapter 10

1. Gratitude for this tale goes to Denny Gillett of Castro Valley, California, who wrote it while attending a residence course for meditators. I have slightly revised a few lines.
2. *On the Bhagavad-Gita*, p. 10.
3. *Ibid*, p. 11.
4. *Ibid.*, p. 13.
5. *Ibid.*, p. 12.
6. *Ibid.*, p. 16.
7. *Love and God*, p. 6.
8. *Ibid.*, p. 9.
9. *Ibid.*, p. 10.
10. *On the Bhagavad-Gita*, p. 16.
11. *Ibid.*
12. *Love and God*, p. 22.
13. David Bolling, "Report from the Source," *MIU International Newsletter*, Vol. 1, no. 1 (February 1972), pp. 9–10.
14. *Ibid.*, p. 11.

Chapter 11

1. Louis D. Brandeis, in *Whitney* v. *California* 274 US at 375.
2. Abraham Maslow, in the preface to Maslow (ed.), *New Knowledge in Human Values,* p. vii.
3. Pitirim Sorokin, "The Powers of Creative Unselfish Love," in *ibid.,* p. 4.
4. John V. Lindsay, graduation address at Manhattanville College, Purchase, New York, reported in *New York Times,* June 1, 1969.
5. Arthur Schlesinger, Jr., "Does American Spirit Reflect a Sick Society?," *Daily Trojan* (University of Southern California), February 13, 1968, p. 5.
6. Leo Tolstoy, *Last Diaries,* Lydia Weston-Kesich (trans.) (New York: G. P. Putnam, 1960), p. 55.
7. Bertrand Russell, transcript of an English television appearance, quoted in *Bertrand Russell Speaks His Mind* (Annandale-on-Hudson, N.Y.: Bard, 1960).
8. D. T. Suzuki, "Human Values in Zen," in Maslow (ed.), *New Knowledge in Human Values,* pp. 100–105.
9. Lewis Mumford, *The Condition of Man* (New York: Harcourt, Brace, 1944), p. 421.
10. Immanuel Kant, quoted in Wade Baskin (ed.), *op. cit.,* p. 330.
11. *I Ching,* Wilhelm/Baynes (trans.) (New York: Bollingen, 1961).
12. Thomas Jefferson, in Paul L. Ford, *The Writings of Thomas Jefferson* (New York: G. P. Putnam, 1899), Vol. X, p. 42.
13. Mumford, *op. cit.,* pp. 422–423.
14. Bertrand Russell, *Human Society in Ethics and Politics* (New York: Simon and Schuster, 1955), p. 225.
15. A. S. Neill, *Summerhill: A Radical Approach to Child Rearing* (New York: Hart Publishing Co., 1960), pp. xxiii–xxiv.
16. *The Science of Being,* p. 184.
17. Vijaya Lakshmi Pandit, in *To Live as Men: An Anatomy of Peace* (Santa Barbara, Calif.: Center for the Study of Democratic Institutions, 1965), p. 58.
18. Thomas Merton, "The Christian in World Crisis: Reflections on the Moral Climate of the 1960's," in *Thomas Merton on Peace* (New York: McCall Publishing, 1971), p. 62.
19. *The Science of Being,* p. 244.
20. *Ibid.,* pp. 245–246.
21. *The Science of Being,* p. 311.

Index

NOTE: *Only major references to Maharishi Mahesh Yogi, Transcendental Meditation and the Science of Creative Intelligence are included herein. Page numbers in italics denote illustrations.*